WALDENSIAN VALLEYS

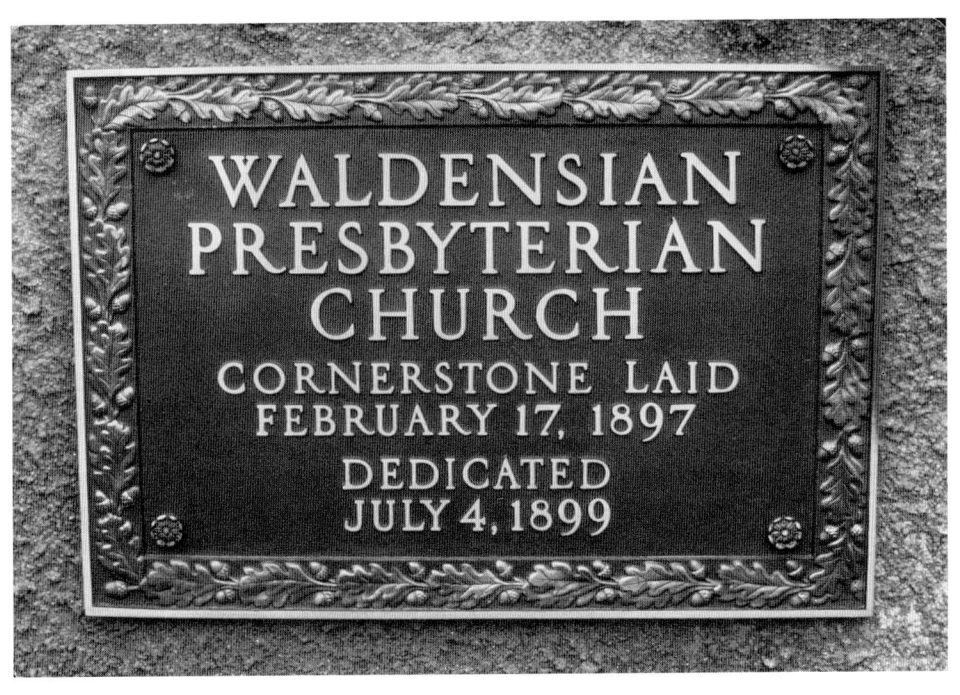

THE FIRST ONE HUNDRED YEARS
1893-1993

HISTORY and HERITAGE
of the
WALDENSIAN PRESBYTERIAN CHURCH

Valdese, North Carolina

1893-1993

Copyright © 1993 by
Waldensian Presbyterian Church
Valdese, North Carolina

Printed in the U.S.A.
by
Delmar Printing

DEDICATION

This history is dedicated to those Waldensians who came to this place one hundred years ago and founded this church and town. As a group, they were poor in worldly goods but rich in the faith that undergirded their lives. Their first act upon stepping off the train on May 29, 1893 was to gather around their pastor to offer a prayer of thanksgiving.

In the distribution of land, the choice area which later became the center of the town was designated as church property. A hastily built, two-story house provided a place for worship until the church was completed in 1899. The force which unified and strengthened the colonists in the hardships of the early years was their trust in God. As He had preserved their forefathers, He would sustain them also and help them prosper in this new land.

We, the descendants of those pioneers, owe them a debt of gratitude for their Christian example, which has given us cause to rejoice in our heritage and to strive to emulate them in our own time. Without the courage and devotion of the Waldensians who settled Valdese, none of the blessings and opportunities we have had here during the past one hundred years would have been ours to enjoy.

MAPS
    Inside front cover: The Waldensian Valleys in Italy
    Inside back cover: 1895 Street Plat of Valdese
                    and
            Current Map of Valdese

Color Presentation
    Sanctuary window with the emblem of the Waldensian Church

TABLE OF CONTENTS

PART I: History of The Waldensian Presbyterian Church

Chapter
1. Waldensian History....................................3
2. Years of Struggle (1893-1900).......................13
3. Building on the Foundation (1901-1917)............37
4. A Time of Transition (1918-1940)...................57
5. Growth and Vitality (1941-1949)....................77
6. Expansion, Involvement, Witness (1950-1968) 93
7. Commitment and Service to Christ and Community (1969-1993)..115
8. The Promise of the Future......................181

PART II: Heritage and People

9. Pastors of the Waldensian Presbyterian Church.....185
10. The Valdese Corporation...........................203
11. Building and Renovation Programs 207
12. Waldensian Customs and Traditions 211
    - The Waldensian Emblem....................211
    - The Waldensian Traditional Dress...........212
    - Baptisms, Weddings, Funerals...............213
    - Waldensian Celebrations....................214
    - Waldensian Food...........................216
    - The Waldensian Dialect....................217
    - Farming and Wine Making 219
    - Social Life 220
    - Boccie 223
    - The Courenta — Waldensian Folk Dance 224

13	Early Organizations	227
14	Church Leaders	231
	Charter Members	231
	Waldensian Presbyterian Church Staff	234
	Elders of the Waldensian Presbyterian Church	236
	Deacons of the Waldensian Presbyterian Church	239
	Sunday School	242
	Women of the Church Presidents	244
	Women of the Church Honorary Life Memberships	245
	Special Awards	246
15	The Second Cornerstone Service	249
	Resources	252
	Index	255

FOREWORD

In May 1989 the Centennial Committee of the Waldensian Presbyterian Church asked the Historical Committee to prepare an account of the first one hundred years of the church as part of the observance of the centennial in 1993. For the past three years, a committee of eleven has worked diligently to research and write this history. As the work progressed, the people and events of the past came alive, and the committee members developed a profound respect for the many who contributed to the growth and nurture of this congregation. Although it was not possible to include the names of all who have given unselfishly of their time, talents, and material wealth to their church, their work was not overlooked nor is it forgotten. It is the sincere hope of the Church History Committee that each reader of this book will be filled with thankfulness for the blessings God has bestowed upon this church.

"Come and see what God has done." Psalm 66:5

Church History Committee

John A. Bleynat
Jewell Pyatt Bounous
Evelyn Pons Bronson
Catherine Rivoire Cole
Catherine Dalmas
Carol Price Felker
Paul H. Felker
Imogene Pons Hudson
Olga Pascal
Naomi Bounous Rostan
Rosalba Pascal Shook

Church Centennial Committee

John A. Bleynat
Evelyn Bounous
Carol A. Perrou Brown
Catherine Rivoire Cole
Catherine Dalmas
Paul H. Felker
Benjamin W. Garrou, Sr.
Hilda Ogle Jones
Edward Pascal
Linda Keenan York

PART I

HISTORY
of the

WALDENSIAN
PRESBYTERIAN
CHURCH

CHAPTER 1

WALDENSIAN HISTORY—Faith of our Fathers

"O Lord my God, in Thee do I put my trust: save me from all them that persecute me, and deliver me." Psalm 7:1

**A short history of the Waldensian Church
from antiquity to the late nineteenth century.**

    A history of the Waldensian Presbyterian Church of Valdese would have little real meaning without a look at the history of the Waldensian Church of Italy. It is necessary to know some of this history in order to appreciate what went into forming the character and beliefs of that group of people who came to Valdese in 1893 to settle the town of Valdese and to found the Waldensian Presbyterian Church.

    The Waldensian Church is the oldest evangelical church still in existence. The church can trace its roots through the records of persecution found in the archives of Europe, as early as the year 1174. This date is 400 years before the Reformation. There are ancient references that would date the beginning back to a much earlier time, at least to the fourth century.

    There is even disagreement as to the origin of the name, Waldensian. One explanation of the name, which seems reasonable, is found in a recommendatory letter from Samuel Miller, Professor of Ecclesiastical History and Church Government in the Theological Seminary at Princeton. The letter was written February 24, 1845 to commend Griffith and Simon Publishers for printing the *History of the Ancient Christians* by Jean Paul Perrin, written prior to 1618. In his letter, Dr. Miller quotes from writings of Robert Robinson, a divine of Cambridge in England, who died in 1795. In his *Ecclesiastical Researches* he gives this explanation:

> From the Latin, "Vallis," come the English, "Valley"; the French and Spanish, "Valle"; the Italian, "Valdesi"; the Low Dutch, "Valleye"; the Provençal, "Vaux," "Vaudais"; the ecclesiastical "Vallenses," "Valdenses," "Ualdenses" and "Waldenses." The words simply signify—valleys—the inhabitants of valleys and no more. It happened that

the inhabitants of the Pyrenees did not profess the Catholic faith. It fell out also that the inhabitants of the valleys about the Alps did not embrace that faith. It happened, moreover, in the ninth century, that one Valdus, a friend and follower of Berengarius, and a man of eminence, who had many followers, did not approve of the Papal discipline and doctrine, and it came to pass about a hundred and thirty years later, that a rich merchant of Lyons, who was called Valdus, because he received his religious opinions from the inhabitants of the valleys, openly disavowed the Roman religion, supported many to teach the doctrines believed in the valleys, and became the instrument of the great conversion of great numbers. All the people were called "Waldenses." (302-303)

In 1847, the publishing firm of Griffith and Simon in Philadelphia began plans to publish the history of the Waldensians written by Jean Paul Perrin. In preparation for this publication they received the letter mentioned above from the Rev. Samuel Miller, D.D., concerning his knowledge of Perrin's history as well as his knowledge of the Waldensians. Miller dates the beginning of the Waldensians to 660 AD or earlier. He further states that the Waldensians were found in France, Italy and Bohemia at about that period. According to Dr. Miller, all these people held basically the same beliefs. They believed in the doctrine of the Trinity, the Divinity of Christ, the vicarious nature of the atonement and justification by the imputed righteousness of Christ. These doctrines were the same as those put forth at a later date by John Calvin. In the centuries ahead, many of the men who persecuted and prosecuted the leaders of the Reformation accused Reformation leaders of being Waldensians or following the Waldensian teachings.

The ancestors of the Valdese Waldensians were located along the French-Italian border in a small area of about three hundred square miles of the Cottian Alps of Italy. This area for many years was under the domination of France. Some of the families had moved into the Valleys hundreds of years ago to escape persecution in France. This helps account for some of the French names found in the area.

In the year 1215, at the Fourth Lateran Council, the Waldensians were condemned for heresy. Prior to this time, they had only been reprimanded and expelled from their communities. This was probably the beginning of serious organized persecution. The first record of a Waldensian being burned at the stake was in 1309 when a Waldensian woman was burned at Pinerolo. During the late 1300's and early 1400's, a series of inquisitions took place against Waldensians in Germany, Austria, Hungary and Bohemia. At one time, 400 people were tried and condemned in Stettin, Poland.

In 1487, the first crusade against the Waldensians in the Alps took place. There had been isolated incidents, but in 1487, Cattaneo, the representative of Pope Innocent VIII, led a full scale war on the inhabitants. Anyone taking part in the war could claim the property of any Waldensian they could kill. This was an open invitation to the rabble to come in, and it led to heavy fighting and much killing and looting. Most of the homes and the vineyards were destroyed or burned. Many of the survivors escaped to the south of Italy.

Martin Luther, in 1517, nailed his 95 Theses to the door of the castle church in Wittenberg, Germany, and the Reformation was under way. During the next few years, some of the Waldensian ministers met with leaders of the Reformation, which led to the synod meeting held in 1532 at Chanforan, Angrogna, in the Waldensian Valleys. At this meeting, the Waldensians officially became part of the Reformation. As their specific contribution to the Reformation, the Waldensians raised the money to support the translation of the Bible into the French language by Olivetan. This was the first complete translation of the Bible into French. Moveable type had recently been invented, and the new printing presses made reproduction practical. Peter Waldo had been responsible for having portions of the Bible translated into the vernacular four hundred years earlier.

There was a fairly large community of Waldensians located around the village of Mérindol, France. Some of the residents had moved in from the valleys across the border in Italy, and some were natives of the area. This was a very prosperous area due to industriousness of the Waldensians. The prosperity became the cause of jealousy on the part of the Roman church and state officials of the area. In 1545, a Roman Inquisitor set out to rid the area of Waldensians. A papal army was sent into the area, and a massacre ensued. Thousands were killed, and several towns, including Mérindol, France, were destroyed.

For hundreds of years, the Waldensians had worshipped in their homes and caves—anywhere they could get a group together. One reason was their belief that church buildings were an extravagance and merely a means for getting money for the priests and hierarchy. However, in 1555, they changed their opinion, and the first church building for the Waldensians was built at Ciabas, in the valley of Angrogna. The building is still standing after 440 years.

The year 1561 brought a peace of sorts. At a meeting in Cavour, Italy, on June 5, a document was signed by representatives of the Waldensians and the Duke of Savoy. Although it was not officially recognized as a treaty, it did arrange for an end to the fighting. This document spelled out for the first time in European history the fact that subjects who practiced a different religion from that of the ruling power possessed officially recognized rights. Up until this time, it had always been the rule, and this was accepted by the leaders of the Reformation also, that the religion of the ruler determined the religion of his subjects. The signing of the document did not end the problems of the Waldensians by any means, but it at least was acknowledged in writing that they had certain rights.

The next fifty or sixty years were somewhat more peaceful for the Waldensians, as the ruling powers engaged in wars in other parts of Europe and persecuted followers of the Reformation in those areas.

The Black Death struck the Valleys in 1630. This was one of the last epidemics of the plague in Europe, but it was one of the most deadly. It began in May of 1630 in San Germano and soon affected all the Valleys. It was estimated that between 8,500 and 9,000 people died, including eleven of the thirteen pastors in the Valleys. The death of these ministers had a far reaching impact on the future of the church. Up until this time, all the pastors had been natives of the area, reared and educated in the Waldensian traditions. When the eleven pastors died, the people turned to Geneva for help. A cadre of pastors was sent to help—pastors who had been trained in the Geneva Academy and who knew little of the Waldensian traditions. They used methods and organizations which were new to the Waldensians but which probably streamlined the operation of the church. The pastors and moderators were given more power than they had previously held. The most dramatic change was the use of the French language in worship. The pastors trained in Geneva did not speak Italian, and although the Waldensians spoke both French and Italian, they had used Italian in their worship services in hopes of influencing their Catholic neighbors. They now began using French in all services and communications. For the next three hundred years, French was the official language of the

Waldensian Church, until the twentieth century when Benito Mussolini forced the use of the Italian language.

By 1655, the wars in the remainder of Europe had calmed, and the authorities could once again return to their favorite pastime of harassing Waldensians. The Massacre of the Piedmontese Easter occurred that year. The authorities had required the Waldensian families to provide room and board for the soldiers. The soldiers were instructed to kill the families they were staying with on Easter morning. More than a thousand Waldensians were slaughtered at that time. In the long run, this act probably helped those who survived, because the brutalities the Waldensians suffered aroused the indignation of the ruling powers of Europe, who protested to the local rulers. In years to come, England and Holland, in particular, provided support for the Waldensians.

The revocation of the Edict of Nantes in 1685 opened the door for more religious persecution. The revocation gave the Duke of Savoy an excuse to tighten his hold on the Waldensians. In January 1686, he revoked the rights of the Waldensians to hold church services. On March 6, the Waldensians resumed their church services in direct defiance of the Duke. This action played right into the hands of Louis XIV of France, who had already stationed Marshal Catinat and his troops at Pinerolo in hopeful anticipation of the Waldensian defiance. The Swiss sent envoys to try to prevent bloodshed, but the Waldensians refused to give up their right to hold worship services. The French Dragoons and Piedmontese militia moved into the Valleys. In six weeks, the fighting was over. Two thousand Waldensians died, and 8,500 were taken prisoner. The rest agreed to renounce their faith. The survivors were scattered over the middle sections of Italy and forbidden to practice their faith. Of those who were imprisoned, 2,000 able-bodied men were sent to Venice to be sold as galley slaves, and others were sent to France. Of 1,400 imprisoned at Carmagnola, 1,000 died within a few months. In another prison, only 46 of 1,000 prisoners survived.

In late 1686, the Duke agreed to permit the surviving prisoners to go into exile in Switzerland. They were to walk across the Alps in the dead of winter. The first group began their trek on January 17, and the last of the thirteen groups arrived in Geneva on March 10, 1687. Of 2,700 who began the march, 2,490 actually completed the trip. Some froze to death, others were lost, and some of the children were kidnapped by hostile peasants along the way, who used them to work and reared them as Roman Catholics. The Swiss, who had negotiated the release, did all they could to ease the suffering. Even many of the guards escorting them from the Duke of Savoy's army tried to help. When the group arrived in Geneva, the entire town turned out to greet them and invite them into their homes. The townspeople attacked the troops who had been guarding the Waldensians when they saw the poor condition of the refugees.

The Waldensians were very unhappy in Switzerland, although the Swiss did everything in their power to make them feel at home. In July 1687, a group plotted to return to their Valleys and set out to do so but were stopped by the Swiss authorities.

In 1688, a revolution in England placed William of Orange of Holland on the English throne. This was the beginning of a better time for the Waldensians. William of Orange was a Protestant and found an opportunity to hurt the French by helping the Waldensians. His emissaries contacted Waldensian leaders and offered money and men to help them regain their lands. An army of 1,000 men, including 600 Waldensians under the leadership of Henri Arnaud, began their march home on the night of August 16, 1689. Arnaud was a Waldensian minister who was born in the French Dauphine. He prepared for the ministry in Switzerland and Holland. He was one of the ministers who had played a leading part in the decision three years earlier to hold services in defiance of the ban on worship issued by the Duke of Savoy and Louis XIV. Arnaud had worked closely with the Huguenots in France and the Valleys, and as a result of this association, he was more militant than the average Waldensian minister.

The army followed a manual written in the 1650's by Josué Janavel, a Waldensian farmer turned guerrilla fighter. He proved to be a good guerrilla tactician. He had laid down severe rules of conduct for the guerrilla fighters. A passage from his manual states: "Whoever in your company swears or blasphemes the holy name of God should be severely punished for his first offence, and if he persists, should be sentenced to death. In so acting you will see that the sword of the Lord our God will be with you."

Janavel further specified that if someone was to be put to death, the execution should not take place until a council of war, composed of thirty or forty leaders, deliberated and pronounced the sentence. There should be no capital sentence if the pastor had no opportunity to prepare and counsel the condemned. It was to be the pastor who designated those who were to carry out the sentence in order that there be no contestation and no offense to God.

Waldensian History

The Waldensian army applied the same rules to all their prisoners. As the army passed through villages, they took hostages to prevent word of their passage from reaching authorities. The soldiers in the "rag-tag" army wore orange ribbons to identify themselves. The officers and men took an oath to obey and protect one another to the death. They fought "hit-and-run" engagements throughout the winter, losing men through battle and defection, until only 300 Waldensians remained.

May 2, 1690 found the small army on a mountainside at Balsiglia facing 4,000 French soldiers in the valley below. The French attacked for several days, and when at last it seemed the men could hold no longer, a fog settled over the area, and the Waldensians were able to escape. A few days later when the Duke of Savoy broke his alliance with France and joined England and Austria, peace was restored to the area.

In 1694, the Duke was forced to issue an Edict of Tolerance which guaranteed henceforth the right of the Waldensians to exist on their lands. The fight for religious tolerance had taken another step forward.

The military mistreatment of the Waldensians ended with the campaign just finished. Now the rulers began a political offensive which went on for another 150 years. What they had been unable to accomplish through force they attempted to accomplish politically.

In 1698, the Duke ordered the expulsion of all French subjects in the area. This included the Waldensians of the area around Pinerolo and the French Huguenots who lived in the area. Altogether about 3,000 people were forced to leave. Although the exile was not as hard as the exile of 1686, it was still difficult. Henri Arnaud was included in the group since he had been born in France. The exiles were sent to the Wurttemberg region of Germany where they expanded the existing Waldensian communities and settled in new ones.

After the completion of the exile of the people from the Pinerolo area, the authorities began working on the Waldensians of the Pragelato area in the northern Valleys. By 1716, the Reformed Christians were forbidden to assemble more than ten people in one place, and in 1721, a decree announced that every new-born baby was to be baptized a Roman Catholic. In 1730, all inhabitants of the Pragelato Valley were ordered to profess the Catholic religion, and no exercise, public or private, would be permitted of the pretended Reformed Religion. Hundreds of people in the area left to join their relatives and friends in Germany. While the church had been subjected to military campaigns, the faith of the people seemed to be strengthened. Now that the persecution took the form of political persecutions, the church seemed to be withdrawing unto itself. The whole area took on the appearance of a ghetto.

The year 1789 brought the French Revolution which had its effect on the Valleys. The Waldensians gladly became part of the Revolution and were given some places of relative importance in the local governments. When Napoleon became emperor in 1804, Waldensians were given the right to their religion, freely and without discrimination. They were once again able to acquire lands and own businesses. However, this did not last for long. They were soon advised that the Waldensian Church was to become a part of the French Reformed Church. This meant they would no longer receive financial help from England. However, it also meant that churches which had been taken from them and made into Roman Catholic churches would now be returned to them; and when Roman Catholic churches were located in a Waldensian community with no Catholic parishioners, these would also be given to the Waldensians. The Waldensian pastors would all be paid by the French government, as was the practice in France. Although the Napoleonic era lasted only about twenty years, it gave the people a taste of what freedom could mean.

After the Napoleonic era ended, the King of Sardinia was returned to his throne, and the Waldensians were relegated to the conditions they had experienced one hundred years before. They were forbidden to import Bibles, there could be no new Waldensian schools established, and a new church at San Giovanni had to have a high fence built around it so that the Catholics would not have to look at it as they passed.

In 1825, a former Genevan soldier turned pastor, Felix Neff, came to the Valleys. He became alarmed at the attitude of the Waldensian leaders who were content to live quietly and not upset the authorities. Neff demanded that the people resume their evangelistic way of life instead of accepting whatever came their way. He was soon chased back into France by the Sardinian government, but the fires he had begun continued to burn. At about this time, an Englishman, General Charles Beckwith, who had been an officer in Wellington's army at the battle of Waterloo and who had lost a leg in that battle, came to the area to recuperate. He read a book about the Waldensian people written by Canon Gilly, an Anglican minister, and became interested. Beckwith encouraged the people to become missionaries of their faith and to stand up for their rights. He helped start a program which within twenty-five years had built a school in every village in the Valleys. By 1848, there were 169 schools operating. Beckwith probably had more positive effect on the Waldensians than any other non-Waldensian man in their history.

The year 1848 was fateful for the Waldensians. A few people in authority were troubled by the treatment of the Waldensians. They began some agitation to try to help them as well as the Jewish minority, who were subjected to the same discrimination. The Waldensian Tavola was so heartened by this effort that they sent a petition to King Charles Albert requesting that he revoke the restrictive edicts denying them civil rights, which had been in effect for so long. On February 17, 1848, the Edict of Emancipation was issued which granted Waldensians the same civil and political rights as the other subjects. The Edict permitted them to attend public schools and universities. However, no change was made as to the exercise of their worship or the operation of their own schools. This was a great step forward and is the reason for the annual celebration observed on February 17. Although the new freedom was greatly appreciated, it took more than 130 years to achieve full religious liberty and recognition by the Italian government.

The foregoing history, which only includes excerpts to show the general climate of persecution and mistreatment of the Waldensians for several hundred years, lets the reader know how the people were tempered and their characters forged by the fire of war and persecution.

After the Edict of Emancipation in 1848, the people lived in peace and prospered. Their numbers grew until the area became so crowded they began to emigrate to other lands. Some went to South America, some to South Africa, and some to the United States. It was this condition that caused the settlers of Valdese to come to Burke County, North Carolina, to find a new home and a chance to earn a livelihood.

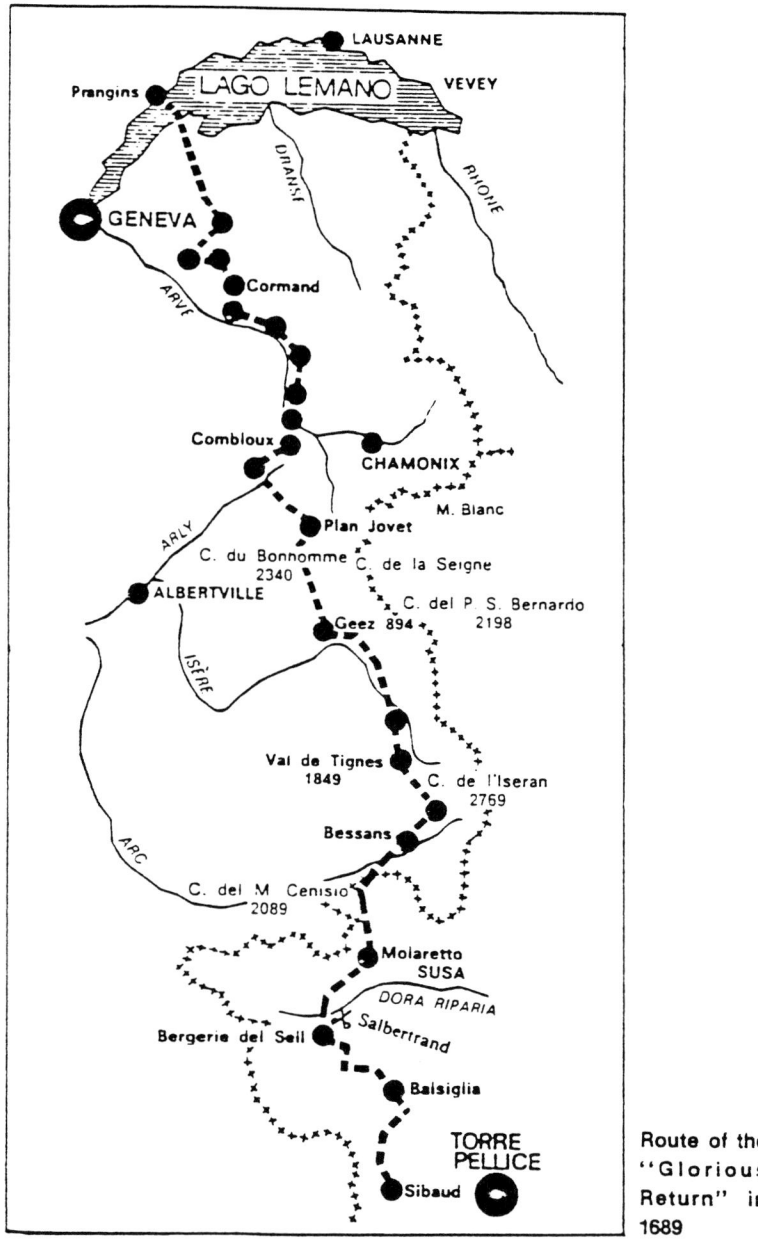

Route of the "Glorious Return" in 1689

This was the route of the 1000 Waldenses, under Henri Arnaud, who fought their way back home from Switzerland. Napoleon said it was the greatest military feat in history. It terminated in the siege of Balsiglia, where the surviving 300 withstood 4,000 troops of Louis XIV of France, under Marshal Catinat, for one whole winter and won back their valleys and liberty.

CHAPTER 2

YEARS OF STRUGGLE—
The Beginning in America
1893-1900

"According to the grace of God which is given unto me, as a wise masterbuider, I have laid the foundation, and another buildeth thereon. But let every man take heed how he buildeth thereupon." I Corinthians 3:10

The story of the first years in Valdese with the problems, fears, hunger, and frustration endured until the people adjusted to their new life and surroundings.

The Waldensian Presbyterian Church in Valdese, Burke County, North Carolina, as it is today, credits its beginning to a group of Waldensians from the Cottian Alps of northwest Italy who desired to leave their ancestral area of historic renown. Increasingly overcrowded conditions since the cessation of oppression, hostilities and persecutions created in them a desire for better living conditions. In the early 1890's, many families made plans to leave the Valleys, to locate in some undeveloped area where cost of land would be less than in their mountains and valleys.

This desire to emigrate came to the attention of an American capitalist and landowner, Marvin F. Scaife, of Pittsburg, Pennsylvania and Morganton, North Carolina. He heard of the Waldensians' need to migrate and proceeded to assist them to emigrate to available lands in Burke County, North Carolina.

In Dr. George B. Watts' book *The Waldenses of Valdese*, he states:

> *Le Témoin*, official organ of the Waldensian Church, reported on November 24, 1892, that the chairman of the Committee of Evangelization, Dr. Matteo Prochet, "received one day in Rome a visit from an American gentleman who discussed the project with him." Moreover, in the same publication is a statement by Dr. Charles Albert Tron, who led the first group to North Carolina, that the venture was initiated in Rome by the Reverend Mr. Buffa, pastor of the Waldensian Church.

> "It was to him," wrote Dr. Tron, "that Mr. Scaife addressed himself when he was in Rome, and it was with him that he remained for a long time in correspondence about the conditions of sale. It was Mr. Buffa who wrote to Dr. Gay when the latter was in America, in order that he might go to the spot and see how things were." This Dr. Gay did, examining the proffered lands and lecturing in Morganton. (16-17)

Dr. Teophilo Gay was traveling in America to collect funds for the Committee of Evangelization of the Waldensian Church.

After many public meetings in the Waldensian Valleys, the first contingent of Waldensians made concrete plans to vacate their ancestral homes. In the spring of 1893, Jean Bounous and Louis Richard were sent to North Carolina to look over the land offered to the group. The new world seemed to offer much promise according to the report of the two delegates who weighed before them both affirmatives and negatives. Nonetheless, the beckoning beam from the lighted torch of the Statue of Liberty was a "golden door" inducement, uplifting the spirit with hope of prosperity.

In May 1893, the first detachment, led by Dr. Charles Albert Tron, left from Turin for Boulogne-sur-Mer. After a wait of six days in this port, embarkation was on the steamship *Zaandam* of the Holland-American Line. After a long and difficult voyage, the passengers arrived in New York on May 26, where they received a cordial welcome from Mr. Scaife, who had completed arrangements for their transportation to Burke County via the Richmond and Danville Railroad.

The party of twenty-nine Waldensians arrived at what is now Valdese during the afternoon of Monday, May 29, 1893. Prior arrangements had been made for their coming, and a large number of citizens of the area were there to bid them welcome. These descendants of a persecuted, evangelical religious group, upon alighting from the train, assembled around a table in a solemn service of thanksgiving. Their leader, Pastor Tron, conducted a short devotional reading from Psalm 103 and bade them to be always faithful to the Lord. The service closed with a hymn and prayer that was frequently interrupted by the tears of the brethren and sisters as reported by their leader. Of the first afternoon in Valdese, Dr. Tron wrote:

> The arrival produced a profound emotion. In spite of the

enthusiastic reception of many warm friends, finding themselves thus alone in the midst of woods, far from their native country, impressed in an extraordinary manner the minds of the immigrants, who did not hesitate to bend their knees in thanks to God and invoke His favor for the newborn colony. To see all the bared heads and the weeping women and children was a scene which cannot be forgotten. (Watts, 22)

This first contingent of twenty-nine individuals, who were to prepare the ground for the coming of many other colonists, included eleven men, not counting Pastor Tron, five women[1] and thirteen children. They are listed as follows:

Jean Giraud, 34.

Jean Guigou, 41. Wife Catherine (née Guigou), 31. Sons: Louis Philippe, 10; Étienne, 7; Alexis, 5. Daughter Naomi, 3.

Jaubert Micol, 40. Wife Jeanne (née Tron), 38. Sons: Jean, 15; Emmanuel, 7; Victor, 2. Daughter Marguerite, 12.

Albert Pons, 35.

François Pons, 24.

Jean Henri Pons, 29.

Jean Refour, 42. Son Jean, 15.

Philippe Richard, 33. Wife Marianna Louise (née Ribet), 38. Sons: Philippe, 9; Étienne, 4.

François Tron, 18. Wife Marguerite (née Garrou), 31.

Jacques Henri Tron, 44.

Pierre Tron, 39. Wife Louise (née Pons), 34. Son Albert, 5. Daughter Madeleine, 3.

Their spiritual leader, Pastor Charles Albert Tron, had the added responsibility of handling the business of the settlers in the acquisition of property through the Morganton Land and Improvement Company.

The responsibility was enormous for their spiritual leader, who did everything in his power to see that reasonably comfortable dwellings could be assigned to respective families. Life in the new world was fraught with much privation, frustration and disappointment, but with steadfast faith and gratitude they survived despite all odds.

The Waldensians, an evangelical, worshipful people, found themselves without a sanctuary in which to congregate in worship, so a hastily constructed meeting house, located at the corner of Massel and Faet Streets, southwest, served the purpose. This meeting house also accommodated meetings relating to community affairs, served as a school facility for the children, a post office and a store. In the beginning, it was constructed primarily to provide housing for the expected contingent of settlers in November.

Pastor Charles Albert Tron immediately organized the colonists' land transaction affairs, and on June 8, 1893, the Valdese Corporation was chartered in the State of North Carolina. The provisions of this charter with all its ramifications and good intent proved incompatible with the highly individualistic nature of the Waldensian people. (See Part II, Chapter 10 for a full explanation of the Valdese Corporation).

The settlers suffered much from a lack of creature comforts in the early days. They sorely missed their "pain quotidien" (daily bread) that they were so accustomed to baking in outdoor ovens. The need for an oven in which to bake bread prompted the Waldensian women to decide on a plan to raise funds. The able-bodied women, with good voices, donned native Waldensian dresses, which consisted of a basic dark dress, a colorful apron, a shawl, and a white, lace-fluted coiffe (bonnet) with ribbon streamers. They walked to visit a church in Connelly Springs, three miles distant, to sing hymns in French and to request an offering. This plan was followed by another occasion at "Big Hill" church (Bollinger's Chapel), where a few welcome coins were added to the "oven fund." This effort was a success, and with the hard labor of the menfolk, the outdoor oven was built and the first loaves enjoyed on June 20, 1893, less than four weeks after arrival! This bread was considered a "benediction from the Lord." Later, until families could be permanently assigned a dwelling, this oven was utilized as a "community" oven available to all. We are told the oven was located on what is now Rodoret Street on a site east of the present post office.

June 1893 was a month of many meetings of the colonists. Much information can be gleaned from the minutes of these meetings recorded in French by Dr. Tron[2]. From the meeting of June 16, 1893, entitled "Constitution of the Colony" is recorded:

> We, the undersigned, here solemnly engage ourselves before God to the following constitution, which we adopt as the foundation for the colony after having seriously examined it. (1) As Christians belonging to the Waldensian Family, blessed miraculously, watched over by the Eternal (Lord), we will strive to be witnesses to the Truth, by our conduct, by our words, by our actions and by our entire lives. (2) We will strive to leave a good impression on all our neighbors and on the inhabitants of this State, who have received us with open arms and who expect much of us, since they see our Church as something miraculous. (3) We engage ourselves to submit to the decisions of the Directorate, and especially to the Pastor, who is its President, accepting its advice and, if need be, its reprimand and its censure.

Further, from the meeting of June 23, 1893, in Article 4 is a statement that attests to the strong ties of the colonists to their heritage:

> The colony considering that its love for the Waldensian Church could never diminish although separated from it by oceans, determines that it will always be one with the Mother Church, and to show its mind and desire, votes the following rule to have a Waldensian minister: From the year 1893 forward, the colony will furnish sufficient flour and vegetables. From 1894 on, each member to pay one dollar and furnish flour for bread. From 1895, two dollars per member.

In essence this agreement was the pastor's salary!

The first elected elder of the Waldensian colonists was Antoine Martinat, on June 26, 1893, who, along with his wife Anne Marie (née Tron) and six children, joined the colonists in mid-June from Ogden, Utah.

In the minutes of July 1, 1893, the locations of the church, the school, the presbytery (manse), the pastor's garden and the cemetery were decided: "They are to be placed on the Valdese hilltop, 120 meters in length and 42 in width, going beside the Morganton Road." It was also decided that the property adjacent to the public buildings and the cemetery would belong to the pastor.

The first cemetery was located directly across from the church on Rodoret Street. Shortly after this first cemetery was established, the church cemetery was changed to its present location at Carolina and Praly Streets. Two children were buried in the first cemetery. The first was Benjamin Tron, born in 1885, died October 19, 1893, the son of Jacques Henri and Marianna (née Micol) Tron. His death was the first in the colony, and his body was never removed from the first cemetery. The second burial in the first cemetery was that of Zeline Fanny Pons, born on June 14, 1894, died on October 20, 1896, daughter of Albert and Jeanne (née Pons) Pons. This child's body was removed to the present cemetery upon the death of her brother Henry (1896-1897), and both are buried in the family plot in the present cemetery. Records show that the second death was that of Henriette Marie Micol, born November 12, 1893, died December 14, 1893, daughter of Jaubert and Jeanne (née Pons) Micol. According to Antoine Grill's genealogical record, this infant's burial was the first in the present cemetery. Mr. Grill's record also indicates that the first death of an adult was that of Margaret Barus Léger, wife of Jean Jacques Léger, on March 8, 1895. She was interred in the present cemetery. These facts show that the present cemetery location was chosen shortly after the first was designated.

Before leaving for Italy to return to his own pastorate, on July 2, 1893, Pastor Tron conducted a service of the Lord's Supper, consecration, baptism and farewell. The baptismal service was for the infant daughter of Antoine Martinat, who was named Amélie, born in Ogden, Utah, December 6, 1892, the first child of the colonists to be consecrated. Pastor Tron's service was concluded with special prayer entrusting the assembled colonists to God and to His care.

During Dr. Tron's stay with the colonists, he called almost daily meetings of the colony. Concerning affairs being settled, he recorded all transactions from the first day. Fortunately these records were continued by succeeding pastors and, in the absence of a pastor, by the elders so that the church has an almost unbroken record from the beginning. Dr. Tron's records are written entirely in the French language, and the original record is entitled *Livre des Procès Verbaux et des Documents se référant à la foundation de la Valdese Corporation. 1893-94 No. 1.* (Book of Minutes and Documents relative to the Founding of the Valdese Corporation).

After the departure of Pastor Charles Albert Tron, the Pastor Enrico Vinay arrived in July 1893 to serve the colonists as their pastor and leader. The pastor's salary of $50 per month was provided by the American Missionary Society of the Congregational Church, which had done considerable work in the North Carolina mountains. This Society also provided a small contribution for the schoolmaster, Michel Auguste Jahier. All this was arranged by Pastor Charles Albert Tron in his energetic efforts to assist the colonists both materially and spiritually.

Separation of church from secular activities was difficult, and the two intertwined. The church was assigned the important duty of treasurer of the Valdese Corporation, and it also had to oversee and organize the public education of the Waldensian children, who were not conversant in the English language.

Pastor Vinay served the colonists barely ten months. During his tenure, he, along with the colonists, endured arduous days in their superhuman effort to uphold morale in spite of many privations and discouragements of the parish. In August of 1893, he welcomed a group of Waldensians from Utah who joined the Valdese colonists, as well as fourteen more from the Waldensian Valleys; also, 178 more from the Valleys in November. All in all, by the end of that year the colonists totaled 225.

December 1893 was memorable for two outstanding events: the visit of Dr. Matteo Prochet and the celebration of the colonists' first Christmas in the New World. Dr. Prochet was a well-known individual for his dedicated services. He was twice knighted by King Humbert for distinguished services to the Italian Republic and was chairman of the Committee of Evangelization of the Waldensian Church. He had been sent to America to raise funds for the work of evangelization of the Church and to visit the colonies in North and South America. He arrived in Morganton on Saturday, December 23, and was entertained in the home of Mr. Scaife. The following day he was taken to Valdese, where he conducted religious services. He was enthusiastically received. At the boundary of the colony lands, he was greeted by over one hundred Waldensian children drawn up in ranks, who sang a song of welcome as his carriage approached. He spent a week in Valdese, taking part in the Christmas celebration; examining the lands, the colony accounts, and the records; visiting all the families; and making plans for the future management of the colony.

This first Christmas celebration in Valdese in 1893 proved a happy occasion. It was arranged by several women of Morganton and other cities. These women came to Valdese on Christmas and

FIRST CHRISTMAS OF THE WALDENSES AT VALDESE — 1893

New Year's Day to distribute gifts. The many donated items consisting of books, toys and articles of clothing were most happily received. Dr. Prochet, who was present at both celebrations, talked to the children as they came forward to receive gifts.

The Presbyterian Church in the United States began to show an interest in the new movement in Valdese. In October 1893, Pastor Vinay attended the meeting of the Synod of North Carolina of the Presbyterian Church U.S., where he was introduced as a member of the Waldensian Synod. Pastor Vinay addressed the assemblage in French. This was the first official interaction between the Waldensian Church in Valdese and the Presbyterian Church U.S.

The first marriage in the parish was conducted by Pastor Vinay before his departure. This wedding occurred on April 29, 1894, uniting John Long, son of Henri François Long and the late Susanne (née Jahier) Long, and Marguerite Gaydou, daughter of Marie (née Baret) Gaydou, widow.

In early May 1894, Pastor Vinay resigned his pastorate and left for California. Pastor Charles Albert Tron arrived shortly after Vinay's departure and remained a month assuming temporary presidency of the colony. He organized a Moral and a Legal Board and attempted to reduce the severe financial burden of the newfound settlement by reducing the land purchase from 10,000 to 5,000 acres. The Legal Board, composed of nine members, three from Morganton and six from the colony, was in charge of the business affairs; the Moral Board, made up of the pastor, the elders and deputy members, was in charge of church affairs and also had to approve the financial transactions of the Legal Board. These two boards met frequently, separately and jointly, until their dissolution at the end of 1894, in conjunction with that of the Valdese Corporation.

In June 1894, the Pastor Barthélemy Soulier arrived with his bride Amélie (née Vinçon) to serve the colonists. First impressions of this young couple were reported as follows to Dr. George B. Watts in 1939:

> We found as a dwelling a hut of wood set upon some pieces of beams, made up of three rooms. Between one board and the next one could see daylight almost everywhere; an almost complete absence of furniture; the largest of our packing cases served as dining table, the smaller ones as chairs. In one corner a wooden bed, equipped only with a soiled mattress filled with straw, hard as wood, in which

> the mice had made their nest! One can imagine what comfort we could have in winter with the west wind! I remember that one morning (and doubtless more than one morning) I found a block of ice in the water pitcher, the loaf of fresh bread frozen, the eggs broken and frozen. — My pastoral duties were but little compared with all my other occupations; I had to serve as public secretary, interpreter, and very often justice of the peace. (52)

Pastor Soulier was a man of great energy, understanding, and foresight. He had been trained at the Waldensian Seminary and had done postgraduate work in Edinburgh, Scotland. He had a thorough knowledge of English, and was a practical man of affairs, intensely in love with his mission. He soon realized that the first organization of the colony was an impossibility and that many changes would have to be made if the venture of this colonization was to succeed. His seven years in Burke County were years of unflinching courage, consecration and untiring effort. During his pastorate, it can be said in all candor, the foundations for the future success of the colony were laid. Years later Soulier wrote to Dr. Watts:

> I worked there (I can say it with complete conscientiousness) with all my might and with the enthusiasm of a first love. I struggled much, suffered much, and received, thanks be to God, many satisfactions. But today my greatest satisfaction is that the colony finally triumphed over all its difficulties. My true and great reward before leaving this world is to know that my work has not been "in vain in the Lord." (53)

VALDESE IN THE SUMMER OF 1894
The large two-story building was built on the corner of Faet and Massel Streets soon after the arrival of the first colonists in May, 1893. It was used for meetings, church services, school, store and post office. The earliest group of colonists spent their first night in the white house on the hill known as the "brick house" because it had a brick chimney. The small house seen between the two railroad signs was the first manse, built on the corner of Rodoret and Massel Streets. The young boy grazing his cow was Louis Philippe Guigou, age 11.

Soulier spent the first few weeks in settling his house, visiting his parishioners, and becoming acquainted with colony affairs. He was not long in calling a meeting of the Moral Board. He informed the Board at this first meeting on July 16 that since the departure of Dr. Tron, the meetings of the two Boards had not been held regularly. He called for a joint meeting of the two Boards for July 21 and reminded the members that their task was a most difficult one, proposing a resolution that each one should exert every effort and

WALDENSIAN CHURCH SUNDAY SCHOOL GROUP — 1894

Right hand corner: Prof. Auguste Jahier, Louise Pons (seated), Esther Tron (seated), Frank Refour (on the ground): Henri François Long (superintendent of the Sunday school), Mrs. François Barus and baby, Louis Long, Stephen Guigou (seated), Rev. Henri Vinay (pastor of the church), Louis Philippe Guigou, Ceasar Pons, Henry Vinay, Margaret Prochet, Judith Pons, Italia Mourglia, (unrecognized), Charlie Long (standing), (unrecognized), Helen Balmas, (unrecognized), Louis Jahier (Sunday school teacher). Top of steps: Frank Pons, Alexandre Pons of the (General) Jean Philippe Pons family, John Peter Pons, Anais Long, Lydia Léger, (unrecognized). Extreme right standing on the porch: Philippe Pons, François Pascal, David Pons, Edward Long, John Pons, Emmanuel Tron, (unrecognized), Lévi Long, Jean Grill, Stephen Richard (the small boy), François Garrou, Jean Louis Garrou, Phillip Pascal. Location: ARNAUD AVENUE between ITALY & RODORET STREET implore help from Heaven. It was decided to hold the Sunday afternoon services in turn in Valdese (area centrally located), the Hill (Bollinger's Chapel area), and Franklin (area of Flat Gap and beyond), with the fourth Sunday reserved for the smaller settlements of Gardiole, Prangins and the Chapel. It was voted to hold one service each month in Italian.

It was early in August 1894, when Pastor Soulier informed the Moral Board that he intended to use the fifty dollars allowed by the American Missionary Association for the pastor's salary for June to buy flour for the needy. On more than one occasion, Soulier purchased flour at his own expense and kept it in the manse to provide for the most desperate cases of need. It had become well known by September in North Carolina that the colony was in dire straits. The Second Presbyterian Church of Charlotte, North Carolina sent its pastor, Dr. Boyd, to investigate. The report to his congregation was that he had seen much suffering. The women of his church sent several large boxes of food and clothing which were received with much joy and happiness in Valdese. Plans for Sunday and day schools were made. On the thirty-first of August, the Moral Board announced that the colony day school would open on the second Monday in September in Valdese.

Michel Auguste Jahier served as teacher of the school in Valdese, which was held in the public building on the corner of Massel and Faet Streets. His small salary was paid by the American Missionary Association of the Congregational Church. Jahier taught under great handicap due to lack of supplies with which to teach and conduct classes to accommodate the different ages of the children. To teach the little ones, he would write on the blackboard, as clearly as possible, words and figures they were to learn to spell and read. In the absence of textbooks, he would write songs, the Lord's Prayer, or some verses of the Bible.

During their first year in Valdese, Pastor and Mrs. Soulier also assisted in the educational program. He conducted classes in English made up of young men and women who desired to go out into the public for gainful employment in other towns, and he wrote a letter to Secretary Ryder of the Missionary Society of the Congregational Church: "My seven or eight pupils give satisfaction." During the fall, Mrs. Soulier started a sewing class for all the girls above eight years of age.

During the months of December, January and February, the colony operated a school in a one-room building which it erected and equipped in Franklin, south of Valdese, near the Laurel Road. Antoine Grill served as master, receiving from Soulier $6 a month given by the treasurer of public education of Burke County.

In addition to Pastor Soulier's multiple duties, he conducted the center school for four months during the school year 1894-1895. The "center" school we assume to be the meeting house located at the corner of Massel Avenue and Faet Street southwest. The church's affiliation with the Presbyterian Church in the United States in 1895 resulted in the end of assistance given by the American Missionary Society of the Congregational Church to the schools of Valdese. This end of assistance resulted in much gratis work by individuals qualified to teach the basics. Michel Auguste Jahier continued his services without pay. Others received minimum pay from church funds. Those qualified to teach, in addition to Pastor Soulier and Professor Jahier, were Antoine Grill, Étienne Perrou and Antoine Martinat. The education of the Waldensian children was of paramount importance in the heart of the pastor and of his helpers. All effort was made to teach the children despite the lack of facilities and the language barrier. The Waldensian children responded readily to instruction and were soon able to join the native children in public school curricula.

From the *History of the Women's Auxiliary and the Women of the Church* by Mrs. Louis Philippe Guigou (Lillian Sweeney), we quote:

> During the year 1895, Mrs. Marguerite S. Grant, a woman of some means, moved to Valdese from Summit, New Jersey. Mrs. Grant was Italian by birth and a convert from the Roman Catholic Church; she was a refined, cultured woman. She befriended the colonists and was beloved by all. Her ability to converse fluently in French enabled her to render valuable assistance to the teachers and those working among the Waldensians. It was she who purchased the "Palmer House" which many years later became the Waldensian Presbyterian Church manse.

In addition to Mrs. Grant's benevolent endeavors among the colonists, she was instrumental in establishing a small boarding and industrial school near Glen Alpine, North Carolina, with the assistance of a brother-in-law. This school was known as the Glen Alpine Spring School, and many Waldensian children were able to attend as boarding students.

Of interest also in the early history of the Waldensian Church in Valdese, Dr. Watts reports in *The Waldenses of Valdese*:

> On Sunday, April 21, 1895, the colony was visited by Secretary Roy of the American Missionary Association. His address to the congregation in English was translated into French by Soulier. He attended the sessions of the Sunday School, the morning service with communion, and the preaching service in the afternoon, noting that all services were in French, with Italian being used interchangeably with it. Secretary Roy was on a tour through the South, where there were many missionary churches with workers, like Soulier and Jahier, under the commission of the American Missionary Association of the Congregational Church. At this time the Valdese church was known as the Evangelical Waldensian Church, the colonists considering themselves a Waldensian congregation in the United States. (64)

From Ippolite Salvageot's diary dated January 1, 1895, through July 31, 1895, we quote: "Sunday, June 9, Fine weather. The congregation voted to put the Valdese church with the Presbyterian Church South." and on Sunday, June 30, "Fine weather. All the colons (French for colonists) signed to be with the Presbyterian Church." This was a momentous decision in the history of the Waldensian Church in Valdese, reached after much consideration and prayer. Inasmuch as the Waldensian Church has a Presbyterian form of organization and the Congregational Church had no representation in North Carolina, it was decided to unite with the Presbyterian Church in the United States. This was the most important step in the history of the church. On July 9, 1895, the Waldensian Presbyterian Church was officially received by Concord Presbytery. The pastor's salary of $50 a month was paid for several years by the Presbyterian Board of Home Missions. It is interesting to note that the identity of the Waldensian settlers as an organized evangelical church group has been maintained throughout its history in the New World by retention of the name "Waldensian" with that of "Presbyterian," hence Waldensian Presbyterian Church.

Ippolite Salvageot, from whose diary much information has been obtained, was from the Waldensian parish of Rora and, with his two sons, Robert and Alexandre, was among the group who came in

November 1893. He was a widower and the only one of the colonists conversant in the English language. His fluency in English was a great asset to the colonists. He was the first Waldensian appointed postmaster in Valdese in 1895 by the Postmaster General of the United States. His diary has proved a valuable source of historical information about everyday experiences of the settlers.

After the dissolution of the Valdese Corporation on January 1, 1895, Pastor Soulier was able to devote more time to church affairs. His first priority was to lead the colonists in building a church. Early in 1895 the congregation decided to begin as soon as possible. It is recorded that in April 1895 an important source of revenue for the colonists was the work, supervised by Soulier, of getting out stone and sand for the future construction of a church and for the enlargement of the manse. By September, the monthly payroll for that work amounted to about thirty dollars; a day's labor was paid at the rate of fifty cents. Funds for paying the wages were taken from monies contributed by individual friends of the colony, collections from certain churches, and from rentals.

Other important decisions were made in 1895 and 1896. The affiliation with the Presbyterian Church in the United States in 1895 gave the Valdese church a much needed source of support from a nearby larger church body. Ties with the Waldensian Church of Italy remained strong, however, and loyalty to the Mother Church influenced many decisions made by the Waldensian Presbyterian Church for several decades. For example, in 1896, the congregation voted to follow the constitution of the Waldensian Church in regards to the examination of newly elected elders and deacons on matters of doctrine and conduct rather than the slightly different policy of the Presbyterian Church U.S.

On December 5, 1896, the practice was begun to elect one elder from each of three districts. The districts were defined as follows: the first district, known as "Chapelle-Colline" or "Chapel," was composed of all the families living south of the railroad; the second district, known as "Ville" or "Town," was composed of all families living to the left of the road that led to "Balsille" (now Laurel Street North), including the families in town; and the third district, known as "Gardiole," was composed of all the families living to the right of the road to "Balsille." At the congregational meeting to elect three elders and one deacon, voting members from each district elected a nominee, and the three nominees were voted on by the entire body of voting members. The deacon was elected at large.

LAYING OF THE CORNERSTONE OF THE CHURCH — February 17, 1897

Voting members were male members of the church, twenty-one years of age and older who had contributed to the church according to their means and had notified the session of their desire to be voting members. A revised list showed thirty-eight voting members at the end of 1896.

In December 1896, the congregation repealed an earlier decision to require new colonists who arrived after the dissolution of the Valdese Corporation to pay any specified sum of money to become church members.

In 1895, the congregation had made definite plans to construct a church. For the next several years, Pastor Soulier traveled extensively to solicit financial assistance which resulted in a gratifying response. He had a detailed drawing of the plans for the church made by a Mr. Munsch, an architect in New York so that a chief mason could direct the building of the church. The work on the church began on December 14, 1896, with the workmen receiving five cents per hour. On February 17, 1897, amid solemn rejoicing and in the presence of many visiting dignitaries and friends from surrounding areas, the cornerstone was laid. The date February 17 was chosen for this ceremony as it represents the Waldensian day of celebration of the issuance of the Edict of Emancipation, which granted to them civil and political liberty on February 17, 1848. Dr. Watts describes the occasion as reported to him:

> The ceremonies began in the wooden chapel with prayer and song. Then the assembly went, two by two, led by two representatives of Bethany Church, Philadelphia, Messrs. Wright and Woodrow, who bore Italian and United States flags, to the spot on which the church was to be erected. After seats had been found on stones, timbers and boards, the service began with prayer, Scripture reading, and hymns. Soulier then preached a sermon appropriate to the occasion, taking his text from Psalm XXXVII, 4-5. Wright placed the cornerstone in position. Within the stone were placed copies of the New Testament in French, Italian and English; a short history of the colony with the names of 120 members of the church; several Italian and United States coins, and a photograph of Pastor Soulier . . . . The Reverend John M. Rose, Jr. (pastor of the Presbyterian Church of Morganton, North Carolina), then preached a historical sermon, stressing the emancipation of the Waldenses on February 17, 1848.

Years of Struggle

> The choir, under the direction of Jean Jacques Léger, sang hymns. The exercises were then concluded by words of thanks by the pastor to those who had come from near and far, a hymn, and the benediction pronounced by Rose. (69-70)

Practically all the work of construction of the church was done by the colonists with intermittent periods of inactivity during 1897 and 1898. Approximately thirty-six men were employed as builders and helpers. The church was completed in late October 1898.

We add this interesting note: the workers employed in the first major enlargement of the sanctuary in 1990-91 were amazed at the size of the stones and of the timbers used in the construction of the original building.

Prior to the completion of the sanctuary, Watts says,

> Soulier made frequent trips to collect funds, and conducted voluminous correspondence with prospective givers. The unpublished "Memoirs" of Hippolite Salvageot contain many references to the Pastor's visits for this purpose: to Morganton, Davidson College, Mooresville, Newton, Connelly Springs, North Carolina; to Richmond, Virginia; and to Philadelphia, Pennsylvania, where he and Mrs. Soulier spent several months from November 2, 1898, during which time he traveled also to Ohio and Michigan. On March 30, 1899, Mrs. Soulier returned to Valdese with an infant son. Soulier was again in his pulpit April 16 and recounted his experiences as collector. (71)

According to Dr. Watts,

> It was several months after the completion of the church that it could be furnished. Many of the furnishings, several of which were gifts, were made in North Carolina. The doors were apparently made in Valdese by the local carpenters. The windows were manufactured in Hickory and arrived in Valdese on September 8, 1898. The pews, which were a gift of the Brigham family of East Orange, New Jersey, were made in High Point. Mr. Snow of the Snow Lumber Company of High Point presented the pulpit. Scaife gave 200 books. A Mrs. Green of Baltimore furnished a communion table. William Wright of the

WALDENSIAN WOMEN IN FRONT OF CHURCH UNDER CONSTRUCTION — FALL 1897
Seated L-R: Marie Pons (Jean) Refour, Susanne Pons (Jean) Pascal, Adèle Bouchard (baby), Henriette Perrou (Etienne) Bouchard, Césarine Jahier (Henri F.) Long. Standing L-R: Marguerite Grill (Antoine) Grill, Louise Pons (Jean Henri) Pascal.

DEDICATION OF THE COMPLETED CHURCH — JULY 4, 1899

> Bethany Church, Philadelphia, gave $85 for the bell, which reached Valdese on August 14, 1899, and was hung in the steeple on the following September 11. William E. Dodge of New York sent $100 and a French Bible. A Mrs. Atkinson of Atlantic City, New Jersey, supplied a communion service, made up of a silver tankard and two silver goblets. (74-75)

Other items donated are preserved in the historical collection of the church. Among the items is a "coffin robe," or throw, used to cover the crude pine boxes for the dead as they were hauled in farm wagons or ox carts to the cemetery. The robe is made of heavy black broadcloth, bound with a silver cord. It has a large "W" embroidered in white in one corner and a "C" in another. It is thought that these initials stand for "Waldensian Church." There is no record of the donor or number of times it was used.

Quoting from Dr. Watts' book: "To the Synod of North Carolina in 1899, the pastor reported that the church 'cost nearly $5,000.' According to Salvageot's 'Memoirs,' however, Soulier announced to the congregation on June 3, 1900, that 'it cost altogether about $6,000'" (75).

The new church building of Romanesque architecture was completed after many hours of contributed hard labor. The Waldenses chose their adopted country's day of celebration of independence from British rule as the date appropriate for the dedication of their church. This event took place on July 4, 1899 before an assemblage from neighboring towns who had come by train, on foot, on horseback, and in carriages. The church was filled when the six pastors who were to take part in the ceremony of dedication arrived and were seated on the platform. After congregational singing in English led by a Waldensian quartet, Soulier pronounced the invocation. The choir, directed by Jean Jacques Léger and accompanied by one of the teachers, Miss Abbott, rendered a hymn. After reading of Scripture, the pastor placed a Bible upon the pulpit. This Bible was a gift from a Mrs. Miller of Newark, New Jersey. The Reverend John M. Rose, Jr. offered the dedicatory prayer. Soulier preached in French and in English. Other pastors followed with laudatory remarks for the Waldensians of North Carolina and of the Waldensian Valleys. Between the remarks of the visiting ministers, there were selections by the school children who sang in English.

On the happy occasion of the dedication, among the six visiting pastors was the Reverend James Alston Ramsay, pastor of the Presbyterian Church of Hickory, North Carolina, who was also Moderator of Concord Presbytery. In addition to addressing the congregation, he presented to the Waldenses an American flag. Also of note, the Reverend Ramsay's son, Julius McNutt Ramsay, Sr., who years later became a resident of Valdese and a member of the Waldensian Presbyterian Church, was the first non-Waldensian elected elder of the church in 1935.

After the dedication of the completed church, Pastor Soulier remained in Valdese one more year. He resigned on June 3, 1900 at a meeting at which he reported that the church debt was paid in full. He was officially transferred from Concord Presbytery to the Waldensian Church of Italy on July 31, 1900. The resignation of the colonists' devoted pastor was accepted with much sorrow. Pastor and Mrs. Soulier proved they were admirably dedicated to their calling. In addition to their devotion to the colonists in their difficult beginning years of adjustment and privation, they, too, suffered great personal loss in the untimely deaths of their two infant sons: William David in 1897, and Willie D. in 1899. Both are buried in the Waldensian cemetery.

Pastor Soulier's farewell sermon was preached on September 16, 1900. He recommended to the grace of God the colonists and his successor. It is recorded that on September 19 the congregation met for the last time under his direction. He addressed to his flock "a warm and touching appeal, in which he exhorted it to follow the Good Shepherd." (Watts, 76). Expressions of gratitude were given for the services of Mr. and Mrs. Soulier. A Waldensian wrote to the editor of *L'Écho des Vallées Vaudoises:*

> Almost the entire colony was present at these two services.... On the day of departure, September 20, 1900, a farewell dinner, that was attended by practically every head of a family, was given in Soulier's honor. Many toasts were offered. The wine which "rejoiced the hearts of the diners" was made from the grapes harvested by the colonists. After the dinner all accompanied Soulier to the schoolroom to await the five o'clock train. His last official act was the balancing of the account books and the turning over to the elders the sum of forty-three dollars. An eyewitness wrote: "The hour approaches. Mr. Soulier gives to each male a farewell kiss. To the women he gives a hearty hand-shake. Mr. Soulier is very much moved.

Tears moisten and redden his eyes. I notice that many men and women also have tears which flow along their cheeks. Some are weeping bitterly .... Mr. Barthélemy Soulier will not forget the twentieth of September, the affectionate demonstration of the Waldensian colonists of North Carolina, the touching farewells and the loving wishes of the crowd which represented the whole colony." (Watts, 77)

This touching expression of affection, esteem and respect was a sincere tribute to the departing leader and pastor who strove to do his duty; by his energy, his perseverance, and his patience, he was able to disentangle the material affairs of the colony and to erect such a beautiful church for the colonists of Valdese, North Carolina.

At a meeting of the Synod of North Carolina on November 13, 1900, the following tribute was paid to Pastor Soulier: "The colony has been greatly blessed under the efficient management and ministry of Brother Soulier. The people now have a beautiful house of worship completed and entirely free from debt." The services of this dedicated pastor left their mark on Valdese for all time to come.

---

[1] All the five women in this group were expectant mothers and gave birth to the following children:
Charles Guigou, born August 13, 1893; died 1964. Son of Jean and Catherine (Guigou) Guigou.
Scafe Henry Tron, born August 15, 1893; died August 10, 1894. Son of Pierre and Louise (Pons) Tron.
Frank W. Richard, born August 28, 1893. Son of Philippe and Marianna (Ribet) Richard.
Henriette Marie Micol, born November 12, 1893; died December 14, 1893. Daughter of Jaubert and Jeanne (Pons) Micol.
Marguerite Junine Tron, born January 21, 1894; died July 4, 1991. Daughter of François and Marguerite (Garrou) Tron.

[2] The translation of the church minutes quoted in this work was done by W.W. Kibler (No. 1) and Dr. Cathy R. Pons, Professor of French at Indiana University, (No. 2) 1987.

CELEBRATION OF THE GLORIOUS RETURN — AUGUST 15, 1900

Location: Below present museum — Pastor Barthélemy Soulier is seated in middle of the group. — First Row (Seated) L-R: Frederic Meytre, (seven boys unrecognized), Pastor Barthélemy Soulier, (six children unrecognized), Margaret Tron, (unrecognized), Jean Refour (Père), Jean Henri Pascal (Gardiole) with son Henry J. Pascal, Marie Pons Refour, François Refour, Jean Refour, Susanne Pons Pascal. Second Row (standing) L-R: Margaret Barét Ribet with infant Césarine Ribet, Alexandre Ribet, Janie Ribet, Ferdinand Ribet, Césarine Léger Meytre, Marguerite Garrou Tron, (unrecognized), (unrecognized), Catherine Guigou Guigou with infant John Daniel Guigou, (next nine unrecognized), Jean (Bobo) Garrou, Marie Pons Garrou with daughter Marianne Garrou, Henri Peyronel, Louise Pons Pascal, Albert Pons, Alexandre Vinay with son Henry Vinay, (next two unrecognized), François Tron (Père), Barthélemy Pons. Third Row (L-R): Jean Pierre Peyronel, Jean Daniel Mourglia, Philippine Odin Mourglia, Catherine Genre-Bert Ribet, Jean Rodolphe Ribet, Jean Jacques Léger, (unrecognized), (unrecognized), Jeanne Tron Pons, Jean Henri Pons, Henri François Long, Césarine Jahier Long, Jean Garrou (Père), Marie Anne Massel Garrou, (unrecognized), (unrecognized), Marie Madeleine Giraud Micol with baby Alice Micol. On white horse: Robert Salvageot

CHAPTER 3

BUILDING ON THE FOUNDATION—
The Best of Two Worlds
1901-1917

"In whom all the building fitly framed together groweth unto an holy temple in the Lord." Ephesians 2:21

The congregation begins the process of Americanization while still remembering their beginnings and the teachings of their fathers.

The departure of Pastor Soulier marked the end of the period of greatest hardship and struggle for survival in the Waldensian Colony. Some of the colonists had left Valdese to find better economic opportunities elsewhere, but the majority had remained and had established themselves on the land they labored to purchase. The town began to grow. The church had been built in the heart of the village.

The turn of the century signaled the beginning of a time of building on the foundation laid in the early years. The new church gave a more worshipful atmosphere to church services and provided space for more church activities. The organization and leadership of the church was strengthened. Financial resources were still meager, but strong efforts were made to build up the church treasury.

Recorded minutes of church meetings are not available from July 1899 to January 1901. It was during this time, however, that discussion began concerning the sale of the lots which had been appropriated to the church at the time of the dissolution of the Valdese Corporation. It was difficult for the church members to agree on the terms of sale. In his "Memoirs," Ippolite Salvageot stated on March 4, 1900, that "Mr. Soulier and Mr. Garrou (Jean, père) resigned as trustees for the church lots, and Jaubert Micol resigned as Deacon." Then Salvageot added on March 31, "Thursday night, a meeting was held here, about one dozen Waldensians, concerning the lots of Valdese. No arrangement could be made. For the present they are to be left as it is now, that is to say, for pasture and going to decay. This is a regular shame for the people of the place."

There was an unsuccessful attempt to elect two new trustees on Sunday, July 1, 1900. It was not until early 1901, after Pastor Garrou's arrival, that these lots began to be sold and the church treasury was built up as a result. In the meantime, some money continued to be raised from these lots by renting them for grazing and by selling the wood.

Pastor Henri Garrou arrived from Italy on December 19, 1900. He joined other family members who had arrived in 1893: his father, Jean Garrou (père) and his brothers, Jean (Bobo) Garrou and François Garrou. His arrival coincided with the festive Christmas celebration at the church. Under the leadership of Mrs. Marguerite Grant and two missionary teachers, Miss Knox and Miss LeDuc, the children presented a program of recitations and songs in French, Italian, and English.

Pastor Garrou found the colony in good condition. In a letter to Dr. Prochet, whose last visit to Valdese had been in 1894, he wrote:

> Almost all the colonists have houses with the first floor of stone and the rest of wood. They have acquired a real talent in the art of house building . . . . All or almost all have fifteen or twenty acres under cultivation . . . . There are some fine vineyards . . . . They have harvested wheat and Indian corn in quantities sufficient for their needs. The greatest difficulty is the lack of trade. To offset this, the young people have to leave the colony to go to various southern cities and even to New York. Things are going well in the church. The services are attended with great regularity. (Watts, 78-79)

Pastor Garrou also noted that many families who had lived on mountain farms had moved nearer to the center so that the colony was more unified.

The first congregational meeting under Pastor Garrou's direction was held on January 20, 1901. At that meeting, two elders were elected, Henri Long from the "Chapel" district and Henri Vinay from the "Town" district. Antoine Grill was elected deacon. Jean Henri Pascal from the "Gardiole" district was also serving as elder at this time.

At the annual congregational meeting on June 2, 1901, the report was given of the sale of four acres of the church land to the owners of the Waldensian Hosiery Mill for $40. The owners were Jean (Bobo)

Garrou, François Garrou, and Antoine Grill. Cash on hand in the church treasury was then $122.62.

Following the sale of this land to the hosiery mill, the church lots were sold rapidly from 1901 through 1903. The lots were numbered, and the name of the buyer of each lot and the amount paid are recorded in the church minutes. The first lots were all sold for $20 each, but later lots were auctioned, with the lowest bid usually set for $20. Some of the property sold for only $50 for three lots, while other lots were sold for as much as $35 each. It is understandable that there was bickering and jealousy among the colonists as they vied for the purchase of these valuable town lots. In February 1902, a dispute over the responsibilities of the trustees and the session in the sale of the lots led to the resignation of both trustees. Later the same year, a disagreement between two elders caused them both to resign. In a few weeks, the only remaining elder resigned, leaving the church with no elders for a short period of time.

In spite of the difficulties, the work of the church went on with regular worship services, Sunday School, day school, classes for catechumens, and additions to the church membership. In his "Memoirs," Ippolite Salvageot wrote on February 17, 1903, "A grand dinner took place at the School House, about 40 Waldensians present, today being the 55th anniversary of the Emancipation of the Waldensians of Italy. The dinner cost about fifty cents each." This was the first record made of a February 17 dinner, a tradition that continues to the present day.

During his brief pastorate, Pastor Garrou did not represent the church of Valdese at the sessions of the Synod of North Carolina. He had been admitted to Concord Presbytery from the Waldensian Church of Italy on April 16, 1902. In the Annual report to the Presbytery for that year, it is recorded:

> Rev. H. Garrou has charge of the important and encouraging work at Valdese. The colony of Waldensians is in a prosperous condition. Two services are conducted each Sunday, and regular Wednesday evening prayer meeting is observed. A good day school is taught by teachers provided by the Northern Presbyterian Church. There have been ten additions to the church during the last year. Brother Garrou writes: "The Waldensians find their best pleasure in their church and they wish to express all their gratitude to the many friends in North Carolina who helped them so kindly in the support of their pastor. Be

yourself our interpreter and tell all our friends that we are not ungrateful to those who love us." (Watts, 82)

At the congregational meeting on May 31, 1903, Pastor Garrou announced his resignation to accept a position at McDonald, Pennsylvania. According to Salvageot, Pastor Garrou's farewell sermon was on Sunday, June 21. He later visited Valdese and served as preacher on several occasions when the pulpit was vacant.

In the months following the departure of Pastor Garrou, the work of the church, both spiritual and secular, was carried on by Elders Henri Long and J. Henry Pascal (Bienvenue) and Deacon Antoine Grill. They led the Sunday services and continued the sale of the church lots. The practice of lending varying sums of money to church members at 5% annual interest was common at this time as another means to earn money for the church treasury.

The search for a replacement for Pastor Garrou was hindered by the small yearly salary of $400, paid in full by the Committee of Synodical Home Missions. In the first two years of the colony, a pastor's salary of $600 and a small salary for teacher Michel Auguste Jahier had been paid by the Congregational Church. The Presbyterian Church in the United States continued to pay the same amount for the pastor's salary after the affiliation with that denomination in 1895. By 1903, the salary had been reduced to $400. A congregational meeting was held on August 2 to find a means to augment the salary. It was decided to collect a voluntary contribution among those present, with a minimum contribution of $2. A sum of $70.75 was collected from thirty-one donors. The name of each contributor and the amount given are recorded in the minutes of the meeting.

MISSIONARY TEACHERS

From as early as 1894, the Waldensian colony in Valdese was fortunate to have several dedicated women to come to Valdese to teach the children and give other assistance. The first was Miss J.C. Palmer, an elderly lady of means and education from Philadelphia, Pennsylvania. She remained in the colony until March 1901, teaching the children and giving aid and advice to the women. Another woman of influence, Mrs. Marguerite S. Grant, came from Summit, New Jersey, in 1895. She was a talented lady of Italian extraction who spoke both English and French. She remained until early 1915.

Beginning with the school year 1896-1897, The Woman's Board of the Presbyterian Church in the United States of America (Northern) sent missionary teachers to conduct a day school for the children of the colony. These young women served under difficult circumstances. They were poorly housed, lacked adequate teaching facilities, and had to overcome language and cultural differences. Their invaluable service in the early struggling years of the colony continued until 1905.

THE WORK OF THE WOMEN IN THE EARLY YEARS

The Waldensian Presbyterian Church owes a great debt of gratitude to Mrs. Louis Philippe Guigou (Lillian Sweeney) for her long service as historian of the Women of the Church. Her *History of the Women's Auxiliary and the Women of the Church* gives a wealth of information about the history of the church not found in other sources. In the early years, records of the women's activities were not kept, except as sometimes mentioned in the session minutes. Mrs. Guigou devoted countless hours collecting material from diaries, news print, and personal contacts to write her account of the history.

Although women did not have active leadership roles in the church in the early years of the colony, they served as a guiding influence in the material growth and spiritual development of the church. Only the bedrock of deep spiritual strength acquired in childhood in the churches in the Waldensian Valleys made it possible for these women to endure the endless toil, the deprivation and the lonely harshness of this new land. Weekly worship provided the sole opportunity for spiritual nourishment and social interaction.

As time went by, the wives of the early pastors, namely Mrs. Barthélemy Soulier, Mrs. Filippo Ghigo and Mrs. Émile Henri Tron, gathered the women in groups for prayer, sewing and English study.

On November 28, 1903, Filippo Enrico Ghigo arrived from Canada to become pastor in Valdese. He was born in Prali, Italy, and educated at the Waldensian Theological Seminary in Florence and at the Universities of Berlin and Leipzig. After two years as a missionary in Switzerland, he served as pastor of Waldensian churches in Uruguay and Argentina. Shortly after going to Canada, he was persuaded by Dr. Prochet to come to Valdese. He preached his first sermon on December 6, 1903.

Pastor Ghigo's work was hindered somewhat by his poor health. The annual spring congregational meeting had to be postponed until October 2, 1904. He was able, however, to provide strong leadership for a full church program, which included two Sunday services, Sunday School, mid-week prayer service, and the Christian Union for the young people.

In her history of the women of the church, Mrs. Lillian Guigou states that the foundation for the women's work was laid by Pastor Ghigo and his capable wife Juliette. There were prayer services and sewing classes for the women. Interest in the education of the children led the women to begin collecting funds for a much-needed school building. Much of Pastor Ghigo's time was spent in acquiring funds to build this proposed school on church property. The school fund grew to $444.59. The fund became unnecessary when the Burke County Board of Education undertook the building of the school on a plot of land directly east of the church. The land for the school was conveyed to Burke County on December 27, 1905. Three hundred dollars of the school fund was given to Burke County, and

CHURCH AND SCHOOLHOUSE — c. 1910

the remainder was transferred to the church treasury in 1910. The two-room school house, which had been enlarged to six classrooms by 1923, was vacated at the opening of the new Valdese High School that year (the building now known as the Old Rock School).

On May 30, 1894, the Valdese Corporation had agreed to deed a lot across from the church to Miss Palmer. She contracted to have built a two-story, five-room frame house. At her death in 1903, she left the house to the Presbyterian (U.S.A.) Board of Home Missions. In 1905, the congregation of the Waldensian Presbyterian Church unanimously authorized the session to buy Miss Palmer's house for $300, without specifying at that time for what purpose the house would be used. The church sold the house the next year to Mrs. Marguerite Grant. In 1917, the church purchased the house again to be used for the manse. This second manse was located on the site of the present museum. The original manse, one of the earliest houses built in Valdese, faced the railroad on the corner of Massel and Rodoret Streets.

Although its affiliation with the Presbyterian Church, U.S. was successful and beneficial, the Valdese church still maintained strong ties to the Mother Church in Italy. Pastors were secured from the Waldensian Church, and its traditions and regulations were observed. At the congregational meeting on May 28, 1905, the congregation voted by a great majority to follow the new regulations of the Waldensian Church. Elder Henri Long opposed the decision and resigned from the session.

At the annual congregational meeting a year later on May 27, 1906, Elder Henri Pascal read a letter from Dr. Prochet asking the church members to increase their contribution to the pastor's salary. The results of this appeal are not recorded. The small salary no doubt influenced Pastor Ghigo to resign that year to go to Scranton, Pennsylvania.

Pastor Filippo Ghigo was succeeded in early 1907 by Pastor John Pons, a native of Massel, Italy, and brother of Albert Pons, one of the first arrivals in the colony. Pastor Pons was educated at the Waldensian Seminary of Florence and had held pastorates in Rodoret, Elba and Sardinia before coming to Valdese. During his pastorate, the Valdese church grew to forty-eight voting members.

Efforts were made to encourage church members to contribute to the pastor's salary. Several men were designated as collectors. In 1908, the sum of $110 was collected to add to the $300 given at this time by the North Carolina Synod's Committee of Home Missions.

In January, 1909, the cemetery was enclosed with a fence. Payment for the fence was made from a cemetery fund and by an assessment of $.75 from each owner of a plot. At about the same time, a pump was installed in the church well.

In 1909, Pastor Pons married Miss Lydia Jacumin, the daughter of Jean Jacques Jacumin and Virginie (née Peyronel), who had arrived in November, 1893. The newlyweds left immediately after their wedding to go to Scranton, Pennsylvania, where Pastor Pons began a new pastorate.

From the departure of Pastor John Pons on October 28, 1909, until December 12, 1913, the Waldensian Presbyterian Church was without a regular pastor. The small salary offered was the principal reason that the search for a pastor was unsuccessful for so long. Elders of the church preached the Sunday morning sermons when no minister was available. Among those who preached often were Jean Henri Pascal (Bienvenue) and Jean Henri Pascal (Gardiole). Morning worship was held every Sunday in spite of the lack of a regular pastor. The elders taught classes for catechumens as well, and these young people became church members.

Mrs. Peter Meytre (Margaret Pascal), who was a young girl at the time, recalls that the years the congregation had no pastor were hard for everyone. Sunday school classes for the children of various ages were held in different areas of the sanctuary, each class having its own teacher. French was used in Sunday school, and the children were expected to recite a new Bible verse in French each week. The Sunday School assembly began and ended with a Waldensian hymn and a prayer. Christian Union meetings, which were in English, were held on Sunday evenings for the young people.

Mrs. Meytre describes the road leading to town (from Gardiole) as being filled with children going to church on Sundays. "We were so happy together," she remembers. The adults did not attend Sunday School as a rule but went to morning worship. The children returned home after Sunday School to do chores and to finish preparing the noon meal. The church bell rang three times on Sunday mornings—once for Sunday School, once to begin morning worship, and again at the end of the service. Mrs. Meytre says that when the children at home heard the last tolling of the bell, they knew it was time to begin cooking the potatoes for Sunday dinner, to be ready when the parents arrived from church.

In the early days of the church, some of the men with fine voices led the singing without instrumental accompaniment. Later Mrs.

Marguerite Grant and the other missionary teachers who had musical training served as directors and accompanists. An organ with foot pedals was used for many years, and later an organ that could be pumped by hand was substituted. About 1909, a French choir was organized with Mrs. Henri F. Martinat (Bertha Stratton) at the organ.

The four years without a pastor were probably the most difficult in the history of the church. Discouragement and disunity grew as time went by. The regular program of the church was carried on, however, through the dedication of the session made up of Elders Jean Henri Pascal (Balsille), Henri Martinat (Pineburr), and Jean Henri Pascal (Bienvenue), and Deacons Antoine Grill and Jean Louis Garrou. These men did not waiver in their faithfulness throughout this trying period.

The services of several ministers were available for short periods of time, and the administration of the sacraments and ordination of church officers were planned accordingly. The Reverend Dugald Munroe, pastor of the Presbyterian churches in Glen Alpine and Marion, supplied the Valdese church for several weeks in the spring of 1910. Former Pastor Henri Garrou installed the officers named above on July 17, 1910 during a visit to Valdese. They were the first church officers elected at large and not by district, for a term of five years. In 1911, the church was supplied for a few weeks by former pastors Ghigo and Pons. Also in June, July, and August 1912, Pastor Ghigo preached regularly, and Pastor Pons occupied the pulpit in January 1913. Dr. C.A. Munroe of Hickory, Superintendent of Home Missions, preached frequently in Valdese during these years when there was no pastor. Small sums were paid to these ministers for their services.

Meanwhile the search for a pastor went on. On August 28, 1910, the congregation voted to contribute $300 to add to the $300 received from the Committee of Home Missions. A subscription list was started, and $145 was raised on the spot. At this meeting, the decision was made to sell the tract of land known as the "Pastor's Farm," which was located between Praly Street, Morganton Road, the Page farm, the Southern Railroad, and the land belonging to the hosiery mill.

The voting members met on February 5, 1911 to elect a pastor. A call was extended to Pastor Pierre Chauvie of the Waldensian Church of Rio Marina, Island of Elba. He refused the call. On December 10, 1911, the voting members decided to call Pastor P.E.

Monnet of Cleveland, Ohio, who also declined to accept.

The discouragement felt by the church members was openly expressed at the annual congregational meeting on June 2, 1912. Quoting from Dr. Cathy R. Pons' translation of the French minutes:

> ... the spiritual life the church is very close to being extinguished for lack of a minister, which would be most regrettable.... Mr. J.H. Pascal of La Gardiole said that he felt he voiced the feelings of all the church, and thanked the members of the session for all their efforts, particularly as concerned the Sunday School, the catechism, and the regular worship service each Sunday. The Moderator responded for the session, saying that the session members sustained themselves by remembering the words of Jesus Christ, "When you have accomplished all that is in your power, consider yourselves still as humble servants." He added that the members of the session appreciated greatly the congregation's expressions of affection and encouragement.

The Moderator was not clearly identified here, but most likely was J. Henri Pascal (Bienvenue), who usually served as Moderator and spiritual leader during this time.

At this same meeting, the congregation decided to send a letter to the Venerable Table of the Waldensian Church in Italy, asking that body to send a pastor soon, one who would be able to speak French and English. Almost five months later, no response had been received to several letters and a petition signed by the church members. Disappointed and frustrated, the session decided to make a last appeal to the Table on October 20, 1912.

An incident in March 1913 clearly showed the disunity resulting from the lack of a leader's influence. Elders Henri Martinat (Pineburr) and Jean Henri Pascal (Balsille) resigned because the session had received an anonymous letter postmarked Connelly Springs, "full of insolence and scorn." The writer soon revealed his identity; consequently, on March 30, 1913, Henri Martinat was re-elected elder. Jean Henri Pascal (Gardiole) was elected elder for the remaining vacancy.

Finally, on March 30, 1913, the congregation met to hear a letter the session had received from the Venerable Table. The Table demanded that the church guarantee the pastor a salary of $600 a year and $80 for travel expenses from Italy. The congregation approved the demands. At a session meeting the following day, the travel allowance was increased to $100. The minutes of these two meetings reflect a sense of relief and joy at the prospect of finally having a pastor.

In addition to directing a regular church program during the four years without a spiritual leader, the session managed the business affairs of the church. It met frequently, often two or three times a month, as the need arose. Congregational meetings were held several times a year. Careful minutes were kept of these meetings.

After the decision was made in 1910 to sell the tract of land on the west side of town known as the "Pastor's Farm," the session auctioned off the wood on the land. No part of the land was actually sold until late 1913. On December 8, 1913, the church sold to a Mr. Upchurch of Morganton ten acres of the farm along the railroad at $40 an acre to build a cotton mill. This $400 brought the total in the church treasury to nearly $2,000. The cotton mill later became Valdese Manufacturing Company.

In October 1911, a committee was given the responsibility of making needed repairs to the manse. Improvements were also made to the cemetery, especially in cleaning the grounds, improving the roads, and adding a gate to the west entrance. In the October 29, 1911 session minutes is found the first record of contributions to benevolent causes of the Presbyterian Church—$5 for Presbytery Home Missions, $4 for North Carolina Synod Home Missions, and $3 for the Orphans' Home (Barium Springs). Each year thereafter, regular contributions were sent from the church treasury. Financial assistance also was given to church families in need. Several loans of money from the church treasury were made to church members.

On October 23, 1913, Moderator Léger of the Waldensian Church in Italy wrote to Elder J. Henri Pascal that a pastor had been secured for the church in Valdese. The congregation met on November 16 to plan a means to raise the $300 required to pay the pastor. A voluntary pledge was instituted, with $200 pledged at the meeting. It was decided to take the remaining $100 from the church treasury.

Pastor Émile Henri Tron and his young wife arrived in Valdese on December 10, 1913. Pastor Tron was born in Massel, Italy. Educated at the Waldensian Seminary and in Edinburgh, Scotland, he was ordained in Torre Pellice, Italy, on September 4, 1911. He had served as assistant pastor in Palermo and Naples and as aide to Pastor E. Comba in Rome.

The session met with Pastor Tron for the first time on December 12, 1913. The minutes of that meeting state:

> Each member gave thanks to God and to the administrators of the Waldensian Church and a heartfelt welcome to our pastor. Pastor Tron thanked the session for having conducted services every Sunday during the four years that this church remained without a pastor, praising the session and the church for not having abandoned the worship services and for having continued the Sunday School without interruption. Pastor Tron said that all this had greatly influenced his decision to come and serve this church.

The coming of Pastor Tron and his wife brought great joy to the congregation as Pastor Tron quickly assumed the spiritual leadership of the church. Wednesday evening prayer services and the Christian Union were resumed. A special service was held in the church on February 17, 1914, to commemorate the 1848 Edict of Emancipation. Pastor Tron possessed a jovial personality which attracted the church members and children. His pastorate was one of warmth and friendship with the congregation.

On March 9, 1914, the session divided the remainder of the "Pastor's Farm" into lots, planned the streets, and gave the streets names. All the lots were to be sold, except for three lots which were to remain church property. At a public auction on April 18, 1914, the session directed the sale of the lots for varying sums, generally between $100 and $175. The lots were paid for largely in cash so that by July 1 a sum of nearly $1,700 had been added to the church treasury.

In the summer of 1914, the first renovation of the church since it was completed in 1899 was begun. It was necessary to lay a new floor, raise it about two feet, and install vents for air circulation. The ceiling was stained with oak stain, and the interior and exterior walls were white washed. The pews were treated with crude oil. A coal-burning stove was purchased. A special fund was collected to install gas lighting. Each member was to contribute $1 or one day's labor to the cost of renovation. With free labor, the sale of old flooring, and contributions, the renovations cost less than $400. The work was completed in early 1915. The financial situation of the church had improved greatly. After payment of all the bills for repairs of the church, over $3,300 remained in the church treasury.

Mr. François Parise with his mule removing dirt from inside the church when the floor was raised in 1914.

The three years of Pastor Tron's stay were marked by change and growth. In December 1914, the Valdese church voted to adopt changes in liturgy recommended by the Waldensian Church in Italy. One change called for silent individual confession of sins and singing after group confession. This practice was discontinued after several months. The decision was also made to take up offerings in the pews rather than at the door, as was the custom. At the congregational meeting on May 30, 1915, the Every Member Canvass proposed by the General Assembly of the Presbyterian Church was approved. These last two changes were not actually put into practice for several years.

Efforts were made to encourage members who were continually absent to attend worship services. Those who continued to be absent after repeated invitations were removed from the list of voting members. The revised roll included forty-nine voting members at the end of 1914. By 1916, the church had grown to fifty-six voting members and 169 total communicants. That year $151 was contributed to benevolent causes of the Presbyterian Church by the church and Sunday School.

On April 2, 1916, Pastor Tron informed the session that he had been called to serve in the Italian Army. He submitted his resignation on April 9. Before his departure, he actively assisted the session in securing Pastor Filippo Enrico Ghigo as pastor for the church.

Pastor Filippo Enrico Ghigo arrived in Valdese on June 7, 1916 to begin his second pastorate of the Waldensian Presbyterian Church. During his brief term of service, the church raised several sums of money for causes of the Mother Church in Italy. The women became more active; in the World War I years of 1916-1917, many engaged in knitting for the Red Cross. A bazaar was held in 1917 in connection with the February 17 Celebration. This event raised $200, which the women sent to Italy for the orphanage at Torre Pellice and for the Waldensian Committee for Assistance of the Military. The Women's Bazaar was an annual event for a number of years and made it possible for the women to give to causes of their choice.

By 1917, the church had increased its contribution to the pastor's salary to $325. Over $300 was given that year to benevolences of the Presbyterian Church.

After June 17, 1917, no minutes were recorded for the remainder of the year. Pastor Ghigo's illness worsened, and he died in an Asheville hospital on December 16, 1917. His widow Juliette and children Anita and Francis continued to live in Valdese.

WALDENSIAN PRESBYTERIAN CHURCH SUNDAY SCHOOL — ABOUT 1915 — First Row L-R: Charlie Pons, Francis Garrou, William Perrou, Henry Long, Emmanuel Pons, Frank Tron, Harriet Martinat, Mary Pascal, Jeanette Garrou (child in front), Louis Vinay, Ermeline Pascal, Elda Pascal, Isabelle Salvageot, Alice Pons, Lena Pons, Mary Louise Guigou. Second Row L-R: Margaret Pascal, Elizabeth Ribet, Louise Gaydou, Leon Guigou, Mary Tron, Nelle Garrou, Lena Salvageot, Mary Martinat, Amandine Bouchard, Mary Grill, Julia Pascal, Susie Martinat, Celine Pons. Third Row L-R: Cesarine Ribet, Christine Mourglia, Annie Garrou, Henry Pascal, Henry Perrou, Helen Long, Anna Bounous, Levi Ribet, Antonio Grill, Rev. Emile Tron, Mary Refour, Marianne Garrou, Janie Ribet, Anita Micol, Emily Parise, Rachel Perrou, Henriette Ribet, Emma Pascal. Fourth Row L-R: Edward Micol, Silvio Pons, Benjamin Pons, Ben Grill, Henri Guigou, Emile Jacumin, Edmond Pascal, Onesime Pons, Frederic Pons, Henry Garrou, Henry Salvageot, Silvio Martinat, John Guigou, Alfred Pascal, Willie Garrou.

CONGREGATION OF THE WALDENSIAN PRESBYTERIAN CHURCH — 1915 — First Row L to R: Pierre Emmanuel Micol, Jean Parise, Sr., Etienne Perrou, Louise LaPise Gaydou Léger, Marguerite Micol Pons and son Willie Pons, Marie Bounous Pascal and dtr. Mary (Bienvenue), Marguerite Grant, Marianne Micol Tron (of White Pine, Tenn.), Catherine Guigou Guigou Garrou, Philipine Odin Mourglia, Isabelle Salvageot Bright (child), Celestine Salvageot Salvageot, Catherine Genre-Bert Ribet, Lena Salvageot Eason (child), Marguerite Baret Ribet, Cesarine Jahier Long, Catherine Ribet Parise, Madeleine Giraud Micol, Marie Pons Refour, Suzanne Pons Pascal, Jeanne Pascal Pascal, Susanne Pascal Pons, Catherine Jacumin Bounous, Catherine Leger Griset, Suzette Bounous Vinay. Second Row L to R: Jean Daniel Mourglia, Jean Rudolphe Ribet, Jean Francois Tron, Antoine Grill, Henry Martinat, Bertha Stratton Martinat, Edith Wine Martinat, Emily Martinat Morrow, Janie Ribet Pons, Marianne Bounous Gaydou, Marianne Garrou Pons, Emily Parise Dentale, Anita Micol Pons, Laura Vigliano Tron, Christine Mourglia Baker, Anna Bounous Refour, Mary Refour Ogle, Jacques Bounous, Ida Pascal Bounous, Madeleine Tron Tise, Jean Jacques Jacumin, Jean Pons, (Bienvenue). Third Row L to R: Daniel Tron, Jean (Bo Bo) Garrou, Jean Garrou (Père), Henri Peyronel, Albert Pons, Barthélemy Bounous, Rev. Emile Tron, Jean Jacques Leger, Jean Henri Pascal (Bienvenue), Pierre Tron, Jean Henri Pascal (Balsille), Francois Perrou, Henri Perrou (Sr.) with son William Perrou, Jean Henri Pascal (Gardiole). Fourth Row L to R: Jaubert Micol, Albert Pons, Charles Martinat, Ernest Martinat, Mary Louise Tron Guigou with Jeanette (Dolly) Garrou Verreault, Henry Guigou, William E. Garrou, Silvio Martinat, Henry Long, Louis Vinay, Benjamin Pons, Emile Jacumin, Henry Perrou, Onesime Pons, John Pons, Silvio Pons.

Building on the Foundation

1915 — 15th OF AUGUST CELEBRATION — JEAN JACQUES LÉGER'S FARM BEYOND FLAT GAP — Seated L to R: Philippe Bounous with son Edwin, Mary Pascal, Julia Pascal, Mary Grill, Amandine Bouchard, Lydia Clot, Elda Pascal, Ermeline Pascal, Emanuel Pons, Henry (Campy) Pascal, Charlie Pons, Helen Long with niece Susie Bleynat, Oscar Clot, standing. First Row L to R: Felix Léger, Victor Léger, Frederic (Dick) Pons, Emily Léger, Catherine Ribet Parise, William (Willie) Pons, Zeline Pons, Margaret Pascal, Rachel Perrou, Anita Micol, Mary Refour, Janie Ribet, Emily Parise, Mary Long, Cesarine Ribet, Louise Gaydou, Henry J. Pascal, Jean Jacques Léger, Louise La Pise Gaydou Léger. Second Row L to R: Etienne Bouchard, Jaubert Micol, Barthélemy Bounous, Jean (Bobo) Garrou, Catherine Guigou Guigou Garrou, John Long, Leon Guigou, Henry Martinat (Hosiery), Henry Guigou, Bertha Stratton Martinat, Mary Parise Léger, Emily Martinat, Emanuel Jacumin, Mrs. Albert Clot and child, Walter Clot, Esther Clot, Felix Bounous, Philip Grill (L-R): William (Willie) E. Garrou, Marie Pons Refour, Rev. Emile Tron, Pierre Emanuel Micol, Rev. Albert Clot, Rev. Noce, François (Frank) Pascal, John Refour. (L-R): Stephen Guigou, Elda Gaydou Bounous, Laura Vigliano Tron, Irma Ghigo Rostan, Jean Pierre Rostan with son Athos, Madeleine Grill, Philippe Grill, Etienne Perrou, Henriette Martinat Pascal, Madeleine Rostan Guigo, Filippo Ghigo, Henriette Long Kraut, Marguerite Baret Ribet, Marguerite Micol Pons, Jean Pons (Bienvenue), Marguerite Grill Grill. (L-R): Jean Henri Pascal (Gardiole), Henri Martinat (farmer), Henri Ghigo, Jean Henri Pascal (Bienvenue), Charles Martinat, Antoine Martinat, Anais Long Bleynat, Albert Bleynat.

CHRISTMAS PROGRAM 1915
(Note the Long Center Pews)
L-R: Anita Micol, Marianne Garrou, Janie Ribet, Marianne Bounous, and Rev. and Mrs. Emile Tron

AUGUST 15 CELEBRATION — 1916
Group enjoys games in picnic area above McGalliard Falls

Building on the Foundation   55

FIRST MANSE AFTER RENOVATION — 1916
Pastor Emile Henri Tron and wife, Laura Vigliano Tron on porch

PALMER-GRANT HOUSE — SECOND MANSE — 1918
This house was built in 1894 by Miss J.C. Palmer, later sold in 1903 to Mrs. Marguerite S. Grant. Sold to Waldensian Presbyterian Church in 1917 to serve as manse.

CATECHUMEN CLASS — MARCH 27, 1915
Standing L-R: Mrs. Emile H. Tron, Henriette Adelaide Ribet, Rachel Perrou, Zeline Fanny Pons, Alice Micol, Cesarine Ribet, Reverend Emile H. Tron, Jean Henri Pascal (Bienvenue). Seated L-R: John Henry Pascal, Frederick Ribet, Henri Philippe Martinat, Jean Henri Pascal (La Gardiole).

CATECHUMEN CLASS — 1916
Standing L-R: Silvio Martinat, Christine Mourglia, Benjamin Grill, Marguerite Louise Pascal, Emma Marguerite Pascal, Mary Martinat, Madeleine Grill, Mary Louise Refour, Reverend Emile H. Tron, Henri Evret Guigou. Seated L-R: Lena Juliette Salvageot, Nelle Louise Garrou, Louise Gaydou, Mary Louise Tron, William (Willie) Emmanuel Garrou.

CHAPTER 4

A TIME OF TRANSITION—From Old World Customs to American Presbyterianism 1918-1940

"For the priesthood being changed, there is made of necessity a change also of the law." Hebrews 7:12

The years of struggle to accept and adapt to the Presbyterian system; the first American minister is called.

On January 27, 1918, the Rev. John Pons, who was serving in Hamilton, Ontario, Canada, was called to begin his second term as pastor. Rev. Pons was one of the most loved ministers. He served the church for two pastorates and then served as supply pastor on numerous occasions. Later the Rev. Pons preached the French service when the church no longer had French-speaking ministers. He was a responsible business and civic leader as well. During his second pastorate, much progress was made.

It was voted at a church assembly on June 2, 1918 to increase the pastor's salary from $625 to $700 per year effective June 1, 1918. At this meeting, it was recommended that the youth begin singing in the church choir, which led to the establishment of a youth choir. Pastor Pons volunteered to practice with them on Saturdays, and Miss Anita Ghigo volunteered to play the piano.

During World War I, seventeen sons of the colony served in the armed forces of the United States.

In July 1918, the three remaining lots of the "Pastor's Farm" were sold. On February 8, 1919, the stone quarry on the "Pastor's Farm" with two acres of land was put up for auction. At $473, Valdese Manufacturing Company was the successful bidder for the property.

On March 8, 1919, the session met to discuss the letter from the Presbyterian Home Mission Committee with reference to Mrs. Ghigo, widow of Pastor Filippo Ghigo. The Mission Committee asked the congregation to assume their Christian responsibility for the widow, Mrs. Ghigo. They cited that the death of her husband had left her almost destitute, and at this time the Mission Committee did not have a place for her to live. They would try to find a place for her as soon as possible. Following a long discussion and considering her present financial straits and the fact that Home Missions would soon find her a place, permission was given to permit her to remain in the manse on Massel Street until September 1 of 1919. Earlier that year at the congregational meeting, the pastor was asked to do everything possible for the education and Christian upbringing of the children of the church, especially striving to preserve French in Sunday School as far as possible.

An event of note in March 1919 was the first formal wedding conducted in the Waldensian Presbyterian Church. Mary Long, daughter of John and Marguerite Gaydou Long, was united in marriage with the Rev. Aurelio Mangione of Plainfield, New Jersey.

Mrs. Juliette Ghigo's request to buy the manse on Massel Street for $1,000 was considered at the June 1 congregational meeting. The vote was sixteen in favor and fourteen opposed. Mrs. Ghigo subsequently withdrew her offer to purchase the manse for the unity and good of the congregation. Later, on September 6, 1919. the congregation voted to sell her the manse for $1,500.

Also on September 6, 1919, the congregation voted to become independent from the Home Missions of the Presbyterian Church in the United States in respect to the pastor's salary. This action would take effect on January 1, 1920, at which time the church would assume all the expenses of its work and became totally self-supporting. An annual subscription of five dollars was imposed on each church member.

Two hundred and seventeen members were enrolled in the church membership. On February 12, 1920, the session voted unanimously to adopt the "Every Member Canvass" and "Goal Pledge" of the Presbyterian church and to go to the envelope method for collection of pledges. The congregation adopted this recommendation on March 7, but it was not implemented until a later date.

In the early 1920's, an English choir was organized with Louis Philippe Guigou as director. It alternated with the French choir which had been organized about 1909. Also sometime in the early 1920's, the old organ was replaced with a square piano. Miss Cesarine Ribet was one of the pianists at this time.

Many changes occurred during the 1920's. As the congregation became more Americanized, it gradually gave up its traditional methods of worship and adopted the Presbyterian form of worship. Most of the celebrations and worship services remained somewhat unique, however, in that they still reflected the customs of the Waldensian Church of Italy.

Christmases of this era were celebrated with a Christmas family night service. A large white pine was decorated with real candles and with garlands of red and green paper. Nuts were wrapped in silver paper and hung on the tree, which was usually located near the pulpit on the right side of the church. A large crowd filled the church. Some of the children recited in French, some in Italian, and some in English. Carols were sung in French. Santa Claus came and distributed bags with fruit, candy, bunches of dried raisins, and nuts.

During these years, Easter was observed with an Easter egg hunt in the afternoon after worship. The hunts were given by the Sunday School teachers for their pupils and were held at the farms of some of the members or sometimes in the cow pasture that the Valdese Manufacturing Company provided for their employees' cows. All the children wore their Easter outfits, including hats.

SUNDAY SCHOOL TEACHERS AND PASTOR 1920 — Seated L-R: William E. Garrou, Rev. John Pons, Emily Pons Erwood, Mary Grill Bertalot, Julia Pascal Bardet, Margaret Gardiol Micol, Silvio Martinat. **Standing L-R:** Mary Martinat, Zeline Pons, Linda Clot, Susanne Giraud Pons, Amandine Bouchard Sanders, Elda Pascal Briggs, Harriet Grill, Madeleine Gardiol Martinat, Aline Pascal, Nelle Garrou Hern, Susanne Martinat.

WALDENSIAN PRESBYTERIAN CHURCH SUNDAY SCHOOL PICNIC HELD AT MICOL'S SPRING ON JUNE 27, 1920 — Back Row Standing L-R: Mary Ann Pascal, Annie Garrou, Julia Pascal, Mary Grill, Frederic Pons, Helen Grill, Henry Garrou, Susie Martinat, Celine Pons, Nelle Garrou, Lena Salvageot, Margaret Pascal, Mary Tron, Zeline Pons, Elda Pascal, Harriet Grill, Suzanne Giraud, Rachel Pons, Emma Pascal, Emily Pons, Rev. John Pons, Antoine Grill. Kneeling L-R: Alice Pons, Lena Pons, Ermeline Pascal, Isabelle Salvageot, Harriet Martinat, Virginia Dare Pons, Elda Clot, Erminia Clot (standing). Seated L-R: Charlie Pons, Henry Salvageot, Leon Guigou, Louise Guigou, (?), Emily Léger, Henry Long, Emmanuel Pons, Frank Garrou, (?), Peter Grill, François Grill, Jr., Willie Pons (lad in back), Louis Vinay, (lad in front?), John Bertalot, Edwin Bounous (in front), Guido Rostan, (child in front?), Ernest Bertalot, Athos Rostan and brother Jean Pierre Rostan, Jr., William Pons, Alexander Vinay, Valdo Clot, Stephen Perrou, Adeline Perrou, Anita Perrou, Madeleine Perrou, Yvonne Rostan, Olga Pascal, Naomi Martinat, Susie Bleynat, Flora Pascal, Rosalie Pascal.

A Time of Transition

Another event was the summer picnic given by the Sunday School teachers for their pupils. One of the members of the congregation remembers a special picnic when the mill lent its truck for the children's transportation. Everyone dressed in their Sunday best. On this particular Sunday, it began to rain about the time the group got to Bridgeport, just west of Valdese. Everyone scrambled off the truck and tried to keep dry under the bed of the truck without much success. As soon as the shower was over, they got back on the truck and proceeded to Asbury Park near Antioch where the picnic was enjoyed.

Reflecting the change from old world customs to modern methods, by 1921 the offering was collected in the pews during the service rather than at the door as the members of the congregation departed.

On July 22, 1921, seeing the need for additional space for growth of the Sunday School, the session voted to build a stone annex to the church (approximately 45' by 28') for use as Sunday School rooms. The men of the congregation, skilled in the laying of rocks and stuccoing, built the annex. As the annex was being built, a central steam heating system was installed in the sanctuary to replace the inadequate pot-bellied stove.

The sanctuary had provided the space for Sunday School, morning service, young people's activities, and mid-week prayer meetings for some twenty-three years. For Sunday School, there was a class in each corner of the sanctuary, one in the chancel, and one in the ante-room on the northeast side.

It is commendable that with a meager budget the men of the congregation were able to build a sanctuary and an annex that have served the congregation of this church for nearly one hundred years with only a few renovations, mostly to the interior.

Interestingly, while the rock masons building the annex were eating lunch, a bolt of lightning hit near the corner of the old schoolhouse, left a ditch along the foundations of the new Sunday School annex, and slightly damaged the corner foundation of the new building.

At the December 15, 1921 session meeting, a decision was made to reorganize the Sunday School under the American plan using the International Lessons which were in English, rather than French or Italian publications. The classes, held in the sanctuary, had served mainly for the teachers' hearing the recitation of scripture verses committed to memory in French by the pupils. After the recitation, the pupils were assembled in the center of the auditorium, and the pastor taught the lesson to the entire school.

From the early years of the church, the seriousness of church membership was strongly impressed upon the children and young people. At about age fourteen, each young person began two years of weekly catechism lessons taught in French by the pastor. At the end of two years, when the young people were examined by the session, they were questioned individually and expected to recite the answers perfectly. On the Sunday they became church members and took their first communion, the pastor addressed each young person with an appropriate verse of scripture. In the solemnity of the occasion, these verses were no doubt imprinted on the hearts and memories of these young men and women.

In the weekly catechism classes, the pastor also instructed the young people about reverence in church worship. They were taught to prepare themselves for worship by offering a silent prayer upon being seated in the sanctuary and also to pray silently at the close of the service. Prayers suitable for these times were memorized by the young people. Many of the older church members still have the cherished memory of observing their parents, after being seated, bend forward, place their foreheads in their right hands, and pray silently for a few moments. As time passed, many of the Waldensian traditions of worship such as this one were no longer observed.

On January 1, 1922, the new annex was dedicated. It was named the C.A. Tron Hall in honor of Dr. Charles Albert Tron, who had led the first settlers to Valdese twenty-nine years earlier. The dedication was a joyous occasion made especially so by the presence of Dr. C.A. Tron. This was Dr. Tron's last visit to the colony. At this time, many of the original group of settlers were still living and were very happy to see Dr. Tron.

**WALDENSIAN PRESBYTERIAN CHURCH
WITH TRON HALL ADDITION — 1922**

Later in the same year at the June 4 meeting of the session, Rev. Pietro Enrico Monnet, a retired Waldensian minister who was born in the Angrogna Valley of the Waldensian Valleys, was thanked for his time and service given to the building of the annex. Rev. Monnet was asked to fill the pulpit during the vacation of the minister.

On April 2, 1922, all communicants who carried out their duties would become voting members, thus giving women the right to vote for the first time.

After the completion of the new C.A. Tron Hall in 1922, the women of the church, then called the Ladies Aid Society, were able to sponsor dinners for church and civic groups. From funds raised by the bazaar and dinners, the women contributed $25 toward the furnishings of Tron Hall and $200 to help pay for the new, modern heating system. That year the young girls of the congregation bought rubber runners for the church aisles.

In 1922, a new procedure was adopted for the Lord's Supper with the members being served in the pews. The women gave the new communion service of individual glasses and containers. This new communion service replaced the old tankard and the two silver goblets, formerly used to serve communion at the altar. In the early years, the men sat on one side of the church, and the women sat on the other side. To partake of communion, the men went to the altar first, two by two, followed by the women. The pastor recited a verse of scripture appropriate to each individual as he or she partook of the bread and drank from a common cup.

During 1922, the change was made from having all services in French to one service a month in the morning in English and the other Sunday morning services in French. The evening service was still in French. This change was effective on the first of July.

That year the Christian Endeavor Society was organized. It met on Sunday evenings in Tron Hall and was enjoyed by the youth of the church. At this time, the number of elders was increased from four to six.

French, which had been the language of the church records, began to be replaced by English in 1922. The first minutes of a church meeting written in English were by the Rev. John Pons on April 14, 1922. From then until 1928, some minutes were written in French and some in English, depending upon the clerk and his ability to write in English. The last minutes in French were written on June 3, 1928 by Elder Henri Martinat (Pineburr). French continued in use in some of the worship services until the time of World War II, when all services were in English. However, French hymns continue to be used during festival seasons and at some weddings and funerals. Until recent times, one circle of the Women of the Church had the Bible lesson in French and as late as 1992 still had scripture and prayer in French.

At a session meeting on April 30, 1923, it was decided to purchase the two lots adjacent to the church, which had been donated to the Burke County Board of Education for the school, since a new school had been built in a new location. It was agreed to buy the lots back for $300 and to allow the local school board twelve months to dispose of the building. On August 5, 1923, it was agreed to sell part of the old school property to the Valdese Shoe Corporation. The lot was 150' x 400' and sold for $1300. The old frame building, which had served as the Valdese school, housed the new enterprise.

It was noted that the skilled Italian workers at the shoe factory from Rochester, New York added to the labors of the pastor. He conducted a Sunday afternoon service for the workers in Italian in addition to the regular morning service in French or English and the evening service in French.

On December 31, 1923, the session voted to buy a clerical robe and to ask the pastor to wear it. (Apparently none of the pastors of the church chose to wear a clerical robe until the 1950's.) The session also voted to enlarge the pulpit area to provide additional

CHRISTIAN ENDEAVOR — 1923 — 1st Row L-R: Ermenia Clot, John P. Rostan, Jr., Evelyn Pons, Adeline Perrou, Margaret Poe, Anita Perrou, Walter Pons, Elizabeth Guigou. 2nd Row L-R: John Stephen Perrou, Athos Rostan, Elda Clot, Louise Guigou, Grace Poe, Willie Pascal, John Harvey Guigou. 3rd Row L-R: Yvonne Rostan, Ida Squillario, Edward Pons, Isabelle Salvageot, Arnaldo Pons, Madeleine Perrou, Alberto Clot, Rosalie Poe.

space for the choir behind the pulpit. A new organ was purchased.

At the session meeting on January 11, 1924, it was decided to accept a mortgage on the land that was sold to the Valdese Shoe Corporation. The three notes payable were as follows: $700 in two years and the other two to be paid soon thereafter.

Mention was made of a new north wall needing to be built to the sanctuary and that nine windows needed to be added. The decision was also made to weatherize the church by adding an attic floor above the ceiling and repairing the windows and the walls to make the building easier to heat and to keep moisture out.

On October 26, 1923, the cemetery was surveyed, and on November 16, one hundred more lots were added. It was voted at the January 11, 1924 meeting of the session to fence the cemetery and to assess the owners of the lots $2 each and to sell the new lots for $10. This would help defray the cost of the fence.

From the proceeds of the bazaars held in 1924 and 1925, the women gave $200 to repair the church and the manse, to install a

WALDENSIAN WOMEN in TRADITIONAL DRESS — MAY, 1924 — Front Row L-R: Amandine Bouchard Sanders, Lydia Jacumin Pons, Susanne Martinat, Mary Grill Bertalot. Back Row L-R: John Tron, Rachel Perrou Warren, Mary Louise Rostan Tron, Lydie Parise Poteet, Marianne Garrou Pons, Margaret Gardiol Micol, Irma Ghigo Rostan, Helen Grill Broverio, Mary Martinat, Susanne Giraud Pons.

fence around the manse, and to place needed carpets in the church.

At the April 29, 1925 meeting of the session, the Rev. Pons asked for an increase in salary. The session, which had been considering this matter for some time, voted to increase his annual salary from $900 to $1500. It was felt that since he was also having to teach at Rutherford College, this increase would enable him to devote full time to the church ministry.

However, at the May 20 session meeting, Rev. Pons tendered his resignation to be effective in the fall of 1925 so that he could devote full time to his teaching at the college. At the congregational meeting on June 7, it was voted to accept his resignation, and the session was empowered to seek a replacement as soon as possible. Consequently on November 22, the congregation voted by secret ballot to call Rev. J.A. Verreault to serve as their pastor.

On January 1, 1926, the Rev. J.A. Verreault began his service to the church. A native of Quebec, Canada, he had most recently

A Time of Transition

served as a missionary among French-speaking families in Louisiana. Rev. Verreault was the first non-Waldensian pastor to serve the church.

On June 6, the session decided to adopt the Presbytery by-laws concerning the election of officers. Also at this meeting the annual "Busy Bee" report of the Ladies Aid Society was read and accepted.

On August 26, 1926, the congregation agreed to invite an expert in window making to give an estimate of the cost of making new windows for the north wall of the church. On November 18, a decision was made not to buy the old building belonging to the shoe factory. This was the same building which had been the school from 1906 to 1923.

During 1927, several changes were made to the church. At a meeting of the session held March 13, the Rev. P.E. Monnet suggested changing the façade of the church to orientate the building from south to north. As Rev. Monnet offered to pay the expenses involved, the session agreed to make the change. Apparently work had begun on a wall which was located behind the church. (The decision to change the entrance of the church from south to north was never carried out.)

Mr. Andrew M. Kistler of Morganton made a generous donation of $500 to be used for the nine windows which needed to be installed. However, the session voted to use the money to pay for work already being done.

On May 9, 1927, it was decided not to accept the proposal of Rev. Clark, representing Concord Presbytery, concerning the possibility of conducting a Daily Vacation Bible School, because most of the congregation would be involved in working in the factories. The custom was begun of presenting New Testaments to catechumens and family Bibles to newlyweds. A new cloth for the Communion Table was purchased.

On August 2, the committee appointed to oversee the repairs to the exterior of the church reported that the metal windows did not fit properly, and the session instructed the committee to see that they were fitted properly. Also, some dissatisfaction was expressed that the money donated by Mr. Kistler had not been used for the nine windows as he requested. The Rev. P.E Monnet's request was granted that the grounds facing the highway be leveled and that windows be properly installed.

The decision was made on September 21, 1927 to install floors in the two small rooms beside the pulpit to make them suitable for

Sunday School rooms. It was also decided to call a tinner each year to inspect and repair the gutters of the church. Plans were made to beautify the surroundings of the church and the cemetery. A fund for this purpose had been started in January of that year.

The Rev. P.E. Monnet donated his library to the church and then financed the building of shelves for the books in the attic area above the present choir loft. The new church library was named for its generous donor, the Rev. P.E. Monnet. A plaque in his honor was to be placed in the library. Later a generous gift from Mrs. Tate of Morganton to the library collection was graciously accepted.

On March 16, 1928, the session voted to begin work in the church bell tower room to adapt that area for use by a Sunday School class. Also considered was the building of a room in the attic of the sanctuary.

At the congregational meeting on June 3, 1928, the assembly arose unanimously to express thanks to member Jean Henri Pascal (Bienvenue) for all the services he had rendered to the church. He had served as elder for twenty-five consecutive years and had recently tendered his resignation as a member of the session.

To enhance the meaning of the Lord's Supper, it was decided to have one Communion service per month rather than two.

On August 7, 1928, the contract was let for the remodeling of the manse (formerly the Palmer-Grant House) for the sum of $3200. After much study, the decision was made to renovate only the first story of the original two-story wood building. The house was also brick veneered, which was made possible by a generous gift from the Ladies Aid Society. Apparently the cost exceeded the original estimate, as it was reported in the fall that the cost for remodeling was $4200; $3000 was paid, leaving a balance of $1200 owed.

A minister from the Moravian church of Winston Salem spoke at the February 17, 1929 supper. The focus of the celebration was the progress that had been made in improving the physical plant of the church in the previous year.

Efforts had been made to organize the women according to Presbyterial guidelines as early as 1924. Finally, Presbyterial records show that in April 1929, Valdese was listed as "an Auxiliary with forty members, contributing to local church work only." In the report of the following year, the women had given ten dollars to the Birthday Offering and ten dollars to Foreign Missions. Mrs. J.A. Verreault, the pastor's wife, was listed as president and as the representative of the group at the Presbyterial meeting held in

A Time of Transition

Morganton in 1931.

In 1930, hymnal racks for the backs of the sanctuary pews were purchased. Priority was to be given to repairing the roof of the church and to repainting and repairing the church interior. New lighting fixtures were installed.

In June 1930, the congregation attended a "Love Feast" at the Moravian Church in Winston Salem. In August, the Moravian Church was invited by the Waldensian congregation to attend the August 15 celebration. This exchange of fellowship between the two congregations continued for a few years.

The practice had been to hold the August 15 service and celebration of the "Glorious Return" on the Sunday nearest the fifteenth of the month at the farms of different members. The families of the congregation attended with their well-packed picnic baskets including their bottles of wine. The dinner followed the worship service. After the service and having eaten their fill, the children and youth of the congregation would play games such as "un, deux, trois, Capitaine Rouge, partez" and other children's games.

On July 8, 1930, the Sunday evening services were temporarily discontinued. The morning services were in English on the first and third Sundays and in French on the second and fourth.

At the December 2 meeting of the session, the Rev. Verreault presented his letter of resignation effective December 30, citing ill health. However, his resignation was not accepted until January 18, 1931. When he resigned, there was much discussion over whether to call a minister from the Waldensian Church in Italy or to call an English-speaking pastor. The older members of the congregation favored a French-speaking pastor, but as none was available at this time, they had to look to Concord Presbytery for assistance.

The years 1931 to 1935 were a period of adjustment for the church and the community. On July 5, 1931, an invitation was extended to the Rev. James H. Caligan to supply the pulpit until May 8, 1932. He was a graduate of Davidson College and of Union Seminary in Richmond, Virginia. He was subsequently unanimously elected to remain and was installed as the regular pastor. All services were conducted in English with the exception of one each month when the Rev. John Pons preached in French.

The Rev. Caligan possessed a charismatic personality. He especially appealed to the youth of the church and organized many activities for them. He and several young men cleared some of the vacant land belonging to the church and built a tennis court for the use of the congregation.

On July 27, 1931, the session decided to rent the manse for one month then discuss with the Rev. Caligan the matter of lodging. As he was unmarried, session members were not sure he would want the manse. However, he did decide to live in the manse. Up until this time most of the session meetings, committee meetings, and some Sunday School classes had been held at the manse. Since the Rev. Caligan was single, he shared the manse with several young men who were teachers in the local school. For that reason the practice of using the manse for various church meetings was discontinued.

Through the persistent efforts of the Rev. James H. Caligan, the Ladies' Auxiliary began to grow and organize. Officers were chosen, with Mrs. Albert F. Garrou (Louise Holloway) as president. Regular monthly meetings were held. The February 1932 Auxiliary minutes note that the women "decided to borrow money to have the church grounds landscaped and a lawn made." In March of that year, the work was carried out by the pastor and the women. For many years afterwards, the women had the responsibility of the upkeep of the church grounds.

At the August 7, 1931 meeting of the session, it was decided that the Christian Endeavor Society would be included in the regular Sunday evening services.

In 1933, Miss Sally Ramseur, from Quaker Meadows, Burke County, North Carolina, was employed to work with the youth during the summer. She was the first Director of Christian Education to serve this church.

On February 21, 1933, the session voted to set aside $1500 in a fund for a future educational building as the Sunday School had outgrown the space available. The Ladies' Auxiliary was asked to donate their surplus money to the future educational building. In January of that year, the Auxiliary had agreed to purchase ten shares of building and loan stock which would eventually be donated for this purpose. The paid-up shares were given to the session in November 1939.

On June 9, 1934, the Rev. J.H. Caligan and Emily Léger, daughter of Humbert and Marie Parise Léger of Valdese, were married. Her grandfather, Jean Jacques Léger, was one of the original settlers in 1893.

On January 1, 1935, the first men's organization was formed, and their first meeting was on February 10, 1935. However, they did not

A Time of Transition 71

BIBLE SCHOOL TEACHERS and PASTOR — 1933
L-R: Francis Ghigo, Essie Devinney (O.H.) Pons, Hazel Coley (Daniel B.) Bounous, Melissa Wacaster (Philip S.) Grill, Anita Ghigo, Irene Tron (James) Weir, Sally Ramseur (Director of Christian Education), Rev. James H. Caligan.

join the Men of the Church of Concord Presbytery until 1946.

In March of 1935, the Young People's Society was reorganized under the guidance of the Rev. Caligan. Also in 1935, the Rev. Caligan proposed a list of ten recommendations to improve the Women's Auxiliary. These included adopting the full plan of work as outlined by the Presbyterian Church in the United States, organizing circles including every woman in the church, and having voluntary offerings instead of set dues. The recommendations were approved, and one result was the formation of three circles from a list of 134 women. Two of the circles were soon combined due to poor attendance. The Auxiliary contributed $4 to help pay for weekly church bulletins, a practice introduced by Rev. Caligan.

On March 31, 1936, it was reported that the number of elders had been increased to eight and the number of deacons to four.

The year 1937 saw the first member of this church go into full-time church work. Jeanette Bounous graduated from Assembly Training School in Richmond, Virginia, and was engaged in church work until after her marriage to Wilson S. Bigham in October 1939.

In 1937, the first church budget was adopted, with a total of

$3,598. There has been an annual church budget since that time. On March 7, 1937, the congregation voted to build the new educational building for which a building fund had been started in 1933.

The Rev. Caligan asked Mrs. George Williams, Jr. (Ruth McQuiston), a talented musician who had moved to Valdese from South Carolina with her husband, to take charge of the church music and to be choir director. Shortly thereafter a beautiful Hammond electric organ was given to the church as a memorial gift.

In April of 1938, Mrs. Williams organized a vested choir. She was assisted for many years by Miss Anita Ghigo, daughter of the late Pastor Filippo Ghigo. The many beautiful organ-piano duets played by Mrs. Williams and Miss Ghigo added much to the church services.

Rev. J.A. Caligan submitted his resignation on April 3, 1938 to be effective May 1. The Rev. John Pons served the church as interim pastor until a replacement could be called.

FIRST VESTED CHOIR UNDER DIRECTION OF MRS. GEORGE W. (RUTH) WILLIAMS, JR. — 1938 — 1st Row L-R: Louise Holloway (Albert F.) Garrou, Bernice Smith (Frederick) Ribet, Jeanette Léger, Marie Garrou, Emily Léger (James H.) Caligan. 2nd Row L-R: Mrs. Paul White, Yvonne Rostan (Hugh) Peeler, Louise Gaydou (J.D.) Guigou, Ruth M. (George W., Jr.) Williams. 3rd Row L-R: John Grant, Julius Ramsey, Sr., Rev. James H. Caligan, John Stephen Perrou, John D. Guigou.

A Time of Transition

In June 1938, the Women's Auxiliary sponsored a Vacation Bible School. A trained worker, Mrs. Askers, was paid $20 for her services for two weeks.

The congregation approved and extended a call to the Rev. Sylvan S. Poet on December 4, 1938. He arrived early in 1939 and preached his first sermon as pastor February 5, 1939. He was a native of Torre Pellice, Italy, and had experience as a pastor in New York and Chicago before coming to Valdese.

During the first year that Pastor Sylvan Poet served the congregation, the much needed educational building was built. On April 30, 1939, the contract was let for the building. It included Sunday School rooms on the first floor and kitchen and fellowship hall on the second floor. Work began in the early summer, and it was estimated that the building would be finished by December 1939 at a cost of $22,454.12. On February 17, 1940, the new educational building was dedicated and named Pioneer Hall in memory of the first settlers. The Rev. Neil McGeachy, Moderator of Concord Presbytery, was the guest minister.

The women were overjoyed to have the use of a spacious dining hall and a well-equipped kitchen. They hoped to use these new facilities to earn money for their projects. However, the Rev. Poet, in discussing the use of the building in a letter to the Auxiliary,

**WALDENSIAN PRESBYTERIAN CHURCH
after the completion of Pioneer Hall in 1940.**

earnestly requested that the women rather strive for the spiritual interest of the church and provide financial aid through free-will offerings. Many of the women who had worked for years preparing meals were relieved at the pastor's suggestion.

Further expenditures for improvement included two new communion trays with covers and two new collection plates which were purchased in 1939.

On July 17 of the same year, the Town of Valdese was notified of the church's policy to reserve the cemetery for members of the Waldensian Church. On August 10, 1939, a motion was made to pay the Town of Valdese the sum of $1,581.31 for street and sidewalk pavement on the streets adjacent to the church.

On October 1, 1939, appreciation was expressed to New York friends of the Rev. Poet for the donation of six pianos for use in the new Sunday School classrooms. Broadcasting of church services over Hickory radio station WHKY began in 1940.

An impressive Easter sunrise service was instituted on March 24, 1940 and continued for several years. The choirs, church members, visitors, and on occasion, groups from other churches united in early morning worship, gathering at the church for prayer and service, then walking in solemn procession to the cemetery where they waited in the stillness for the sun to rise slowly over the horizon. This service was very inspiring, and members of the congregation who experienced it have never forgotten.

Sincere appreciation was extended to Robert O. Huffman of Drexel Furniture for the furnishing of the ladies' parlor in Pioneer Hall. On July 15, 1940, flagstone was used to pave the walk between the Pioneer Hall and the church to the Main Street.

The rotation method of election of officers was adopted March 16, 1941. The April 6, 1941 meeting of the session recommended that folding doors be placed in the Sunday School assembly room and that partitions be placed in the C.A. Tron Hall.

On June 16, 1941, the Rev. Poet submitted his resignation to accept a call to Middletown, New York effective August 1. On July 6, 1941, a meeting was called for July 13, 1941 to accept the resignation of the Rev. Poet and to elect a pulpit committee. Members of the congregation were reminded of the debt still remaining on Pioneer Hall.

During June and July 1941, the French service was broadcast on Sunday afternoon over Radio Station WHKY Hickory. At this time, the church still had French and English choirs and services in French and English.

A Time of Transition

1940

Some of the surviving members of the first group of Waldensians who alighted from the train in Burke County (later Valdese) on May 29, 1893. L-R: Louis Philippe Guigou, Victor Micol, François Tron, Alexis Guigou, Catherine (née Guigou) Guigou Garrou, Emmanuel Micol. Not pictured are: Jean Henri Micol, Marguerite Micol (Jean) Pons, François Pons, Jean François Refour and son Jean Refour, Philippe Richard and spouse Louise (née Ribet) Richard, sons: Philippe Emmanuel and Etienne Richard; Albert Tron, Madeleine Tron (Frank W.) Tise. Total: Seventeen Surviving Members.

First Formal Church Wedding
April 29, 1919
Mary Long and Rev. Aurelio Mangione

CATECHUMEN CLASS OF 1929
L-R: Athos Rostan, Rosalie Pascal, William F. Pons, Margaret Pascal, Rev. Joseph A. Verreault, Yvonne Rostan, Valdo Pierre Rivoire, Ida Emma Squillario, Henry Barthélemy Pascal.

CHAPTER 5

GROWTH AND VITALITY—
World War II and the Post-War Years
1941-1949

"But grow in grace, and in the knowledge of our Lord and Savior Jesus Christ. To him be glory both now and for ever. Amen." II Peter 3:18

Full acceptance of Southern Presbyterianism. The impact of the war years and the vitality and growth of the early post-war era.

Dr. Watson Munford Fairley was called as temporary pastor to serve for three months. He preached his first sermon on October 5, 1941. Dr. Fairley had retired from his pastorate in Raeford, North Carolina on June 1, 1940 due to ill health and had moved with Mrs. Fairley to their home at Montreat. After coming to Valdese, he became so well loved by the congregation that his supply pastorate was renewed every three months until the limit set by the synod was reached in 1945.

Under the leadership of the Fairleys, new vitality was seen in the life of the church. Church activities were expanded and giving increased. These were the World War II years when much attention was given to remembering the men in military service and to contributing to the war effort.

Dr. Fairley worked to increase participation in the work of the church. Soon after his arrival, he organized a Men's Bible Class with twenty-two members. In turn, Mrs. Fairley started a Women's Bible Class with twenty-four members.

In 1942, the church budget was $5,500. The Every Member Canvass resulted in pledges of $6,575. For the first time, the church furnished envelopes for the collection of pledges. The rotary system for the election of elders and deacons was adopted in 1941 and put into effect a year later. An Educational Committee was appointed by the session to advise and assist the Sunday School superintendent and teachers. In 1942, a number of Advance Movement Goals were adopted to promote family worship and to increase Sunday

School and church attendance. The nursery for young children was enlarged to encourage parents to attend worship services.

The year 1943 saw an emphasis on activities for children and young people. A Girl Scout troop was sponsored by the Women's Auxiliary, and the church began sponsoring Boy Scout Troop No. 1. In May, 1943 Mrs. George Williams and Miss Anita Ghigo organized a junior choir for girls between the ages of twelve and eighteen. A two-week Vacation Bible School was sponsored by the Women's Auxiliary in June. Dr. and Mrs. Fairley presented thirteen books on missions to the Sunday School library, which was reorganized by Mrs. Wade H. Stemple. Funds were given by the Sunday School and Auxiliary circles to buy books for the library.

The need for renovation and restoration of the church sanctuary had become evident by this time. In January 1943, an architect was recommended, but due to scarcity of workmen and materials during the war years, work was not begun until 1945. A building fund campaign was started in September 1943. By the end of 1944, $15,000 had been set aside for this work.

In January 1944, the session approved a donation of $150 to Valdese General Hospital to maintain a "charity bed." The budget for the following year included $600 for this purpose. In February 1944, the session voted to include the Apostles' Creed in the worship services. This was a departure from the teachings of the Waldensian Church, which opposed any liturgical form of worship. Some of the older members were not pleased but did not oppose the decision.

The session decided in September 1944 to reserve the remaining space in the cemetery for members of the Waldensian Presbyterian Church. The town was asked to provide a cemetery for the community. A commission was appointed to formulate a plan for operation of the church cemetery. The price of a full lot was set at $100; half lots were priced at $50 and individual plots at $25.

The Rev. John Pons, who had served the church two terms as pastor and who had continued to supply the pulpit and preach in French as long as his health permitted, died on November 11, 1944. A memorial service, sponsored by the Eastern Star and conducted by Dr. Fairley, was held for this faithful servant of the Lord in the church on December 10.

In December 1944, the first full-time janitor, Mr. Emmanuel Perrou, was employed. By the end of the church year, there were 445 enrolled members. The budget for 1945 was $19,692. Dr. Fairley's allowed time as supply pastor ended in the summer of 1945. The Fairleys retired to their Montreat home, but Dr. Fairley continued to fill the pulpit frequently.

FIFTIETH ANNIVERSARY CELEBRATION, 1943

On June 20, 1941, a committee made up of Lee Ribet, chairman; the Rev. John Pons, secretary; and Antoine Grill, treasurer, was named to provide for the erection of a suitable memorial in honor of the pioneers who settled Valdese in 1893. The cost of the monument, to be located on the property of the Waldensian Presbyterian Church, facing Highway 70, was to be shared by Burke County, the Town of Valdese, and the citizens and friends of the community.

On the afternoon of October 27, 1943, the monument was dedicated in an impressive ceremony planned for the church lawn but held in the school auditorium due to inclement weather. The dedication address was delivered by the Honorable J. Melville Broughton, Governor of North Carolina. Other guests included the Honorable Cameron Morrison, former United States Senator and Governor; Judge Sam J. Ervin, Jr.; and North Carolina State Representative A.B. Stoney. Also taking part in the program was J.D. Brinkley, Sr., mayor of Valdese; John Long, first mayor of Valdese; Dr. Watson Fairley, pastor of the Waldensian Presbyterian Church; Rev. John Pons and Rev. J.A. Verreault, former pastors; and Rev. M.I. Harris, pastor of the First Baptist Church, Valdese.

Music was provided by the Valdese and Drexel High School Bands and the Junior Choir of the church. Boy Scouts and Girl Scouts led the Pledge of Allegiance. A letter of greeting from President Franklin D. Roosevelt was read.

The monument is inscribed as follows: "To The Waldensian Colony from the Cottian Alps who settled here first in 1893, numbering in all 427. In recognition of their Christian Ideals, Integrity, Industry, and Good Citizenship this Monument is erected by the Town of Valdese and Burke County, commemorating The Fiftieth Anniversary of their Arrival." The word "Waldenses" is carved on the front and back. On the back are the dates "1893-1943."

Following the ceremony, dinner was served in Pioneer Hall by the Women's Auxiliary to the honor guests and other officials.

Monument Erected to Commemorate the Fiftieth Year of the Founding of Valdese — Dedicated October 27, 1943

On October 31, 1943, the Sunday following the dedication of the monument, Antoine Grill, venerable leader in the spiritual and economic life of the colony, presented to the church a carefully prepared genealogy and history of Waldensian families who had settled Valdese. He had been greatly assisted in this work by Henry Martinat (Pineburr). This valuable document representing thousands of hours of research and writing had been photocopied by the North Carolina Department of History.

THE WOMEN'S AUXILIARY, 1941-1945

With the coming of Dr. and Mrs. Fairley in October 1941, the Women's Auxiliary of the Waldensian Presbyterian Church began a new era of growth and vitality. Although the leadership and organization had grown stronger during the pastorates of Pastors Caligan and Poet, a matter of concern for Mrs. Fairley when she came was the fact that the Auxiliary was not a legally constituted organization. The committee appointed to draft a constitution and by-laws was composed of Mrs. L.P. Guigou (Lillian Sweeney), chairman; Mrs. Joe Hern (Nelle Garrou), Mrs. Leon Guigou (Nell Saunders) and Mrs. Wade H. Stemple. According to the February 19, 1942 executive board minutes, "The constitution and by-laws which were approved were read by Mrs. Fairley." With their adoption, the Auxiliary became a legally constituted institution of Waldensian Presbyterian Church.

Following the suggestion of Mrs. Fairley, Monday was the day selected for Auxiliary meetings to avoid conflicts with meetings of other organizations in the community. The bazaar in December 1941 was the last one held by the Auxiliary, due to a gradual lessening of interest in the once popular money-making event.

In March 1942, the Auxiliary treasury showed a balance of $607.60. The women voted to donate this amount to assist in the payment of the debt remaining on Pioneer Hall. At the end of the 1941-42 year, the Auxiliary had seven active circles, including the newly organized French Circle for those who spoke French and patois. The amount budgeted for 1942-1943 was $523.

The Auxiliary historian, Mrs. L. P. Guigou, reported that "much valuable data and material had been collected and filed." She recommended that a standard minute book be used and that records should be kept carefully and dates recorded. Mrs. Guigou stated in her history that "The closing of the year 1941-42 might be called the beginning of a period of reconstruction." Under the very efficient and forceful leadership of Dr. and Mrs. Fairley, the Auxiliary began to show signs of being shaped according to the plan of the General Assembly of the Presbyterian Church in the United States.

Three delegates attended the Auxiliary Training School held at Montreat in July 1942. No mention had been made of attendance at the conference in earlier years. That year, reports were given of projects undertaken by the individual circles, including providing for local needy families, "adopting" a child at Barium Springs Home for Children, and purchasing a desk for the Sunday School office. Also in 1942, in the report of the French Circle, the first mention is made of the "Home Circle." These were women who, because of age or illness, could not be active circle members. A special work of the French Circle over the years has been to visit these women on a regular basis. Mrs. F.H. Pons (Iola Britt) served as president in 1942.

Mrs. Fairley assumed the presidency of the Auxiliary in 1943 and served two years. The term of office gave her an excellent opportunity to instruct the women in the use of parliamentary law, in which she excelled. The historian notes that there was also much improvement in records kept by the Auxiliary and the circles. A special project for 1943 was the purchase of robes for the newly formed Junior Choir. In September, the "Advance Movement" goals of the church were studied at a dinner for Auxiliary officers and Sunday School teachers. Throughout the year, a number of interesting presentations were made by the Secretaries of Causes. It was a busy, productive year.

The year 1944 began with eight circles and 192 women in membership. At the Auxiliary meeting on April 17, the historian, Mrs. L.P. Guigou, read a sketch of her partially completed history of the women's work of the Waldensian Presbyterian Church from 1893 to 1942. Her work was officially adopted. The polio epidemic of the summer of 1944 prompted the Auxiliary to send $25 to the Infantile Paralysis Committee.

On September 26, 1944, at the District I Group Conference held in Newton, Mrs. Fairley was recognized with an Honorary Life Membership. Later, the Auxiliary in Valdese presented the Honorary Life Membership Pin to her. Mrs. Fairley was the first in the Waldensian Presbyterian Auxiliary to be so honored. A biographical sketch of the life and work of Alice Rollwage Fairley is included in Mrs. L.P. Guigou's history.

Receipts for the year 1944 were $1,245.33. Of this amount, $587.82 was given to benevolences and $617.75 to the church building fund. That year for the first time a sum of $25 was set aside by the Auxiliary for the purchase of flowers for the sanctuary, especially during the winter months. For many years, Mrs. L.P. Guigou had provided the flowers for worship services. Annual reports were made for the first time. The circles had a membership of 186 women.

Mrs. O.H. Pons (Essie Devinney) became president in 1945. That year, priority was given to the needs of Barium Springs Home for Children. Efforts were also directed to wartime needs. Dr. and Mrs. Fairley left Valdese during the summer of 1945. The Auxiliary officers prepared a set of Resolutions which were sent to the Fairleys as a token of appreciation for their work in the Waldensian Presbyterian Church.

Growth and Vitality

WAR TIME CHURCH ACTIVITIES (1941-1945)

It is appropriate to follow the preceding sketch of the Women's Auxiliary with an accounting of the church activities of the World War II years, for it was largely the women who addressed the special needs of that period of time.

As early as 1941, the Auxiliary kept in touch with the servicemen from the church. Bibles and packages were sent to them. Mrs. Joe Hern (Nelle Garrou) sent home-made candy to the men throughout the war years. In June 1942, the women placed an honor roll of servicemen in the church vestibule with the plea "Pray for them daily." In September 1943, the Auxiliary sent a contribution to the Jacksonville, North Carolina Presbyterian Church to assist in their work with servicemen.

In 1944, a large service flag with sixty-nine stars representing the servicemen from the church was presented by Mrs. L.P. Guigou in honor of her son John Harvey Guigou, who was serving in the Air Force. This flag now hangs in the museum. Beginning on May 1, 1944, the church bell tolled each evening at six o'clock calling citizens to prayer for God's protection of our men and for peace. Also that month, the session voted to send $50 to the Defense Service Council to aid servicemen.

Beginning in 1944 and continuing for several years, the Women's Auxiliary collected clothing, food and other necessities to send to people in the Waldensian Valleys, who had suffered greatly during the war.

The mothers of the church who had sons serving in the armed services were honored by Mrs. L.P. Guigou when she presented to the church two large flags, one American and one Christian. On VE Day, May 8, 1945, when hostilities ceased in Europe, the church bell tolled on and on. There was much loud rejoicing in the streets of Valdese. Many found their way to the church sanctuary for prayer and thanksgiving. Finally, on August 14, 1945, when hostilities ceased with Japan, all could look forward to their sons coming home to a world at peace.

On June 14, 1945, the Rev. Albert Bonner McClure, Sr. was called as pastor of the Waldensian Presbyterian Church. He preached his first sermon on October 7, 1945 in Pioneer Hall due to renovations of the sanctuary. The Rev. McClure was installed pastor by a commission appointed by Concord Presbytery.

World War II had just ended, and the men were returning home from Europe and the Pacific. The Rev. McClure stressed the importance of contacting the young men returning from service and inviting them to attend church and welcoming them with open arms. He also urged the Women's Auxiliary and the circles to continue sending packages of clothes, supplies and money to the Waldensian people in Italy who were still suffering from the devastations of war.

On July 23, 1945, a committee was authorized by the session and diaconate to secure the services of an architect and a builder to remodel the manse. Two rooms were added to the front of the house, a bathroom was added, the house was painted, and other repairs were made to make the manse more comfortable and convenient for the pastor and his family. In a joint meeting of the session and the diaconate on November 5, 1945, the treasurer was authorized to pay for all repairs to the manse from the church building fund.

Second Manse remodeled in 1928 and again in 1945

During his ministry in Valdese, the Rev. McClure placed much emphasis on the youth of the town. He had such a strong feeling of love and concern for young people that he devoted quality time to their welfare, and he worked diligently to mold them into good citizens. He helped provide entertainment for all the teenagers in town at the Valdese Community Center on Fridays, and he went on

Growth and Vitality

many high school field trips as a chaperon. He knew everyone by his first name and had nicknames for many people.

Under the direction of Mrs. George Williams and Miss Anita Ghigo, the Junior Choir began to grow. Special attention was given to the choir which had an enrollment of thirty. To accommodate the enrollment, tiers of seats were placed at the left and right sides of the pulpit. Mrs. Williams and Miss Ghigo did numerous things to stimulate interest and participation in the Junior Choir. Each fall when the choir began its new year, the two leaders would do something special for them. Once they entertained the choir with a picnic on the lawn at Mrs. Williams' house. That does not seem like much to teenagers now, but it meant a lot in the mid-forties because there was very little social life except for what the church offered. Every event was thoroughly enjoyed.

The directors also took the choir to compete with other North Carolina church choirs at state meets held either in Statesville or Charlotte. The Waldensian Junior Choir always made a good showing. Many of the Junior Choir members sang solos, played instrumental solos and duets, and took charge of the church music during the summer months. From these musical experiences, many of the choir members continued to participate in music activities in college.

Since the late 1940's, special recognition has been given each spring to the graduating high school seniors for their work in the music department of the church. The students are presented choir pins and certificates. This recognition of youth at the close of their high school years has continued as a way to thank them for their years of service to the church.

The need for a director of religious education in the church was recognized. Mrs. C.W. White accepted this position on a part-time basis. In March 1946, Rev. McClure expressed his desire to resume the custom of presenting a Bible to couples married in the church.

It was evident that more land was needed for the cemetery; therefore, on April 21, 1946, the church purchased two and one-half acres adjoining the present cemetery from Louis Ferrier at $200 per acre. Later that year, The Reverend Guido Comba, treasurer of the Waldensian Church of Rome, visited Valdese to report on the living conditions and health of relatives and friends in Italy. Not long after his visit, the Women's Auxiliary, the circles and friends sent three hundred boxes of clothes weighing 1600 pounds and $2000 to the Waldensian Valleys. This aid continued for several years.

In 1947, a Historical Collection Committee was organized to gather and preserve items brought by the colonists from Italy or used in their pioneer days in Valdese. A room in the Charles A. Tron Hall was set aside for the museum. The committee members were Mrs. L.P. Guigou (Lillian Sweeney), Mrs. John D. Guigou (Louise Gaydou), Mrs. Ben Pons (Marianne Garrou), Mrs. Edward Micol (Marguerite Gardiol), Mrs. Albert Garrou (Louise Holloway), Antoine Grill, John Pascal (Gardiole) and Henry Philip Martinat (Pineburr). In December of that year, chimes for the organ and an amplifier for the church tower were donated as a memorial gift.

Mrs. Louise Gaydou Guigou displaying early Museum Collection 1944

On November 2, 1947, the original builders of the church (those still living) were honored at the morning worship service, and the building committee members who had worked for two years in the renovation of the sanctuary were also honored for their diligent work. In the renovation, the entire outside of the sanctuary and Tron Hall was stuccoed. On the inside, new stained glass windows bearing the seals of various ancient Reformed churches were installed. The chancel area had a divided pulpit with choir area on each side of the archway. Before, there was a single pulpit in front of the arch. Wood-paneled screens were installed across the front of the church around the pulpit, lectern, and choirs. New pews were also installed as well as a new concrete floor covered with an oak floor and then carpeted. Recessed radiators were placed in the walls under the windows to give more space in the side aisles. The cost of the renovation was $52,473.91.

The church budget for 1948 was $14,524. The membership had increased to 492 with 259 in Sunday School. During this same year, we had two guest speakers: Mrs. Catherine Anderson, secretary of Waldensian Aid Society in New York, and the Rev. Alfred Janavel from the Waldensian Church in New York.

In January 1949, there was a rededication of the sanctuary and a dedication of its furnishings. The Rev. McClure presided at this service and burned the cancelled note of $7,000 representing the balance due.

The Rev. McClure received a call in September 1949 to accept the superintendency of the Barium Springs Home for Children at Barium Springs, North Carolina, and he asked that his pastoral relations with the Waldensian Presbyterian Church be dissolved effective January 10, 1950.

This was a sad time for the Rev. McClure, his wife and four children, as well as for the church. The congregation would miss his graciousness, his fantastic sense of humor, and his radiant personality. A farewell party was given in his honor on Christmas Eve, 1949.

At the last session meeting presided over by the Rev. McClure, he expressed his desire that the church would purchase the remaining tract of land in the church block and name the entire block "Little Waldensian," making it a garden spot for all who have been and are yet to come. On January 8, 1950, he preached his last sermon.

Centennial Anniversary of Edict of Emancipation of February 17, 1848
Celebrated February 17, 1948

**Anniversary Banquet Celebrating the 100th Year
of the EDICT OF EMANCIPATION
February 17, 1848 — February 17, 1948**

(Among those pictured above are many of the original 1893 pioneers). Seated L-R: Frederic Peyronel, Daniel B. Bounous, Antoine Grill, John (Bobo) Garrou, John Henry Pascal (Balsille), John Henry Pascal (Gardiole), Reverend Albert B. McClure, John Long. Standing L-R: Alexis Guigou, Julius Grisette, Henry F. Martinat, Jean Pierre Rostan, John Refour, Louis P. Guigou, Marie Ferrier (James Henry) Pascal, Susanne Long (Eli) Bertalot, Irma Ghigo (JP) Rostan, Catherine Anderson Beattie (Secretary of the American Waldensian Aid Society for over 13 years), Louise Gaydou (John D.) Guigou, Helen Pascal (Aldo F.) Martinat, Henry P. Martinat, Juliette Rosso (Filippo E.) Ghigo, François Pons, Henry F. Garrou, Frank Pascal, Albert F. Garrou, Benjamin Perrou.

CHANCEL CHOIR — c. 1949

1st Row L-R: Anita Ghigo, Patricia Melvin (W. Harold) Mitchell, Jeannine Garrou, Marian Morrison, Pauline Ribet (Wm. T.) Eanes, Vivian Ogle (Harley) Coffey, Bertha D. (Louis) Deaton, Ruth McQuiston (George W., Jr.) Williams — Director. 2nd Row L-R: Doris Campbell (Edward) Garrou, Clementine Perrou (William) Butler, Bernice Smith (Frederick) Ribet, Jane Caudell, Vera Berry (M. Haynes) Rutherford, Mildred Smith (R. L.) Pyatt, Elfie Bounous (George) Grill. 3rd Row L-R: Robert Gorley, Edward Pons, Helen Crow, Barbara Bounous (Leroy) Wall, Rosalie Grana (Hedrick) Powell. 4th Row L-R: Benjamin Perrou, Robert Micol, Kenneth Bumgarner, Frank Goode, John Stephen Perrou, Jr.

Growth and Vitality 91

JUNIOR CHOIR — c. 1950

1st Row L-R: Margaret Perrou, Louise Ann Verreault, Maxine Briggs, Gwendolyn Garrou, Joan Goode, Gwendolyn Pons, Ann Long, Joan Hall, Lorraine Perrou, Catherine Baker. 2nd Row L-R: Beverly Tron, Junine Tron, Joan Rutherford, Jeanne Grana, Mildred Searcy, Julia Lee Ribet, Anne Dare May, Harriette Pons. 3rd Row L-R: Jenelle Searcy, Rheta Micol, Peggy Jane Perrou, Ruth Williams, Peggy Benfield, Doris Searcy, Mary Ann McCarley, Louise Perrou, Betty Giraud, Anaise Bridges, Weeta Searcy.

**JUNIOR CHOIR MEMBERS WITH REV. ALBERT McCLURE
1947**
L-R: Imogene Pons, Margaret Garrou, Pauline Ribet, Bernice Ribet, Josephine Perrou, Rosalba Pascal, Doris Pons, Helen Crowe, Emily Micol, Ann Frazier.

First Recipients of Junior Choir Pins
June 1949
Rosalie Grana and Barbara Bounous

CHAPTER 6

EXPANSION, INVOLVEMENT, WITNESS
1950-1968

"If any man serve me, let him follow me; and where I am, there shall also my servant be: if any man serve me, him will my father honor." John 12:26

A growing awareness of our obligation to our fellow man.

The 1950's were a good time for churches in general. The world was recovering from a tragic world war, and there was worry about the beginning of another conflict in Korea. People were turning to religion to find meaning for their lives. The people of Valdese were no exception. Church attendance and church membership were on the rise. People were open to new and expanded programs.

In December of 1949, the Women of the Church had begun regular visits to Broughton Hospital under a program started by the hospital chaplain, the Rev. A.W. Lippard. The Rev. W.R. Smith III, YMCA secretary at Davidson College, had been selected to serve as supply minister until a new minister could be called.

At a meeting on February 5, 1950, the congregation of the Waldensian Presbyterian Church voted unanimously to extend a call to the Rev. Walter H. Styles, pastor of Black Mountain Presbyterian Church, to serve as pastor. His first worship service was on March 12, 1950.

During a congregational meeting held at 2:30 P.M., February 26, 1950, a baptismal font matching the new church furnishings was dedicated as a memorial gift.

The Women of the Church hosted the Concord Presbyterial, April 24 and April 25. A total of 427 women from throughout the presbytery attended.

Elder George W. Williams, Jr. attended the 90th meeting of the General Assembly of the Presbyterian Church U.S. held in Harrisonburg, Virginia in early June 1950 as a commissioner from Concord Presbytery.

The church sponsored the building of a Scout Hut for Troop 1 of the Boy Scouts at the corner of Carolina and Massel Streets. The

WALDENSIAN WOMEN IN TRADITIONAL DRESS — 1953 —
1st Row Seated L-R: Mary Grill (Henry) Bertalot, Irma Ghigo (Jean Pierre) Rostan, Adèle Grill (John Daniel) Pascal, Harriet Vinay (John) Long, Ida Gardiol (Armando) Menusan, Madeleine Rostan (Emile) Squillario, Marie Ferrier (James Henry) Pascal, **2nd Row Seated L-R:** Madeleine Grill, Jeanne Pons (François) Perrou, Judith Pons (Daniel B., Sr.) Bounous, Marie Bounous (John Henry) Pascal, Elda Gaydou (Philip) Bounous, Louise Rivoire (Laurent) Rivoire, Margaret Gardiol (Edward) Micol, **3rd Row Standing L-R:** Marie Meytre (Jacques) Meytre, Susanne Long (Eli) Bertalot, Lydia Martinat (Philip) Rostan, Ida Pascal (James Henry) Bounous, Jeanne Berger Bertalot (Frederick) Meytre, Jeanne Pascal (Jean Henri) Pascal, Madeleine Pons (Henry) Curville, Marianne Garrou (Ben) Pons, Louise Gaydou (John Henry) Pascal, Susanne Menusan (John Louis) Rostan, Louise Gaydou (John D.) Guigou, Mary Refour (Marshall) Ogle.

hut was built on the railroad right of way. The building was funded in part by $4,000 taken from the church's building fund.

In anticipation of need for additional space for the educational program, a committee was appointed to document those needs and make recommendations. As a result of this study, at a meeting November 26, 1950, the congregation approved the establishment of a building program and the appointment of a Finance Committee and a Building Committee.

Expansion, Involvement, Witness

NURSERY SUNDAY SCHOOL CLASS — 1952 — Louise Perrou, Connie Hastings, Susan Deal, Harvey Jones, Jane Perrou, Bobby Martinat, Sharon Hudson, Marilyn Stiff, Jimmy Brinkley, Susanne Pascal, Claudia Pons, Betty Giraud, Evelyn Stiff, Cindy Stiff, Louise Grill, Charles Grill, Donald Brittain.

KINDERGARTEN SUNDAY SCHOOL CLASS — 1952 — Left Table L-R: Johnnie Gardner, Linda Burns, Rachel Micol, Benny Perrou, Toni Perrou, Vera Rutherford, Lucy Zimmerman, June Rostan, Mary Alice Powell, Elizabeth Garrou. Right Table L-R: Butch Pascal, Brooks Styles, René Dickerson, Paul Hastings, John Bleynat, Vivian Ogle Coffey, (unrecognized), Kathy Jones, Don Henry Martinat, Kenny Rector.

A celebration of the 103rd Anniversary of the Edict of Emancipation of the Waldenses with the Rev. J.P. Zaccara, pastor of Broome Street Presbyterian Church of New York and member of the Board of Directors of the Waldensian Aid Society as speaker, was held Friday, February 16, 1951. The pictorial plates of the church being sold to raise money for Waldensian Aid were made available.

At a joint meeting of the session and diaconate on July 13, 1952, the officers agreed to pledge $6,000 to the Mid-Century Development Program of Union Seminary in Richmond. The money was to be paid over a period of five years.

An important congregational meeting was held March 1, 1953. At this meeting, a budget for nine months was approved. The fiscal year of the church was changed to conform to the calendar year effective December 31, 1953. A report from the Building Committee was received and approved unanimously. The report authorized the committee to plan a campaign to raise between $125,000 and $150,000. It was also authorized to solicit funds for enlarging the sanctuary as well as expanding the educational facilities. The committee was authorized to borrow money as needed. A report in the April 5, 1954 church bulletin stated cash and pledges totaling

SUNDAY SCHOOL CLASS — 1952 — 1st Row L-R: John Stephen Perrou, Jr., Jenelle Searcy, Weeta Searcy, Alton Pons, Louise Ann Verreault. 2nd Row L-R: Dale Eugene Bridges, Joan Hall, Ruth Williams, Julia Lee Ribet, Catherine Baker.

$79,740 had been received, and this raised the total in the building fund to $106,661. The authorization to enlarge the sanctuary was withdrawn because the architect felt it was impractical.

Miss Nancy Stikeleather of Statesville, a senior at Flora MacDonald College, arrived June 15, 1953 to serve as church secretary and Director of Religious Education for the summer. The church bulletin for August 16 reported the church picnic had been postponed due to the polio epidemic.

The Building Committee, at a congregational meeting February 14, 1954, requested approval to execute a contract with Herman-Sipe of Conover, North Carolina in the amount of $111,553 plus approximately $13,000 for the heating contract. It also requested authority to make changes as necessary and permission to conduct a campaign during March 1954 to raise the additional funds needed to construct the new Educational Building. Approval was given by the congregation.

Youth Sunday was observed January 31, 1954, and at the session meeting on February 28, 1954, Rev. Styles expressed pleasure at the way the youth had handled the worship service. He was especially happy over the decision of one of the youth, Gregory Grana, to enter the ministry.

Miss Mary Ruth Marshall of Hickory, a graduate of Montreat College with a Bachelor of Arts degree in Christian Education and Church Music, began work the first week of June 1954 as church secretary and first full-time Director of Christian Education. She continued in this capacity until her resignation August 30, 1956.

The fifties brought a method of making buildings more comfortable in summer—air conditioning. At a July 25, 1954 joint meeting of the officers, it was decided to proceed with installing a refrigerated air conditioning system in the sanctuary at a cost not to exceed $5,000.

Moderator Styles brought a suggestion from the diaconate to the session at its October meeting that the diaconate be increased from twelve to fifteen members. This was unanimously approved at a congregational meeting November 21, 1954.

The church received a rather large bequest from the estate of Louis Bounous in 1954. This gift is still returning an annual income to the church. Louis Bounous was the son of Jean Bounous, one of the two scouts sent to North Carolina in the spring of 1893 to find suitable land for the colony. Jean Bounous joined the colony in 1902 with his family. Louis Bounous became the superintendent and vice-president of the Valdese Manufacturing Company.

GROUNDBREAKING FOR EDUCATIONAL BUILDING — MARCH 17, 1954 — L-R: George W. Williams, Jr., Rev. Walter H. Styles, John Alex Guigou, John D. Guigou, Henry F. Garrou, W. Harold Mitchell, J. Armand Verreault, Emmanuel Perrou.

Church with Completed EDUCATIONAL BUILDING
Dedicated January 16, 1955

Expansion, Involvement, Witness

The year 1954 brought an effort to unite the Presbyterian Church U.S., the United Presbyterian Church, and the Presbyterian Church U.S.A. Meetings were held during late 1954 and early 1955 to study the plan of union. The Presbyterian Church U.S. voted against the plan later in 1955.

January 16, 1955 brought the official use of the new Educational Building. Figures showing the church growth and activity for 1950 through 1954 were released.

	MEMBERSHIP		BUDGETS			
Year	SS	Church	Benevolences	Current Exp.	Building	Total
1950	299	531	8,025	11,041	2,436	21,502
1951	300	551	8,832	10,575	14,209	33,615
1952	319	558	12,102	13,893	15,400	41,395
1953	299	574	8,718	14,648	18,007	41,373
1954	329	608	10,598	18,202	28,375	57,175

Sunday School enrollment on January 16, 1955 was 336. The average weekly attendance during 1954 had been more than 210.

The General Assembly of the Presbyterian Church U.S. adopted a program for 1955-56 called "Forward With Christ." Each church appointed a committee to establish goals for the particular church during the year. The Waldensian Presbyterian Church adopted the following goals:

1. Fifty new members
2. An average of 300 present at church
3. Enrollment gain of ten percent and an attendance gain of fifteen percent for Sunday School
4. Reach ten percent more youth
5. Twenty-five percent increase in enrollment and attendance in Men's work
6. Women's work—enlist more women, continue study and service
7. Emphasize tithing

At the session meeting July 24, 1955, it was reported that the total cost of the Educational Building had been $147,387.11. Pledges totaled $80,000. A special program of tithing during September, October and November to help the church budget and building fund was adopted.

In an attempt to meet a need for kindergarten care for children in Valdese, the session appointed a committee to study the matter and make recommendations. The committee reported on November 27, and they were instructed to proceed with plans to open a kindergarten. The kindergarten opened Monday, January 9, 1956 with Mrs. Frederic H. Pons, Sr. (Iola Britt) as director. Classes were held from 9:00 to 12:00, Monday through Friday, and were limited to twenty children. Classes were held on the first floor of the Educational Building. Fees were set at $15 per month.

At the meeting of Concord Presbytery on January 17, 1956, the Rev. Walter H. Styles was elected commissioner to the General Assembly to be held in Montreat, May 31 to June 6. He was also elected chairman of the commissioners from Concord Presbytery.

In 1956, the 108th Anniversary of the Edict of Emancipation was celebrated with special entertainment by the Youth Team dancing the Courenta. This group had won several awards participating in Folk Dance Festivals in Asheville and Virginia Beach.

COURENTA DANCE TEAM — Performed for the February 17th Celebration in 1956 — 1st Row L-R: Pamela Briggs, Frances Bounous, Dianne Tron, Janet Micol, Mary Louise Pascal, Gigi Grill, Sandra Gilreath, Linda Grana, Rachel Micol. 2nd Row L-R: Harold Murray, James H. Rostan, Albert Pascal, Paul Weir, Bart (Bartholomew) Bounous, Steve Rostan, John P. Rostan III, Brooks Styles, Albert Perrou. Accordian Player — James H. Pascal.

Gregory Grana appeared before the session on March 18, 1956, giving his reasons for entering the ministry and asking for the endorsement of the session. The session gave advice and encouragement and unanimous endorsement. Gregory was the first member of the Waldensian Presbyterian Church to seek to enter the ministry. He was examined at the meeting of Concord Presbytery held in Valdese, April 17, 1956.

A series of special services was conducted by the Rev. John D. Smith of First Church, Morganton, North Carolina, March 24 through 28, 1957. The title of the services was "Built On the Rock."

Elder John D. Guigou represented Concord Presbytery as a commissioner to the General Assembly held at South Highland Church in Birmingham, Alabama, April 25-30, 1957. He reported to presbytery on July 23 at a meeting at Lees-McRae College, Banner Elk, North Carolina.

Church membership on December 31, 1957 was listed at 593. Sunday School enrollment was 335 with an average attendance during 1957 of 210.

October 13, 1957 was observed as Churchwide Laymen's Day. Elder George W. Williams, Jr. presided, and W. Harold Mitchell delivered the sermon.

The congregation passed a resolution during the congregational meeting held November 3, 1957, requiring a two-year period between terms of those serving on either the session or diaconate.

The Rev. Mr. Styles announced at the morning worship April 4, 1958, that Miss Yvonne Raftelis, upon graduation from Assembly Training School in Richmond, Virginia, had accepted the position of Director of Religious Education. Her work began June 1, 1958.

Mr. Styles left May 5 for two weeks of study at Union Theological Seminary, Richmond, as a Tower Scholar.

The year 1958 was an eventful year for the Women of the Church. The organization, consisting of ten circles with 222 active women, presented eight folding tables for use in Pioneer Hall. The Women hosted the fifty-second annual meeting of the Women of the Church of Concord Presbytery, November 5 and 6.

With deep regret, the congregation concurred with the Rev. Mr. Styles' request that his pastoral relationship with the church be dissolved effective December 15, 1958. The action was taken at a congregational meeting called for this purpose at the close of the morning worship November 23, 1958. Mr. Styles accepted the pastorate of Faith Presbyterian Church in Tallahassee, Florida. The worship service of December 14, 1958 marked Mr. Styles' 415th sermon delivered to the church and ended eight and three quarter years of pastorate. An interesting note is that during his pastorate, forty-two spouses of members who had held membership in other churches became members of the Waldensian Presbyterian Church.

Dr. George E. Staples, Minister of Students at Davidson College, Davidson, North Carolina, began service as stated supply on January 11, 1959. He commuted each Sunday and was available when needed. Dr. George Staples completed his service as supply pastor on May 3, 1959, and a covered dish dinner was held in Pioneer Hall in his honor. On this date, it was announced that the debt on the Educational Building had been paid, and the church was now debt free.

A congregational meeting held on March 29, 1959 heard a report from the Pulpit Nominating Committee. The committee nominated the Rev. J. Clyde Plexico, Jr., pastor of the First Presbyterian Church of Cartersville, Georgia, to serve as pastor. The nomination was unanimously approved. Mr. Plexico, his wife Miriam, and children Sandra, Clark and Dale moved to Valdese the first week of May. His first sermon was on May 10, 1959. The sermon subject was "The Coming of God in Power." A reception to welcome the Plexico family was held May 17, and Mr. Plexico was officially installed as pastor July 26, 1959.

A congregational meeting was held April 5, 1959 to hear the report of the officers' recommendations on the building of a new manse. The congregation approved the appointment of a committee to: (1) Acquire a lot of their choosing in a suitable residential area; (2) employ an architect; (3) prepare plans and specifications; (4) prepare a plan of financing; and (5) report to the congregation as soon as possible. The committee reported on July 26, 1959 at a congregational meeting which authorized them to proceed with the construction of a manse on North Laurel Road at an estimated cost of $50,000.

May 31, 1959 marked the end of Miss Yvonne Raftelis' service as Director of Christian Education. She left to be married to the Rev. Thomas Miller, a Presbyterian minister. The congregation expressed its sincere appreciation for her service and wished her well in her future life.

The worship bulletin for June 21, 1959 noted that Miss Elizabeth Steele of Statesville, North Carolina, would serve as Director of Christian Education for the remaining summer months. Miss Steele worked until September 1, 1959 when she returned to college.

The church bulletin for September 6, 1959 announced the first practice for a group of children's choirs. The Cherub, Melody, Junior and Youth Choirs were to begin practice that week. These choirs with slight changes have remained a part of our music program to this day.

The first officers' retreat was held at Camp Grier on Friday evening, September 11, 1959 and Saturday morning, September 12. Elders, deacons and their wives attended the retreat where long range plans for the church were discussed.

A Dial-A-Prayer telephone line was installed at the church, and service began September 20, 1959. A recorded prayer and thought for the day was heard when the number was dialed.

In preparation for a week of spiritual enrichment services, cottage prayer meetings were held in thirteen homes on Thursday, October 15, 1959. The services were conducted by the Rev. Dr. S.W. Dendy, pastor of First Presbyterian Church of Dalton, Georgia.

In October 1959, plans were made to present a live Christmas scene on the church lawn. Volunteers were asked to assist in preparing for this presentation. This ministry has been expanded and improved and has been enjoyed each year since it began.

Philip H. Garrou, chairman of the Manse Building Committee, reported on November 22, 1959 that contracts had been signed for the construction of the manse. The total cost including land was to be $50,241.76. Construction would take approximately eight months. The manse was dedicated in a service held at the new manse on Sunday, September 18, 1960.

New Manse on Laurel Road — Dedicated September 18, 1960

December 6, 1959 brought the dedication of new hymnals, donated as a memorial gift.

Ann Long Hern (Mrs. Joe Hern, Jr.) was employed as the first part-time church secretary in 1959. She served until July 1962. Hazel Coley Bounous (Mrs. Daniel B. Bounous, Jr.) began work as part-time secretary in 1962. It was not until 1974 that a full-time secretary was employed.

The session meeting of January 24, 1960 was a notable one in the life of the church. The second young man in the history of the church announced his decision to be a candidate for the ministry. Joseph A. Verreault III, grandson of a former pastor, Rev. J.A. Verreault, was received as a candidate by Concord Presbytery on July 19, 1960. He entered Union Theological Seminary at Richmond, Virginia during the fall of that year.

FRENCH CHOIR AT FEBRUARY 17th CELEBRATION — 1960
Front Row L-R: Madeleine Pons (Henri) Curville, Elda Gaydou (Philip) Bounous, Evelyn Pons (Leroy) Bronson, Madeleine Rostan (Emile) Squillario. Back Row L-R: Henri Curville, Peter A. Meytre, Marian Morrison, Maxine Briggs Hightower, John Alex Guigou, Catherine Rivoire Cole, Louise Gaydou (John D.) Guigou, Olga Pascal, Marie Ferrier (James Henry) Pascal, Frances Micol (Edward) Pascal, Rosalba Pascal (Kenneth) Shook, Ruth McQuiston (George W., Jr.) Williams, Director; Nell Saunders (Leon) Guigou.

The announcement was made March 20, 1960 that Miss Shirley Gilliam, student at Presbyterian School of Christian Education at

Richmond, would be coming to work as Director of Christian Education upon graduation. She began work July 7, 1960.

A Men of the Church Fall Rally was held at Barium Springs Home for Children on Tuesday, September 13, 1960. W. Harold Mitchell was installed as President of the Men of Concord Presbytery, and John A. Bleynat was installed as secretary.

A presbytery-wide meeting was held at Statesville High School Auditorium at 8:00 pm Thursday, October 6, 1960. The meeting was the kick-off for "Evangelism Emphasis" proposed by the General Assembly. A cavalcade from Valdese attended the session. Cottage prayer meetings were held Thursday, October 13, at 7:30 pm in twenty-one homes to support the week of Spiritual Enrichment Services scheduled for October 16-23. Guest minister was the Rev. Dr. Harry K. Holland from First Presbyterian Church of Marietta, Georgia.

During the installation and ordination service for church officers held January 1, 1961, the congregation dedicated itself to "A New Commitment in a New Century." The new commitment was to a greater emphasis and participation in evangelism. The year 1961 marked the beginning of the second century of the Presbyterian Church in the United States (Southern).

Mr. Plexico left January 23, 1961 for two weeks of intensive study as a Tower Room Scholar at Union Theological Seminary in Richmond, Virginia.

The statistical report for December 31, 1960 showed 622 communicants on roll. This was the largest membership in the history of the church as of that date. A total of $60,515.66 was reported as the giving of the church. Average Sunday School attendance during 1960 was 226.

A series of special services began on Palm Sunday, March 26, 1961 with the Rev. Mr. Plexico as speaker. Good Friday services were held from 12:00 to 3:00 P.M. with different speakers from the local churches. Short services were held every twenty-five minutes during the three hours.

The Waldensian Presbyterian Church hosted a meeting of Concord Presbytery Tuesday, April 18, 1961.

The September 10, 1961 worship bulletin announced a series of meetings to be held in various homes of the congregation. The meetings were to be in a different home each week and were designed to afford the area members of the congregation an opportunity to meet and talk with the pastor in small groups.

REUNION OF WALDENSIANS AT THE ALBERT F. GARROU HOME — SEPTEMBER 9, 1961

L-R Seated: Henry Pascal, Ben Pons, Dr. Robert Pascal, Jean Pierre (JP) Rostan, John D. Guigou, Louis Philippe (LP) Guigou, Frederic (Dick) Pons, Alexis Guigou, Benjamin Grill, Irma Ghigo (JP) Rostan, Helen Barker (Alexis) Guigou, Lydia Jacumin (Rev. John) Pons, Marianne Garrou (Ben) Pons. L-R Standing: Louise Johnson Grill (Henry) Grill, Henriette Rostan (Michael) Grana, Olga Pascal, Lydia Parise (Clarence) Poteet, Louise Gaydou (John D.) Guigou, Bertie Cook (Henry) Pascal, Lillian Sweeney (LP) Guigou, Iola Britt (Dick) Pons, Catherine Dalmas, Henri Curville, Bernice Smith (Frederick) Ribet, Madeleine Pons (Henri) Curville, Jeanne Pons (Frank) Perrou, Mary Refour (Marshall) Ogle, Ida Pascal (Jacques Henri) Bounous, Apollonie Barus Hill, Henriette Vinay Lavanchy (John) Long, Marie Hill, Marianne Bounous (Pierre) Gaydou, Madeleine Rostan (Emile) Squillario, Hilda Ogle (Wayburn) Jones, Annie Marie Garrou (Ben) Grill, Catherine Meytre (Philippe) Rostan, Margaret Gardiol (Edward) Micol, Celestine Allio (Jean-Pierre) Dalmas, Rachel Perrou (Marshall) Warren, Catherine Guigou, Madeleine Gardiol (Silvio) Martinat, Madeleine Grill, Ruth Coulter (Ferdinand) Ribet, Henriette Martinat (Auguste) Pascal, Jean Barus, Susanne Menusan (Jean Louis) Rostan, Henriette Jacumin (Jean) Barus, Jannie Jacumin (Arthur A.) Deal, Augustine Jacumin Parise (Jess Lee) Maltba, Hilda Whitener Yoder (Albert F.) Garrou, Albert F. Garrou. L-R Back Row Standing: Ferdinand Ribet, Henry Vinay, Jean Peyrot, Ernest Ribet, Frank Pascal, James Henry Pascal, Maurice Rostan (standing behind Frank Pascal).

Expansion, Involvement, Witness 107

The October 29, 1961 worship bulletin reported that representatives of West German television visited Valdese and our church during the week. They were preparing a television show on the world's great religions, and a portion will feature the Waldensian Church of Italy. Scenes of the town and church were filmed. The meeting of the Tuesday Evening Leadership Class was filmed. The French Choir provided hymns for background music.

A change in election procedures was approved at the congregational meeting of November 26, 1961. Church members nominated double the number of men needed for elders or deacons. The following Sunday the required number receiving the highest number of votes were elected to office by acclamation.

The session voted on February 10, 1962 to participate in the support of a missionary to Japan in the amount of $3,000 annually. The missionary was Miss Lois Grier Moore, an educational missionary.

Miss Shirley Gilliam, Director of Christian Education, presented a plan to the session on March 4, 1962 for a future caravan of the Youth Fellowship members to tour various churches, schools, colleges and seminaries of the Presbyterian Church to learn more about the work of the church. The caravan was originally scheduled for the first week of July, 1962 but was not carried out until May 30 through June 7, 1963, due to problems in getting organized. The cost was borne by the members of the Youth Fellowship.

The worship bulletin for May 20, 1962 carried the announcement of the installation of a new Allen organ. The new Allen electric organ was dedicated at a worship service held at 5:00 P.M, September 23, 1962. The organist at Christ Church in Charlotte, North Carolina, Mr. Richard Van Sciver, gave a recital. Mrs. Dorothy Lowdermilk Harwell was soloist.

A new program was offered the youth of the church in June of 1962, which gave the first opportunity to participate in a Vocational Guidance program through a local church program and the Presbyterian Guidance Center at St. Andrews College. This program has been offered to the youth of the church each year since 1962 with great success and meaning for the participants.

The September 1962 issue of the Presbyterian Survey carried a feature article on the Waldensian Church. Also in September, approximately twenty-five officers and their wives attended a retreat at the Waldensian Club House on Mineral Springs Mountain. After an evening meal, the program of the church, the

Covenant Life Curriculum, and evangelism were discussed. The retreat ended with the observance of the Lord's Supper. At a session meeting on September 23, the session agreed to a study of the Covenant Life Curriculum to prepare for its use in the local church. A committee was appointed to conduct an evaluation and study of the material.

During 1962, a new road was built into the Waldensian Cemetery approaching from the south side. All roads in the cemetery were paved.

The Waldensian Presbyterian Church participated in a new program providing a chaplain for Valdese General Hospital. Local church ministers served as chaplain one week at a time. The Rev. Mr. Plexico served the first week of the new program. The church planned for two services for Easter Sunday at 9:30 and 11:00 A.M. in 1963.

At a meeting on May 19, 1963, the congregation approved a plan to conduct a special fund drive the last two weeks of June to raise money to liquidate the debt on the manse. The amount currently budgeted was diverted to the Presbyterian Development Fund until a total of $19,000 was paid. There would be no capital fund programs accepted until after 1966.

At the May 19 worship service, Shirley Gilliam announced her resignation effective June 25, 1963. She resigned to accept a position with Covenant Presbyterian Church in Charlotte, North Carolina as a youth worker. Her resignation was accepted with regret.

Mr. Donn W. Wright, a student at Columbia Seminary, began work June 16, 1963 as summer Director of Christian Education. The worship bulletin for June 30, 1963 reported Mrs. John Heilman (Margaret Garrou) had been employed to direct the weekday kindergarten.

The committee to study the Covenant Life Curriculum made its report to the session August 25, 1963. The committee recommended the adoption of the curriculum to begin October 1, 1963. The session approved the recommendations.

Two morning services were begun on October 13, 1963. The first service was at 8:45 A.M. with music by the Youth and Boys' Choirs. The second service was at 11:00 A.M. with music by the Chancel Choir. This worship arrangement continued through December of 1963. The early service was discontinued with the statement that it would be studied again in March.

The session at its January 19, 1964 meeting endorsed Gregory Grana for appointment as a foreign missionary. The session stated in their judgment he possessed such qualifications for this work as would render his appointment proper and good.

During the session meeting March 1, 1964, a motion was made and approved to begin planning a day of recognition for Mrs. George Williams (Ruth McQuiston), who had led our church music program for approximately thirty years. The event was held on May 3, 1964. A special program of favorite anthems was given. Mrs. Williams was given a plaque and a charm for her bracelet. The congregation was privately canvassed, and the Ruth M. Williams Music Scholarship Fund was set up and announced on that day. This scholarship continues to assist young musicians with their college training.

Also during the March 1 meeting of the session, the Rev. Clyde Jones, a Baptist minister residing in Valdese, was employed as Director of Christian Education for a period of six months. Mr. Jones was a graduate of Baylor University and Southern Baptist Theological Seminary. He was under the care of the Presbytery's Commission on the Ministry preparatory to becoming a Presbyterian minister. The session, at its September 9 meeting, extended the employment of the Rev. Clyde Jones as Director of Christian Education.

The April 26, 1964 worship bulletin contained several interesting announcements. Concord Presbytery met Tuesday, April 21, at Back Creek Church. Mr. Plexico was elected moderator-nominee for the July meeting of presbytery. Also, April 26 marked the beginning of a week of special services led by Dr. F. Crossley Morgan. Fifteen home prayer meetings were held the prior week to prepare for this series of services.

The moderator announced at the May 10 meeting of the session that our sponsored missionary, Miss Lois Grier Moore, would not be returning to the mission field. As an alternative, it was suggested that the church support the Rev. and Mrs. Gregory Grana as missionaries for a total of $7,200.

July 26, 1964 marked a historic first for the Waldensian Presbyterian Church. A commission from Concord Presbytery came to Valdese to ordain Gregory Grana as an Evangelist. This was the first ordination of a son of this church. His parents were Michael and Henrietta (Rostan) Grana. It was a unique circumstance which permitted his ordination in his home church. Since he was not being installed to serve a particular church, it was possible to hold the service in his home church. The Rev. Grana and his wife, the former Janice Timmons, were to go to the Belgian Congo as Evangelistic and Christian Education Missionaries. They left the United States August 13 for Belgium for one year's study. While in Brussels, their son Andrew was born on October 28, 1964.

The congregation approved a new election procedure on September 16, 1964. In the future, the retiring elders and deacons would serve as a nominating committee. The committee would nominate twice the number to be elected. The third Sunday of September would be the election day for elders and the second Sunday of October the election day for deacons.

During the congregational meetings to elect officers in 1964, two very significant events took place. At the October 11 meeting, Mrs. J. Laird Jacob, Sr. (Jeanne Verreault) was elected an elder, and at the October 25 meeting, Mrs. Leroy Bronson (Evelyn Pons) was elected a deacon. These were the first two women elected as officers in the Waldensian Presbyterian Church. Both were daughters of former pastors of the church. Mrs. Jacob was the daughter of the Rev. J.A. Verreault, Sr., and Mrs. Bronson was the daughter of the Rev. John Pons. Their election was made possible by a change in the Book of Church Order, approved at the General Assembly earlier in 1964, providing for the election of women officers. Prior to this time, women had not been permitted to serve as church officers.

Elder Jeanne Jacob made history again by attending a meeting of Concord Presbytery with Mr. Plexico at Davidson College Church on January 19, 1965. She was the first woman elder to represent the Waldensian Presbyterian Church at a presbytery meeting and the first woman elder to attend a meeting of Concord Presbytery.

Concord Presbytery met October 20, 1964 at Lees McRae College, Banner Elk, North Carolina. Mr. Plexico served as Moderator during the meeting. He was also elected a commissioner to the General Assembly scheduled to meet in Montreat, North Carolina in April of 1965. At an adjourned meeting of presbytery held in Statesville, North Carolina, on October 27, Mr. Plexico was elected Chairman of the Commissioners to General Assembly.

The Rev. Clyde Jones tendered his resignation as Director of Christian Education at the session meeting December 6, 1964. Mr. Jones resigned effective December 31, 1964 in order to pursue his studies. His resignation was regretfully accepted.

In 1964, John Stephen Perrou, Jr., who held membership in this

Expansion, Involvement, Witness

church as a youth, was ordained to the gospel ministry at the Cedar Rock Baptist Church in Castallia, North Carolina. He was the son of John Stephen and Mary Margaret (Mackie) Perrou. He was a 1963 graduate of the University of Tennessee and received the Master of Divinity Degree from Southeastern Baptist Seminary at Wake Forest, North Carolina in June 1968.

Miss Elizabeth Jean Lunsford arrived the first week of June 1965 to serve as our summer Director of Christian Education. She was a recent graduate of Montreat-Anderson College.

The session called Donn Wilson Wright to serve as our Director of Christian Education and Assistant Minister at the session meeting August 26, 1965. Mr. Wright had served as summer Director of Christian Education in 1963. He moved to Valdese on September 1 and began his work on Thursday, September 2, 1965. He was received by Concord Presbytery, Tuesday, October 19, at its meeting in Mt. Mourne, North Carolina, and was ordained in Valdese, October 31, 1965. Donn Wright was the first Assistant Minister to serve the church.

Also at the August 26, 1965 meeting, the session voted to discontinue the weekday kindergarten program. This action was taken due to lack of enrollment and in accordance with the by-laws under which the kindergarten operated.

On September 1, 1965, Mr. R.L. Pyatt began work as business manager for the church. He was to oversee the maintenance and upkeep of property and supervise the non-professional staff. He served in this capacity until December 31, 1966. His service to the church was appreciated.

The minutes of the session meeting October 17, 1965 record the fact that Mr. and Mrs. J.P. Rostan, Sr. gave to the church the property on the east side of the church bordering South Italy Street. The deed was filed November 5, 1965. This action gave the church ownership of the entire block bordered by Main, Italy, St. Germain and Rodoret Streets. This was the realization of a dream expressed by the Rev. Albert McClure at his last joint meeting of the officers on January 8, 1950 prior to assuming his duties at Barium Springs Home for Children.

December 1965 initiated the first dramatized Christmas scene. Prior to this time, the scene had used live actors but only in stationary poses. The dramatized production has continued each year and has been an important event in the life of our youth and a meaningful service to the community.

The church library was relocated in the room next to the church secretary's office in December 1965. The statistical report for 1965 showed 689 communicant members. Benevolent giving totaled $36,049, and current expenses totaled $40,589. There was $13,760 given to the building fund for a grand total of $90,398. The Sunday School enrollment was 311.

On February 20, 1966, the Rev. Gregory Grana, assisted by Dr. Francis Ghigo and others, led a French worship service. A total of 348 people attended this service.

The worship bulletin for March 5, 1966 announced that repairs were being made to the sanctuary floor, and services would be held in Pioneer Hall for the month of March. The session approved borrowing up to $15,000 for the repairs. The work done included: (1) Installing a footing drain system and waterproofing all underground walls of the sanctuary, Tron Hall and Pioneer Hall; (2) Removing the oak floor in the sanctuary which was on concrete and replacing it with lightweight concrete; (3) Repainting the sanctuary; (4) Replacing all rotted baseboards, floors, and other woodwork in Pioneer and Tron Halls.

The session at its meeting March 27, 1966 approved plans presented by the Rev. Donn Wright for making the old manse building into a Christ-centered coffee house for the young people. He was authorized to proceed with plans. The chairman of the Planning and Research Committee reported there seemed to be little interest in building a museum. The committee suggested postponement for the present. The possibility of converting Tron Hall into a museum was discussed but no action taken.

The worship bulletin for July 10, 1966 announced the opening Friday night of the Maze Coffee House. "The Maze is open to all fifteen years of age and older who are interested in conversation. The Maze will be open on Tuesday, Wednesday and Thursday nights."

The session meeting of September 26, 1966 brought action on the proposal made March 27, 1966 concerning renovating Tron Hall for a museum. The Museum Building and Planning Committee had furnished more specific plans on June 17, 1966 for the renovation. These plans were adopted, and the diaconate was instructed to take steps to implement the plans in accordance with the guidelines furnished by the Museum Building and Planning Committee.

A year-end report stated that the Rev. and Mrs. Gregory Grana were now in Nashville, Tennessee. He was serving as Candidate

Secretary of the Board of World Missions. The Granas were unable to go to the Belgian Congo as planned due to the health of their son Andrew. A daughter Lisa Marguerite was born June 9, 1966.

The statistical report for 1966 showed 677 communicants. Sunday School enrollment was 316. Benevolent giving was $38,948.76, current expenses were $46,920.15, and the building fund amounted to $19,447.25, for a grand total of $105,316,76.

The worship bulletin of September 3, 1967 reported: "Contracts have been signed with Guy Frye and Sons to renovate Tron Hall for a museum. Plans have been approved by the Historical Committee and the Museum Building Committee. All present partitions will be removed and glassed partitions installed along each wall. There will be glass cabinets in the center of the room. The cost will be $8,000."

The congregation was called to meet September 24, 1967 for the purpose of considering a recommendation by the session that the congregation review the procedure for election of church officers. The recommendation was not explicit enough, and the congregation asked the session to appoint a committee to recommend a more detailed plan. At another meeting called for October 8, the congregation received a more detailed procedure and approved the plan. The plan was a combination of congregational nominations and the use of a nominating committee.

The session met on October 22 and received the resignation of the Rev. Donn W. Wright as Assistant Minister and Director of Christian Education to be effective October 31, 1967. Mr. Wright resigned to accept the position of Assistant Minister of Trinity Presbyterian Church, Nashville, Tennessee. The resignation was regretfully accepted.

At a meeting of Concord Presbytery on October 17 held at Northminster Church, Hickory, Elder Edward Pascal was elected to serve as commissioner to the General Assembly to be held in May 1968 in Montreat.

The worship bulletin for December 17, 1967 contained a notice that a steering committee was elected to plan the celebration of the seventy-fifth anniversary of the founding of Valdese. The statement did not mention who elected the committee, but it was evidently the town council. Named to the committee were Gerald Baker, Chairman; Walter Boone, Sebren Cannon, Evelyn Bronson, Haynes Rutherford and Howard Wilkie.

The seventy-fifth anniversary included Heritage Sunday, which was observed May 26, 1968, with the Waldensian Presbyterian

Church participating in the community observance. Special music was presented during the morning worship, and during the evening, a community service was held on the high school football field. Senator Sam J. Ervin, Jr. spoke on "Religious Freedom and American Democracy." Numerous events were held during the year to commemorate the beginnings of the town. One of the events which began during the year and continues to this day is the outdoor drama, *From This Day Forward*, written by Fred Cranford, a Valdese native. The drama tells the story of the early history of the Waldensian people and the founding of Valdese. The 1992 season marked the twenty-fifth consecutive year of the production.

The statistical report for 1967 showed 693 communicants with 295 enrolled in Sunday School. Benevolent giving was $36,856, current expenses $56,486, and the building fund $9,511, making a total of $101,853.

The session at its meeting March 24, 1968 called Mr. Ray Waters, a student at Louisville Theological Seminary, to serve as summer assistant. He worked in Valdese from the last week of May through the first week of September 1968. His wife Patsy worked as assistant in the music program.

The worship bulletin for April 14, 1968 announced the schedule of services for Easter week. Morning worship services were to be at 8:45 and 11:00 A.M. These dual services continued through the month of May. The April 21 bulletin announced that Concord Presbytery would meet in our church April 23, 1968. The chancel choir and elders participated in the worship service.

At a congregational meeting, the Rev. Mr. Plexico requested the congregation concur in asking Concord Presbytery to dissolve his pastoral relationship with the Waldensian Presbyterian Church effective August 20, 1968. The congregation concurred with regret. The Rev. Plexico left Valdese to accept the pastorate of Metairie Ridge Presbyterian Church, New Orleans, Louisiana. He had completed just over nine years and three months as pastor of the Waldensian Presbyterian Church. The session was authorized to appoint a pulpit nominating committee to begin work immediately to secure a minister.

On August 18, 1968, a special union service was held at First Baptist Church to recognize Mr. Plexico's service to the community and his church. The service was planned by the Methodist and Baptist ministers of the community. There was special music by the combined church choirs of the town.

CHAPTER 7

Commitment and Service to Christ and Community 1969-1993

*"Commit thy way unto the Lord,
trust also in him; and he shall bring it to pass."*
Psalm 37:5

An expansion of our commitment to Christ's church and to the needs of our community.

January 1969 ushered in a period of numerous changes. The church took on a new interest and direction with the arrival of a new minister, the Rev. Paul H. Felker; his wife Carol Price Felker; and three sons, Mark, Alan and Eric. Mr. Felker assumed the pastorate of the Waldensian Presbyterian Church on January 16, 1969.

One of the first acts of the new minister was to start in February a monthly newsletter, which by the second edition was identified as the *Waldensian Herald*. It included information about the various programs of the church, listed births, deaths, new members, and other newsworthy items. This service was appreciated by the congregation and proved to be such an asset that the *Waldensian Herald* continues in use twenty-three years later.

The traditional celebration of the Emancipation of the Waldenses was held in Pioneer Hall in 1969 with Mr. Harold Noyes, Executive Director of the American Waldensian Aid Society, New York, as guest speaker. This became a memorable evening because of the snow which began falling during the program. By the time the snow ended late the following day, it had reached a depth of twenty-three inches, the deepest snow in the memory of most of the congregation. It necessitated the cancellation of Sunday services and paralyzed the community for several days.

Following the bad winter, the Easter season was welcomed by all. The ecumenical Easter Sunrise service on April 6 in the Waldensian Presbyterian Church Cemetery was well attended. The youth choir provided music for the service. A breakfast, prepared by the Men of the Church, was served afterwards in Pioneer Hall. The church provided worship services at 8:45 A.M. and 11:00 A.M. in the sanctuary. The special offering of the day amounted to $1,900.95 and went to the American Waldensian Aid Society. The society has functioned since the turn of the 20th century with the expressed purpose of raising funds for the benevolent programs of the Waldensian Church of Italy, maintaining communication between Americans of Waldensian descent, preserving Waldensian heritage, and planning tours by dignitaries of the Waldensian Church of Italy.

Miss Rachel Micol, member of the church and daughter of Mr. and Mrs. Robert Micol (Frances Deal), and a graduate of East Carolina University, was hired as temporary Director of Christian Education for the summer of 1969. She did a most acceptable job planning various youth activities. Following her summer's work, she entered Presbyterian School of Christian Education in Richmond to prepare to be a Director of Christian Education. Rachel was the second member of this church to attend that institution. That summer, twenty- six children and youth attended camps and conferences at Camp Grier, the presbytery camp. Three young people attended the World Mission Conference at Montreat.

The church had expressed a desire to again become partial supporters of foreign missionaries. With the help of the World Mission Board, we were able to secure two missionaries who were

THE HULL FAMILY 1969 Dr. and Mrs. Walter Hull, Missionaries to Zaire with daughters Leigh Anne and Maria

going to the mission field. Dr. and Mrs. Walter Hull and their daughters, Leigh Anne and Maria, came from the Mission Conference in Montreat to visit in the church before they left for language school in Brussels, Belgium. The family was warmly received by the church, and mission emphasis was to take on new significance in the life of the church.

The Historical Committee saw the need of a consultant to help with the organization of artifacts displayed in Tron Hall. Consideration was also given to building a separate structure to house the historical collection. Dr. Thomas Spence of the Presbyterian Historical Foundation in Montreat served as consultant and provided the group with excellent advice.

In August 1969, the congregation was honored to have a son of the church, the Rev. Gregory Grana, to conduct a morning worship service. He was then serving on the staff of the Division of World Missions, Nashville, Tennessee.

Youth began to play a special part in the worship services. On December 14, they presented a Christmas Vesper Service. On December 21, they joined the Chancel Choir in presenting their cantata. They also played major roles in the annual production of the outdoor nativity scene.

The December 1969 issue of *Presbyterian Life*, a publication of the United Presbyterian Church, USA, featured a cover picture and four-page article on Valdese and the historical drama, *From This Day Forward*. In addition to group pictures, individual pictures were shown of Mrs. John D. Guigou (Louise Gaydou) in the church museum, actor John Heilman, drama director Gigi Grill, and town leaders Valdo Martinat and J. P. Rostan, Sr. A picture of the church was also included.

Waldensian Presbyterian Church, feeling a close kinship with the presbytery, was honored to have six members of the church serving on presbytery's committees. The end of the year 1969 saw the congregation adopt a budget for 1970 for $92,655.14. The church ranked second in benevolent giving in Concord Presbytery with $35,447 in 1969.

In January 1970, the congregation welcomed the Rev. Ford G'Segner to serve as Minister of Education and Assistant Pastor. In February, he was ordained by a commission from Concord Presbytery. The young minister was a graduate of North Georgia College and Columbia Theological Seminary. His wife, the former Susie DeLoach, and daughter Donna accompanied him. Because of his youth, ability and understanding, he soon established a close relationship with the youth of the church.

The annual observance of the Waldensian Emancipation of 1848 was a highlight of 1970. Dr. Robert Pascal presented the program, a slide presentation of the Waldensian Valleys, in which he showed slides of the villages, homes and many relatives of the original settlers of Valdese. His program was entitled "A Tour of Ancestral Villages and Churches."

In 1970, the Valdese Ministerial Association planned and executed a series of Holy Week services in which our church participated. Planned for the noon hour, they were designed to secure attendance not only of retired individuals but also of employees of the industries on their lunch hour. The site of the old Colonial Theatre, abandoned for years, was chosen to appear non-denominational. Services were conducted by area ministers and musicians. Attendance was excellent, but the site was hardly conducive to worship as rats scurried over the feet of the worshippers. The result was that in succeeding years the services have been held in the sanctuary of the Waldensian Presbyterian Church, which is the church most centrally located in town. These services have continued for two decades, being held in the First Baptist Church and the First United Methodist Church on two occasions when our sanctuary was being renovated.

Under the direction of the Minister of Education, THE MAZE, a youth center housed in the old manse across the street from the church, was reopened. It opened in March and became a gathering place for youth for Sunday School and on several nights a week.

In April 1970, we were honored with a visit by the Moderator of the Waldensian Church of Italy and his wife. Pastor Neri Giampiccoli addressed the congregation at a special meeting. That was a particularly lovely spring, with the dogwoods and azaleas in full bloom. The Giampiccolis were enchanted by the beauty of our area and reveled in the dogwood trees which they had never seen.

In August 1970, Rev. Felker served as a fraternal delegate from the Presbyterian Church, U.S. to the Waldensian Synod meeting in Torre Pellice, Italy. Rev. and Mrs. Felker were treated like royalty as they visited historical sites, toured the ancestral villages of Valdese natives, toured numerous church institutions, participated in numerous worship services, met with church officials, and enjoyed the celebration of the Glorious Return. The Vice Moderator and Mrs. Achille Deodato planned the tour and accompanied them.

Commitment and Service to Christ and Community

One of the highlights of the fall was the church retreat in September at Camp Grier in Old Fort, North Carolina. Families and individuals were in attendance with some camping out or staying in their travel trailers, while others lodged in the dormitories. One hundred fifty-seven attended.

In the fall of 1970, a new cemetery entrance was constructed. Built of yellow Roman brick with the name of the cemetery on a special marker, it became a worthy addition to the sacred spot. It was given as a memorial gift.

A new program was introduced into the Adult Division of the Church School that fall. The three classes established were: (1) Uniform Lesson Cooperative Series, (2) Covenant Life Curriculum, and (3) Adult Response — a class which looked at contemporary issues and the appropriate response by Christian adults. Again the church hosted the Union Thanksgiving Service. The church also broadcast worship services for a month over the local radio station WSVM.

Word was received that the church sponsored missionaries, Dr. and Mrs. Walter Hull, had completed their year of language study in Brussels and had begun their service in Zaire. The church demonstrated its support of the missionaries by several worthwhile projects. The Men of the Church provided a camera and film for them. To aid the Hulls in their hospital work, between $4,000 to $5,000 in sample drugs was collected from area drug stores, packed in drums and made ready for shipment by December 12, 1970. The Women of the Church provided their services to remove the drugs from individual packages and group like medications in larger containers.

The annual celebration of the Waldensian Emancipation was held on February 15, 1971 with Rev. Paul Felker showing slides of the tour he and Mrs. Felker had made the previous year to the Waldensian Valleys. His review included pictures of Waldensian churches and institutions they had visited in Rome, Florence, Milan, the Waldensian Valleys, and the tour of Reformation sites in Geneva, Switzerland. In April, Rev. and Mrs. Felker journeyed to Princeton, New Jersey to give the same program to the Waldensian Aid Chapter in that city.

In 1971, a special project was designed to focus attention on world hunger. Members of the congregation engaged in a Day of Prayer and Fasting on Maundy Thursday. That night, they gathered in Pioneer Hall for a rice supper followed by a communion service.

Never had a small bowl of rice tasted so good to those who participated in the event.

Within the Synod of North Carolina, there was to be restructuring of some of the presbyteries in 1971. The new presbytery in our geographic area was to be composed of Concord, Winston Salem, and Kings Mountain Presbyteries. The organizational meeting was held in Gastonia with Rev. Felker, Rev. Ford G'Segner, and Elders Edward Pons and John Bleynat in attendance. The name of "Covenant" was first chosen for the new presbytery. That was later changed to Concord because of the long history of that former presbytery. Barium Springs, North Carolina was chosen as the site of the presbytery offices.

This year brought about changes in our music program. Mrs. George Williams (Ruth McQuiston) retired in May 1971 after thirty-six years as the organist and choir director. She was recognized on May 30 during the worship service, given a plaque expressing appreciation for her years of faithful service, and honored with a set of diamond earrings.

On June 20, 1971, Steven Lee Mowery, a native of Salisbury and a 1971 graduate of Appalachian State University with a B. A. degree in Choral and Piano Music Education, was installed as the first full-time Music Director of the church. His presence in the church led to a strengthened musical program. The five existing vocal choirs benefited greatly from his direction.

The annual Men's Convention of the Presbyterian Church, U.S., held in Atlanta in 1971, was attended by Rev. and Mrs. Paul Felker. One of the key note speakers was Georgia Governor Jimmy Carter, who was later to become the President of the United States.

Over a period of months, the Women of the Church had become interested in making Chrismons to be used on a tree in the church. In February, Mrs. Harry Spencer, of Virginia, who originated the idea and drew the designs for the Chrismons, visited with the local women and gave them instructions on how to begin the project. Many women and a few men worked diligently over the months to fashion exquisite symbolic designs of gold and white to decorate a tree at Christmas. The tree was placed in Pioneer Hall and was first displayed at a special service on December 12, 1971, during which the Christian meaning of the designs was explained.

The year 1972 was off to a good beginning. Rachel Micol, a member of the church and student at Presbyterian School of Christian Education, requested that she be allowed to come under the care of the session in anticipation of her graduation and serving as a Director of Christian Education. With joy and pride, the session approved her request. On June 11 of that year the church was the scene of Rachel's marriage to the Rev. Huw Christopher, a native of Wales, who had just graduated from Union Theological Seminary, Richmond, Virginia. Their first pastorate was in the Washington Presbyterian Church, Washington, North Carolina.

Music had long been a strength of the church. Each week, there were over one hundred people involved in the choir programs. The musical program was to be further enhanced by a memorial gift of handbells. Steve Mowery, church Music Director, began a handbell training program. In May 1972, the vocal choirs and handbell choir gave a musical production entitled "My Faith Should be a Happy Thing." The handbells began to provide a wonderful new dimension to the music.

A terrible tragedy struck our town in late May 1972 when an underground fallout shelter accidentally exploded, killing five children who had been playing there. Two of those were from the church: Jean Garrou, daughter of Mr. and Mrs. J. Edward Garrou, and Michael Powell, son of Mr. and Mrs. Hedrick Powell. This event saddened the whole community and led to the town establishing a memorial park, "Children's Park," located on Highway 70 East at Micol Creek. A community-wide memorial service to the five children was conducted on June 5, 1972.

A great honor came to one of the fine Christian women of the church in June. Mrs. Laird Jacob, Sr. (Jeanne Verreault), an elder, was elected to serve as a commissioner to the 112th General Assembly of the Presbyterian Church U.S. meeting at Montreat. She was the first woman from Concord Presbytery to be so honored.

In August, the church received a beautiful gold trimmed white brocade funeral pall, given as a memorial gift. In the early years of the church, a black funeral pall had been used, but that was retired later and placed in the museum. For several decades, a funeral pall was not used. With the gift of a new pall, the practice was again readily accepted by the majority of the congregation.

In October of 1972, Rev. and Mrs. Felker gave new linen communion cloths, which she had made by hand. They were bound in a gold and white brocade tape bearing the wheat and grapes motif, which had been purchased in Rome. The cloths were given by the Felkers in appreciation for the privilege of touring the Waldensian Valleys. On the same date, the Boys Choir was dressed in new choir robes, donated by interested members. They were white cottas over wine cassocks, all of which were made by faithful women of the church.

In the fall of 1972, there was a change of organists. John Bridges, who had served faithfully for several years, resigned to assume other duties. James Benton Brinkley, Sr., a very talented member of the church, was hired as the new organist.

Under the direction of the Christian Education Committee, a new program of weekday Christian education called Youth Club was inaugurated the fall of 1972. The program, which provided an opportunity for recreation, choir, Bible study and dinner, met every Wednesday during the public school year. Children in grades one through twelve were involved, including a good number of non-Presbyterians. Youth Club has proved to be one of the outstanding programs of the church providing Christian witness and training. It was flourishing twenty years later with some of the same effective teachers and leaders.

A decision was made to have a Wednesday night Bible Class taught by the minister. It was held at 5:45 P.M. each Wednesday to accommodate any adult who had just completed teaching in the Youth Club or who wished to attend the Chancel Choir at 7:00 P.M. It received a good response, but it soon became evident that the greatest number of participants were senior citizens. Little did the staff and Christian Education Committee know in 1972, that the class would be continuing twenty years later with some of the original participants having studied almost the entire Bible.

A highlight of the Christmas season for many years has been the Christmas Cantata given by the church choir. In 1972, the cantata was a portrayal of the story "Raphael" with an original score by our music director, Steven Mowery. It involved five choirs, soloists, and was enjoyed by 350 people packed into the sanctuary. Thank goodness the fire marshall did not check the facilities at that time!

The Waldensian people in Valdese have always been closely tied to their history. In 1947, the pastor, the Rev. Albert McClure, appointed a Historical Committee to collect and arrange for a place "to preserve anything relating to the early settling of Valdese." For a time, items were collected in a room over the sanctuary. Then in 1955, they were displayed in a small room in Tron Hall. The museum collection grew, and by 1962, the session had approved a building fund for a museum. By 1965, $5,000 had been collected for the purpose. Tron Hall was renovated in 1968 as a temporary

Commitment and Service to Christ and Community

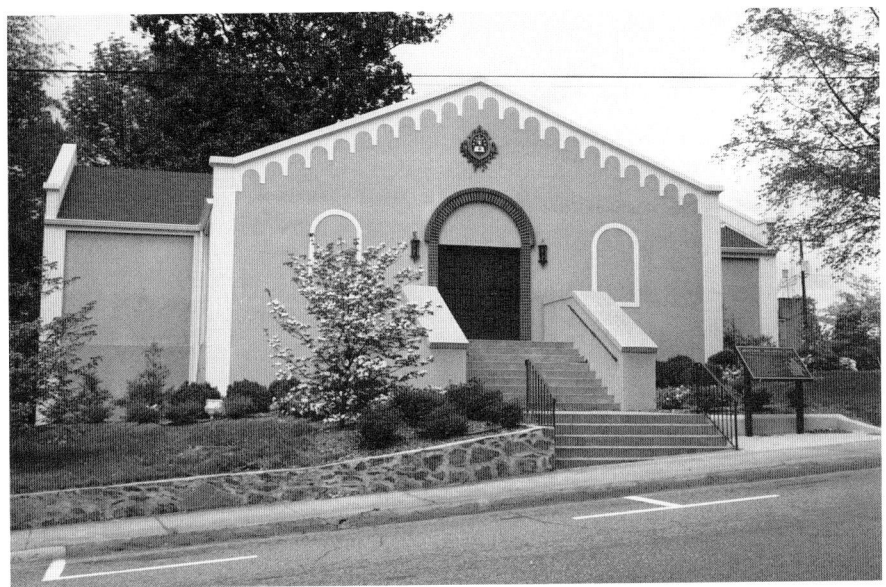

Waldensian Museum — Completed in 1974

setting for the collection. In 1971, the Historical Committee requested and received permission from the session to begin preliminary plans for a new museum building. It had been decided that rather than make the structure a part of the church complex, it might be more advantageous to locate it on the corner of Rodoret Street and St. Germain Avenue where the old manse stood. Plans were submitted to the congregation on February 11, 1973 and received unanimous approval. A financial campaign was launched with the announcement that Mrs. John P. Rostan, Sr. (Irma Ghigo), Mr. and Mrs. John P. Rostan, Jr. (Naomi Bounous) and the Waldensian Bakeries offered a challenge gift. The campaign was very successful and netted $104,310 in cash and pledges. Construction began in July of 1973, and the building was used the first time for the February 17 celebration in 1974.

In 1973, a memorial gift made possible the purchase of robes for the Chancel Choir and Les Jeunes Chanteuses. The robes chosen were royal blue with white stoles; they added much to the beauty of the worship services.

The year 1974 began with two important speakers. First, the church was honored with a visit from Dr. and Mrs. Walter Hull, missionaries to Zaire. Everyone was happy to renew friendships with them and to learn about their medical work there. Dr. H. C.

Doris and Edward Garrou as he works on replica of the Waldensian Emblem for Museum

Olga Pascal in kitchen area of Museum

Evans, president of Lees-McRae College, preached on January 27.

The celebration of the Waldensian Emancipation was conducted in the basement of the new museum. The highlight of the program was a movie which had been produced in Valdese in the 1930's, showing workers leaving the schools and plants, and street scenes. Valdo Martinat, demonstrating his phenomenal gift for remembering names, gave narration of the scenes and identified the vast majority of the people.

One of the church elders, John A. Bleynat, was honored by serving as moderator of Concord Presbytery at the spring meeting.

In June 1974, the church began its summer schedule. Sunday School was omitted, and the worship hour began at 9:30 A.M. Grades one through three were taken to the Educational Building for a reading program. This practice of early worship during the summer was to continue for some years. Pentecost was observed with a special service and the reception of eight youth uniting with the fellowship of the church. On July 5, children and youth of our church were invited to a "Sanctified Seed Spit" (watermelon feast) on the church lawn. This activity was part of the recreational and musical programs of our church. As was the custom, a variety of recreational activities was planned for our children and youth throughout the summer. The second annual music conference was held at the Methodist Campground in July. The children and youth, under the direction of Steven Mowery, gave a production of the contemporary musical, "It's Cool in the Furnace," which made a big hit with the church audience.

During the summer of 1974, the congregation was pleased to have the services of Ann Garrou, one of its young adults, a student at Davidson College, who served as the summer Director of Christian Education.

During the month of August 1974, two new staff persons were secured. Miss Kathy Newton, a South Carolina native and graduate of Presbyterian College, became the Director of Christian Education. Mrs. K. P. Floyd (Dianne Smith) became the first full-time secretary, replacing Mrs. Dan B. Bounous, Jr. (Hazel Coley), who had served as part-time secretary for a number of years. Both of these staff persons were to serve several years and become integral parts of the life of the church.

On February 9, 1975, the church received a very special and unusual gift, a replica of the Liberty Bell, one-fifth the size of the original. It was prominently displayed and used for the call to worship. It has a very distinct tone which lingers in the air. The bell commemorates the 200th anniversary of the Declaration of Independence in 1776 and was cast by the White Chapel Bell Foundry of London, which cast the original bell. It bears the inscription of the original, "Proclaim liberty throughout all the land unto all the inhabitants thereof." After the service on February 9, the bell was placed on permanent display in the museum. James Edward Garrou, a craftsman in the congregation, fashioned a beautiful walnut pedestal for the bell.

The annual observance of the Waldensian Emancipation Proclamation was an outstanding event in 1975 with Pastor Aldo Sbaffi, moderator of the Waldensian Church of Italy, as speaker. He had earlier presided over the 800th centenary of the Waldensian movement in Italy. His address before this congregation was entitled "The Waldenses — Their Present and Future." His enchanting personality charmed not only the congregation, but also members of the East Burke High School with whom he also spoke on another occasion. At the conclusion of the morning worship, the congregation moved in a processional, led by the dignitaries and choir, to the museum. There a brief dedication service was conducted by the moderator and our minister. Dr. Sbaffi visited the church again in 1977.

Also at the February 17 celebration in 1975, Dr. George B. Watts, Professor Emeritus of Davidson College, was honored for his work

Dr. George Byron Watts Honored at the 1975 February 17 Celebration

in writing the history of the Waldensians. A plaque which was placed in the Waldensian Museum in his honor reads as follows:

> In Honor and Appreciation of
> our Friend
> George B. Watts
> Teacher, Historian, Author and Man of God
> for compiling and writing the history
> of the Waldenses recorded in two volumes,
> *The Waldenses in the New World* and
> *The Waldenses of Valdese*
> Presented by the
> Waldensian Presbyterian Church

In April 1975, the North Carolina Presbyterian Historical Society recognized the achievements of the church in preserving the Waldensian heritage of the members. Several members of the church were present at the awards banquet held in Raleigh.

On Good Friday, the church was blessed by a very impressive Tenebrae service with music written by the music director, Steve Mowery. "Tenebrae," meaning "deepening shadows," features music and scripture portraying in a dramatic fashion the closing events in the life of Christ. That year the Easter Sunrise Service was conducted by the Presbyterian church only and followed by breakfast. The dual Easter services were very impressive with trumpets accompanying the hymns and choir.

In May 1975, under the auspices of the Valdese Ministerial Association, a series of ecumenical services were held. The town was honored to have as the speaker, Rev. Dr. John Anderson, pastor of the First Presbyterian Church, Dallas, Texas. The preaching mission had as its theme "The Gospel for Today's World." The series was well received by the churches of the area.

In August, the drama *From This Day Forward* played to full houses, with many of the visitors touring the Waldensian museum prior to viewing the drama. The August Waldensian Festival continued to be a success with the church serving a wonderful Waldensian meal and providing a booth for baked goods and crafts. As was the yearly custom, a brief worship service conducted in the church told visitors the history of the "Glorious Return of the Waldenses in 1689."

In October 1975, Rev. Felker began a course of study, one week each quarter for three years, which would lead to a Doctor of

Ministry degree. The graduate study, offered by McCormick (Presbyterian) Theological Seminary in Chicago, Illinois was being taught at St. Andrews Presbyterian College, Laurinburg, North Carolina. As a part of that venture, the pastor would be conducting various projects and programs through the local church to develop skills and improve ministry.

Upon the resignation of the organist James Benton Brinkley, Sr. in 1975, Mrs. Carol Stewart was employed. She held a degree in music from Appalachian State University.

The Director of Christian Education, Kathy Newton, planned a special program in November, a "Christmas Craft Night." Members of the congregation displayed in Pioneer Hall their crafts and talents including paintings, needlepoint, carving, ceramics, wood crafts, and foods. This festive occasion put everyone in a holiday mood.

The heritage of the Waldensian Presbyterian Church was highlighted by several events in 1976. On February 15, the formal dedication of the Waldensian Museum was held at the conclusion of the morning worship service. This ceremony celebrated the debt-free status of the $110,000 building and its furnishings. The building had been in use since its completion in 1974. The congregation rejoiced at the completion of the museum, which will witness for generations to come to the faith and perseverance of the Waldensian colony in Valdese.

On August 15, 1976, a bronze plaque was placed over the cornerstone of the church, noting the laying of the cornerstone on February 15, 1897 and the dedication of the church on July 4, 1899. Made possible by an anonymous donor, this plaque is significant to the history of the church. After the enlargement of the sanctuary in 1991, the marker was relocated from the south side of the building to the west side.

Another event related to Waldensian heritage was held the weekend of September 25 and 26, 1976. On Saturday, the Women of the Church honored the members of the French Circle at the home of Mr. and Mrs. Albert F. Garrou (Hilda Whitener Yoder). A photograph of the gathering is in the museum. On Sunday, September 26, at the morning worship service, the women of the French Circle were recognized for their faithfulness, devotion, and service to Christ, this church, and His people. In honor of the French Circle, the Women of the Church presented a large print pulpit Bible in the Revised Standard Version.

Commitment and Service to Christ and Community

FRENCH CIRCLE MEMBERS HONORED — SEPT. 26, 1976
1st Row L-R: Marie Parise (Humbert) Leger, Lisette Rivoire Masi, Marie Ferrier (James Henry) Pascal, Annie Garrou (Ben) Grill, Harriet Vinay (John) Long, Irma Ghigo (J.P.) Rostan, Elda Rostan (John) Tessore. 2nd Row L-R: Lydia Jacumin (Rev. John) Pons, Emily Parise (Salvatore) Dentale, Jeanne Pons (Francis) Perrou, Prosperine Heritier (Gilbert) Ribet, Marianne Pons (Clement) Pons, Louise Gaydou (John D.) Guigou, Frances Ullman (Victor) Micol. 3rd Row L-R: Zeline Pons, Louise Achino (Ernesto) Achino, Pauline Grill (Charles) Guerico, Irene Pascal Sturman, Helen Pascal (Aldo) Martinat, Rachel Perrou (Marshall) Warren, Adèle Bouchard (Albert) Tron.

Miss Ann Garrou, a rising senior at Davidson College and daughter of Edward and Doris (Campbell) Garrou, served as a Youth Delegate to the 116th meeting of the General Assembly of the Presbyterian Church, U. S. The meeting was held at Stillman College, Tuscaloosa, Alabama on June 11-19, 1976. Ann reported to the congregation on her role at the assembly during the morning worship on July 18.

The August 15 anniversary of the Glorious Return of 1689 was observed with two worship services in 1977. A number of out-of-town guests attended, including a contingent from the Waldensian Church of New York City. Rev. Alfred Janavel, pastor of that church, assisted in the worship services. A special time of fellowship was enjoyed with dinner under the trees on the south lawn of the church. The Felix Canal family and others from New Jersey entertained the gathering by singing several French and Italian hymns and songs.

A long-range planning committee had been appointed to study the needs of the church buildings. On October 2, 1977, the committee presented to the congregation proposals for the renovation and improvements of church facilities. The estimated cost would be $274,573. The congregation approved the project.

The Sunday before Christmas, a musical reading, "The Coming of the King," was presented by the pastor with Steve Mowery at the organ. A highlight of the Christmas season of 1977 was the revival of a tradition observed in the early years of the church. Each child was given a bag with fruit, nuts, raisins and candy. The youth requested that bags also be presented to those of the congregation

YOUTH CHOIR IN WALDENSIAN DRESS — c. 1977
1st Row L-R: Sherry Pons, Carmen Watts, Bea Picou, Amy Hern, Alan Bonner. 2nd Row L-R: Eric Felker, Lori Church, Ben Hanks, Kim Wilkinson, Vickie Neale, Wesley Garrou. 3rd Row L-R: Willie Garrou, Donna Garrou, Bo Garrou, Michelle Bleynat, Carol Ann Guigou, Caroline Perrou, Mitchell Guigou.

aged seventy or older. Christmas worship was held on Sunday, December 25, with everyone enjoying the singing of traditional carols.

In February 1978, neighborhood meetings were held to acquaint the congregation with the proposed renovation needs of the church. Members of the Renovation Finance Committee and the Building Committee were present at the meetings to answer questions. These meetings led to pledges for the construction program.

On May 21, 1978, the musical "Joseph and the Amazing Technicolor Dreamcoat" was presented by the children and youth choirs.

The Rev. Paul H. Felker received the Doctor of Ministry degree from McCormick Theological Seminary on June 27, 1978. The graduation ceremony was held at St. Andrews Presbyterian College at Laurinburg, North Carolina. A number of family and congregational members were present for the occasion.

Mr. and Mrs. David Dickey, students at Princeton Theological Seminary, assisted in the worship service on August 6, 1978. The congregation rejoiced that Ann Garrou Dickey had been called to the ministry. At the time, Ann was being processed for candidacy under the care of Concord Presbytery.

Miss Kathy Newton completed her work as Director of Christian Education on August 13, 1978. She had served the church since August 1974. She continued to live in Valdese while she was engaged in graduate study at Appalachian State University. At that time, Steven Mowery, Music Director, also assumed the duties of directing the Christian Education program.

The renovation work began in Pioneer Hall in early August 1978. It was to include a new heating/cooling system of heat pumps for all the buildings. While expensive to install, it proved to be cost effective since the buildings were zoned and placed on time clocks. Thus, areas would be heated or cooled only when they were in use. The program included painting and carpeting various areas and refurbishing the sanctuary. The congregation was shocked that the committee would place royal blue carpeting in the sanctuary, but soon discovered that the color enhanced the stained glass windows and wondered why it had not been done earlier.

For the first two months of 1979, Sunday morning worship services were held in Pioneer Hall while the sanctuary was being renovated. In January, it became necessary for the Building Committee to recommend to the session and diaconate that funds for the renovation be increased from the estimated $295,573 to $350,000.

The request was approved.

Ann Garrou Dickey was received as a candidate for the gospel ministry at the meeting of the Presbytery of Concord in Winston Salem, North Carolina, on January 26, 1979. She became the first female candidate for the gospel ministry from this congregation.

Dr. Francis Ghigo, professor of Romance Languages at Davidson College, was the guest speaker for the February 17 Celebration in 1979. Dr. Ghigo was the son of Pastor Filippo Ghigo, who served the Waldensian Presbyterian Church in the early 1900's. At the dinner, Dr. Ghigo talked about his boyhood memories of growing up in Valdese, about the older Waldensians, and especially about the "patois," which was the common language in the early days of the colony. In late 1979, Dr. Ghigo's book, *The Provençal Speech of the Waldensian Colonists of Valdese, N.C.*, was published and made available for purchase. The book was a revision of his master's thesis completed in 1937 at the University of North Carolina, Chapel Hill. Upon his retirement, he decided to publish his work, which will be invaluable to the preservation of the "patois" spoken by the original Waldensian settlers.

The Worship Committee of the session recommended that cushions be purchased for the sanctuary pews and that the choir seats be re-upholstered. The recommendation was approved. The Worship Committee was designated to seek funds of approximately $2,000 to cover the cost of the project. The cushions would be blue velvet to match the color of the carpet.

Upon the completion of the church renovation project, a re-dedication service was held on April 1, 1979. It was a service of thanks and praise to God for His mercy in enabling the congregation to refurbish the sanctuary and to renovate the educational buildings. Rev. Felker preached on the theme "Remembrances" and led the congregation in a litany of rededication.

April 12, 1979 was the wedding day of Miss Kathy Newton, former Director of Christian Education, and Steven L. Mowery, Music Director of the church. Young men of the church served as groomsmen and young women of the church as honorary bridesmaids. The wedding festivities were a happy time for the whole church.

Special services were held May 6-9 with Dr. Moffett Swain of Lenoir as guest minister. The theme of her sermon series was "Women in the Church." Each year a series of special services is conducted in the church in the late spring or early fall.

On May 12, 1979, new Presbyterian hymnals, *The Hymnbook*, were presented to the church as a memorial gift.

Dr. Paul Felker served as a commissioner from the Presbytery of Concord to the General Assembly of the Presbyterian Church, U.S. in Kansas City, Missouri, May 18-June 1, 1979.

The Church Personnel Committee recommended to the session on June 24, 1979 that the number of elders and deacons elected each year be increased from five to six, beginning with the class of 1982. This recommendation was approved by the session and the congregation.

In honor of the twenty-fifth anniversary of his ordination as a minister in the Presbyterian Church, U.S., Dr. Paul H. Felker was presented a silver Revere bowl on July 15, 1979 at the morning worship service. The presentation was made by Dr. Benjamin W. Garrou. At the service, a letter from Dr. Clements E. Lamberth, Jr., General Presbyter and Stated Clerk of the Presbytery of Concord, was read, commending Dr. Felker's work.

On October 28, 1979, Steven Mowery submitted his resignation as Director of Music and Christian Education to be effective July 15, 1980. Mr. Mowery was to begin a four-year course of study for a Doctor of Ministry degree at Union Theological Seminary, Virginia, in the fall of 1980.

As one of his many labors of love for the church, James Edward Garrou designed and built portable tables for use by the handbell choirs.

In November 1979, the prospects of the church's sponsoring a refugee boat family from Vietnam were first discussed. Several years would be spent seeing the project to its fulfillment. The sponsorship of the Tran family would become one of the most heartwarming, rewarding acts of Christian love experienced by the congregation in the history of the Waldensian Presbyterian Church.

In January 1980, a resolution was presented to Commander Edward L. Bleynat expressing the congregation's gratitude for his outstanding work for two years as coordinator of the renovation of the church buildings. Also, as an acknowledgment of his efforts, a gift of $1,000 was given by the church to Lees-McRae College, his alma mater.

At the morning worship service on January 13, 1980, two generous memorial gifts were presented to the church — pew Bibles and a new silver communion service. The communion service contained ten stackable trays each for bread and wine.

On March 30, 1980, the session met to examine Steven Mowery as a candidate for the gospel ministry. He would later be taken under the care of the Presbytery of Concord.

Moderator Giorgio Bouchard, of the Waldensian Church of Italy, and Dr. Charles Arbuthnot, Director of the American Waldensian Aid Society, visited in April as part of a three-week tour of Presbyterian Churches in the United States.

Ann Garrou Dickey received the Master of Divinity degree from Union Theological Seminary in Richmond, May 30, 1980. She and her husband David, a graduate of Princeton and Union Theological Seminaries, accepted a position as co-pastors of the Grove Presbyterian Church, Keenanville, North Carolina, and the Smith Presbyterian Church, Pink Hill, North Carolina. A large contingent of family and friends journeyed to Ann's ordination and installation service and David's installation. Dr. Felker was honored to preach the ordination and installation service of this outstanding young woman. As a token of love from the session of the Waldensian Presbyterian Church, Ann was presented a gold necklace and pendant bearing the emblem of the Waldensian Church. The pendant had been purchased in Italy.

On June 8, 1980, Steven Mowery was honored for his outstanding service to the church for nine years. He was presented a plaque and a gift of health insurance for his four years of study in seminary. After the morning worship service, a farewell dinner was held on the grounds for Mr. and Mrs. Mowery. Others honored that day were the parents of the couple and recent new members of the church.

On June 13, 1980, John Mode assumed part-time responsibilities as choir director. John was serving as a public school band teacher. This was to be the beginning of a long and happy relationship with the choirs and church.

A new Waldensian history, *The Waldensians: The First 800 Years*, by Giorgio Tourn, was received and made available for sale. It was recognized as the first comprehensive history of the Waldensian faith to be published in recent decades.

A group of ninety-six from the church and community traveled to Torre Pellice, Italy, in the Waldensian Valleys, from June 28 to July 3, 1980. A crowd of over one hundred Waldensians greeted them, and the Waldensian Church choir sang French hymns. The group was officially welcomed by the mayor of Torre Pellice; mayor pro tem Edward Pascal in turn presented the mayor the "Resolution of

Friendship" the Town of Valdese sent to the people of Torre Pellice. On June 30, a special thanksgiving service was conducted by Vice Moderator Taccia of the Waldensian Church. Ernest Jahier gave an address in patois, and Hilda Jones presented a plaque which depicted the Waldensian Presbyterian Church of Valdese. The group toured many of the villages and churches in the Valleys, discovered family homeplaces, and met cousins they had never seen. Participants in this trip presented a monetary gift to the area churches as a token of their appreciation for the warm hospitality extended to them. The money was applied to the translation of Giorgio Tourn's book into Castigliano for the benefit of Waldensians in Uruguay and Argentina.

September 1980 can be remembered as a month of generous giving. Dr. Walter Hull, missionary to Zaire, requested $3,000 to ship to Zaire an X-ray unit which had been donated by the Valdese General Hospital. The session approved his request, and the congregation responded by providing the funds. On another occasion, a breakfast was held to assist with the medical expenses of a member of the church who had a terminal illness. Also, a memorial gift of property at Beech Mountain was given to be sold and used for a brick patio at the sanctuary entrance. Another monetary gift of $3,000 inaugurated a pipe organ fund.

On November 2, 1980, a memorial plaque to Miss Sylvia Brown was placed in the hallway of the preschool department. Miss Brown had served as a Sunday School teacher most of her life and was in the preschool department for twenty years. Her small estate was left to be used for the preschool department. Various toys and equipment were placed there from her bequest. The memorial plaque should be a reminder of Sylvia Brown's life of faithful service to the church.

In November 1980, the Pulpit Search Committee recommended that a call be issued to the Reverend John C. Parse as Associate Pastor with special responsibilities in Christian Education. At the time, Rev. Parse was serving the Canton Presbyterian Church, Canton, North Carolina. He moved to Valdese in January 1981 with his wife Kathy and children Andy, Christie, and Julianne. The Rev. Parse was installed as Associate Pastor on February 8, 1981 by a commission from the Presbytery of Concord. A reception in Pioneer Hall that afternoon welcomed the Parse family to the Waldensian Presbyterian Church. The family quickly became active in the life of the church.

Miss Noelle Garrou, daughter of Victor and Ann Garrou, was elected as one of five members of the Concord Presbytery Youth Council. On May 24th, a musical program, "Down by the Creek Bank," was presented by all of the children's choirs.

Organist Mrs. Steve Stewart (Carol) resigned her position on October 11, 1981 after six years of service on the church staff. On November 8, Mrs. Fern Abernathy was hired as interim organist and on December 13 became the permanent church organist.

In November 1981, a brass candelabrum was placed in the church parlor as a memorial gift. The next year, Circle 1 of the Women of the Church purchased a water color by Miss Olga Pascal which depicts the arrival of the first twenty-nine Waldensians in Burke County. It, too, was a memorial gift and was hung in the parlor.

The "Museum 2000 Fund" was established by the Historical Committee in November 1981. The money in this fund cannot be used until after the year 2000. The purpose of the fund is to assure that the future needs of maintaining the museum will be met. Lawyer W. Harold Mitchell serves as administrator of the fund.

A mission request by Dr. Walter Hull was in the forefront at the beginning of 1982. A campaign was started to raise funds to help purchase a Land Rover for transportation on the rough roads on the mission field in Zaire. Then in May, 190 medical books were shipped to Dr. Hull at Good Shepherd Hospital in Zaire. The staff of Valdese General Hospital paid the shipping costs.

The benevolence of the church was further experienced that year when a gift of $1,000 was given from benevolent receipts to the capital funds campaign of Queens College. Personal pledges of $19,000 were made also to a "Time to Grow," Church Development Campaign of the Presbytery of Concord.

In February 1982, a gift of eight large print hymn books, for use by those with visual difficulties, was given as a memorial gift. Later in the year, an evergreen tree was given as a memorial and planted on the main street lawn of the church.

Mrs. John D. Guigou (Louise Gaydou) was recognized on February 28, 1982 for her faithful service of sixty years as a member of the church choirs.

The congregation was saddened by the belated news of the death of Dr. George B. Watts on May 7, 1981. Dr. Watts, a former professor of French at Davidson College, had spent much time doing research in Valdese and had made many friends. His initial interest in the Waldensian people in Valdese grew to include all

Waldensians who had immigrated to North and South America. That research resulted in the publication of his book, *The Waldenses in the New World*, in 1941 and his 1965 book, *The Waldenses of Valdese*. Dr. Watts brought together a wealth of information gathered from several sources and many persons in Valdese to give the town and church its first published history. The Waldensian Presbyterian Church owes a great debt of gratitude to Dr. George B. Watts for his work.

An announcement was made on May 30, 1982 that the book *A History of the Waldenses* by the Rev. John Pons had been reprinted and was on sale in the museum. The books were donated to the museum by the family of the Rev. Pons.

On June 27, 1982, the long-awaited Vietnamese refugee family arrived in Valdese under the sponsorship of the Waldensian Presbyterian Church. The Tran family included two young adults and two teenagers—a sister, Thu, and her three brothers Chung, Long, and Thanh. The girl and the youngest boy spoke some English which assisted greatly in their becoming acclimated to new surroundings. Their politeness and gratitude won the hearts of everyone. Mrs. Evelyn Stiff, Chairperson; the Glenn Yoders, Commander Edward Bleynat, the John Heilman family, the Hugh Fletcher family, and many others in the congregation helped the family adjust to American ways. The family proved to be very diligent in study and faithful in work, which created pride among those who helped them so much and the congregation at large. The three young men have earned Bachelor's degrees, and Thu earned an Associate's degree from a community college. Each has earned a responsible position in life. The three older siblings have become American citizens.

Special services on September 26-28, 1982 were led by Rev. Ann Garrou Dickey and Rev. David Dickey, pastors of the Grove and Smith Presbyterian Churches in Keenanville and Pink Hill, North Carolina. The congregation rejoiced to have this clergy couple to conduct the series of sermons.

The congregation rejoiced that a former member, Joseph A. Verreault, son of Mr. and Mrs. Armand Verreault, and grandson of the former pastor, Rev. J. A. Verreault (1925 - 1931), was ordained as a minister in Blue Ridge Presbytery in Halifax Virginia in September 1982. He had completed his theological training at Union Theological Seminary in Richmond, Virginia some years before seeking ordination.

The year 1983 saw the production of the first pictorial directory of this church. Much work went into the publication of the directory which proved to be an asset to everyone.

In a desire to enhance the worshipful attitude produced in the sanctuary, members of the congregation donated paraments in seasonal colors and with appropriate embroidered symbols for use in the sanctuary. Later on, the ministers were to get matching sets of stoles for seasonal wear.

On February 13, 1983, Mrs. Lydia Pons, widow of the Rev. John Pons, celebrated her 90th birthday. The family gave an open house in her honor.

On May 29, we noted the 90th anniversary of the arrival of the Waldenses in Burke County. Alexis Guigou, the sole survivor of the original settlers, was 95 years old at the time.

In June 1983, a momentous event occurred in Presbyterian history. The United Presbyterian Church U.S.A. and the Presbyterian Church U.S. became one denomination—the Presbyterian Church (U.S.A.) at a historic meeting in Atlanta, Georgia. This union was a result of much prayer, work, and negotiations over a long period of years. Thus, the local church is now a part of the new denomination.

Several events of importance occurred in June 1983. A new Kawai upright piano was purchased for use in the choir room. It was given in memory of two church members. Also that month, new election procedures were approved conforming to the new denominational requirements and congregational preference. The regulation specifies, "A diversified nominating committee will select nominees for elder and deacon. Officers elected serve for a period of three years and must be out of office for two years before returning to office. The slate of nominees must be twice the number of vacancies."

Since 1982, the congregation had expressed great concern for the elderly of our community, that they might have adequate retirement housing. Initiated by the Service Committee of the church and approved by the session, a board of directors was established to seek a site and government funding for apartments for the elderly. In September 1983, governmental approval was granted for a loan of $813,000 for constructing thirty apartment units. The site chosen was on Church Street N.W., and the name chosen was "AGAPE Retirement Housing." The original intent was that many of our own people might use the facilities, but because of governmental regulations only persons with limited income could utilize the apartments. This venture was to become one of the greatest projects of the church and would meet the need of people who would otherwise not have adequate housing in a caring community. The project required $10,000 seed money, which was loaned from church funds and repaid after the project was complete and operating.

In November 1983, ten youths and two adults journeyed to Washington, D.C. for a three-day experience of working with the homeless, a project of the Church of the Pilgrims. Rev. Jack Parse headed the project, which was a tremendous experience for the youth as well as a culture shock.

December was a busy month for the church. A workshop for officers and officers-elect was held on December 4 with the Rev. Clements Lamberth, Executive Presbyter of Concord Presbytery, acquainting the officers with the structure and expectations of the new denomination. In addition, the officers received their committee and visitation assignments for the coming year. At a congregational meeting on December 11, the proposed budget for the coming year was approved. In accordance with the new Book of Order, the congregation also voted to approve the incorporation of the church, as required by the Book of Order.

A big step was taken in 1984 when the diaconate was given permission to purchase a fifteen passenger van for church use. This had been a long-time dream of the youth and other organizations. The blue Dodge van became a wonderful asset to the programming for youth and eliminated much of the use of individual cars.

Many people of the congregation had longed for a pipe organ to replace the electric organ. Interested individuals requested permission of the session to conduct a "quiet campaign" to raise funds for a pipe organ. Under the direction of William D. Schubert, the chairman, funds were solicited and in a three-week period, $90,000 was raised or pledged. A special Selection Committee was chosen, chaired by John Mode, Music Director. A number of churches were visited to assess the qualities of various instruments. Finally, a decision was made to order from the Lewis and Hitchcock Organ Company of Virginia. It would be eighteen months before the instrument would be completed and installed.

At the request of the Burke County Historical Association, the process was started to get the Waldensian Presbyterian Church placed on the Historical Register. With the help of the association, the application was completed and the designation as a historic site was made in October 1984.

The Service Committee of the church held its semiannual spring and fall clothing drives in 1984, with a ton of clothing collected. Items were sorted by Mrs. Melany (Bounous) Grill and others and distributed to various institutions including Broughton Hospital, Grandfather Home for Children and Burke United Christian Ministries. This has been one of the outstanding service projects of the church.

In recent years, Mother's Day had been chosen for the Women of the Church to present Honorary Life Membership Awards to deserving women of the congregation. In 1984, Presbyterian Women not only named three women to receive the honor, but recognized all twenty-one other living recipients of the award at the morning worship on May 13. Each year since then, at least one woman has been honored with such an award. (A complete list of Honorary Life Membership recipients can be found in Part II, Chapter 14).

A group of visitors from the Waldensian Valleys came to visit August 2-13, 1984, under the direction of Pastor Giuseppe Platone of Angrogne, Italy. The congregation entertained these guests with special meals at the church and in private homes and took them to visit the mountains of North Carolina, Reynolda House and Old Salem in Winston-Salem, and the Biltmore House in Asheville. Many warm friendships were established through these events.

The summer highlight for seven of the Boy Scouts from Troop 192 was their journey to Camp Philmont Scout Ranch near Cimmaron, New Mexico for a three-week camping trip. Chaperoned by Scoutmaster Steven Morrow, the boys were Jerry Burgin, Jr., Henry Garrou, Victor Garrou, Jr., Andy Parse, Greg Henderson, Jimmy Tipton, and Shawn Whisenant. Upon their return, several of the boys related their adventures to the church and several civic organizations. It was truly a lifetime experience for those young men involved. Boy Scout Troop 192 is sponsored by the Waldensian Presbyterian Church.

August featured the annual observance of the Waldensian Festival with the church providing the brief worship service, tours of the museum, the craft booth and Waldensian meal for the public. The festival has become quite a cosmopolitan affair with visitors from afar. In attendance at the worship service on August 12, 1984 were seventy-eight visitors from five other states, including Massachusetts and California, and other countries, including Italy, France, and former residents of Romania and Viet Nam.

**Strengthening The Church Committee Presentation
September, 1984**

Over the years, the museum had received an increasing number of artifacts which could not be displayed properly in the main floor area. September 1984 marked the opening of the lower floor of the museum with new displays, depicting the agricultural work, industries, and municipal areas of the community. Two displays of particular interest proved to be the wine-making equipment and the armed forces uniforms worn by members of this church.

The year 1985 saw some dramatic events and some "life changing practices." In establishing the membership of the various committees for that year, it was discovered that we did not have a male deacon who worked in town and could be on call as chairman of the Cemetery Committee. Mrs. Mary Louise Hatley, deacon, was asked to be the first woman to chair that committee. She readily agreed to accept the responsibility and wound up chairing the all-male committee with great ability. The committee, which not only oversees the maintenance of the cemetery, the selling of lots, and the placement of graves, also directs funeral traffic at the church and cemetery. When Mary Louise asked the pastor if she was to direct the traffic, he facetiously said, "Of course, that is part of YOUR job." Being the feminist she is, each time there was a funeral, there was Mary Louise directing traffic. She was to serve a three-year term as chairman of that committee and another term later. How can one not respect such a lady?

The year started off with a good Christian gesture on the part of the congregation with the reception of a special offering of $3,244 for famine relief in Ethiopia.

The annual observance of the Waldensian Emancipation Proclamation was held February 16, 1985 in Pioneer Hall with a covered dish meal. Fred Cranford, Assistant Superintendent of Burke County Schools, was the guest speaker. His subject for the occasion was "The Waldenses — Their Incredible Beginnings." During the program, the Historical Committee presented him with a plaque commending him for his authorship of the outdoor drama *From This Day Forward*, which has been produced every year since 1968.

At the morning worship the next day, a special offering was received for an improvement of the Waldensian Hospital in Torre Pellice, Italy. A $6,000 check to that cause was presented to the Rev. Frank Gibson, Executive Director of the American Waldensian Society, when he preached in the church on April 28. 1985.

Two church members, in honor of their fiftieth wedding anniversary, presented a monetary gift with which new Cherub Choir robes were purchased. The robes were "Carolina blue" with white collars.

On April 1-5, 1985, the church was scheduled to host the traditional community-wide Holy Week noonday services. They were discontinued after the service on Maundy Thursday because of a great disaster in our geographic area. An elderly gentleman living off Highway 18 south of Morganton allowed a brush fire to escape his control. The result was that hundreds of acres of timberland were burned as fire swept northward over High Peak and Mineral Springs Mountains, jumping Interstate Highway 40 and threatening the entire town of Valdese. The drought of the season made the woods like a tinderbox, and winds of 45 miles per hour spread the flames rapidly. It was only by the grace of God that the fires were brought under control at the site of the Waldensian Presbyterian Church Cemetery, which served as a buffer to further spread of the fire. It was not until several days later that the fire was brought under complete control. In the immediate area of Valdese, Mineral Springs, High Peak Mountain, and Shady Grove community, thirty-five homes were destroyed. Mr. and Mrs. Robert Micol of this congregation lost their home.

The Red Cross and Salvation Army immediately moved into the area to assist the victims of the tragedy. The Service Committee of the church had just begun its spring clothing drive. The following Monday, it began to make clothing available for the fire victims. As announcements were made over the radio about the availability of clothing, others brought additional clothing for distribution. Soon the first floor of the Educational Building was like a clothing warehouse without space for the volunteer workers to move about. Rev. Felker arranged for the free use of a vacant store where the clothing was then relocated and made available for distribution. Men and women of the church, under the direction of Mrs. Melany Grill, clothing chairperson, volunteered countless hours to arranging, sizing, and distributing clothing to the hundreds of people throughout the county who came for aid. After all their needs were met, there was a sale of clothing at very low cost to other needy families. Proceeds from that venture brought $700 for the victims of the disaster. Still there remained two truck loads of clothing which were finally sent to West Virginia to the needy people of the Appalachian area. This was truly an example of people practicing the gospel admonition ". . . inasmuch as ye have done it unto one of the least of these."

Easter Week 1985 Clothing Relief for Victims of Forest Fire — Service Committee Volunteers — Melany Grill and Jane Lane

During the same time, the minister was receiving monetary gifts, not only from the congregation but also from compassionate

Dedication of AGAPE Retirement Housing — December 15, 1985 — L-R: Committee members: John A. Bleynat, Evelyn Stiff, Rev. Paul H. Felker, Hal Harrison, Barbara Baker Freiman (consultant), Hugh Fletcher, Betty Bumgarner Garrou, Julius ("J") A. Grisette, Hilda Ogle Jones, Jerry Wilkinson, Louis E. Vinay, Jr., James C. Farris

Section of Agape Apartment Complex

Christians throughout the state of North Carolina. He organized the "Valdese Christian Aid Society" composed of the ministers of the eight community churches and a lay representative from each. That organization assisted needy families in finding lodging and receiving aid through the Red Cross. It also distributed over $34,000 to assist those families. This venture proved to be one of the greatest ecumenical experiences of the Valdese community.

At the April 1985 meeting of Concord Presbytery, Tracey Burns, one of our high school students, was elected to the Presbytery Youth Council. This was a position of responsibility which called for planning presbytery youth activities. She took her duties seriously, contributing her gifts to the task and earning recognition and honor for herself.

May 1985 was an eventful time due to the ground breaking of the AGAPE housing complex of thirty apartments. A thunderstorm made the Church Street site a quagmire for those present. James Farris was serving as chairman of the Board of Directors. There was great rejoicing as the facility was dedicated for use on December 15, 1985.

A series of Special Services was held beginning September 29, 1985. This was a spiritual highlight for all as we welcomed in turn, four clergy sons and daughters of this church: Rev. Dr. Gregory Grana, the Rev. Ann Garrou Dickey, the Rev. Joseph Verreault, and the Rev. Dr. Steven Mowery. Another highlight was special music provided by former member Mrs. Rita Pons Reich.

In 1984, the session had approved the installation of heavy duty playground equipment costing up to $2,000. It was placed, in September 1985, on the south-east quadrant of the property and included a concrete area equal to half a basketball court, which served double duty for shuffle board. The play areas were to become wonderful assets not only to the church, but to the community, with many non-members using the facilities during times they were not scheduled for church use.

The musical highlight of the year came with the Chancel Choir presentation of Handel's *Messiah* on December 22, 1985. The choir with orchestral accompaniment provided a memorable occasion for all who were present.

The annual observance of the Emancipation of the Waldenses held on February 15, 1986 was simpler than some years. A musical program was presented by Les Jeunes Chanteurs and the Youth Handbell Choir. The highlight of the evening was when two

NEW PLAYGROUND EQUIPMENT INSTALLED SEPT., 1985
Dr. Felker and Linda Rostan — First Kids on the Slide

members of the Historical Committee were given special recognition for their faithful and devoted service to the museum through the years. Reece Scull made fun of the "bossiness" of the two in working with others in the museum to achieve their standards of excellence. Mrs. Naomi Bounous Rostan and Miss Olga Pascal received plaques of honor and a standing ovation. They were primarily responsible for the creation and design of the numerous displays in the Waldensian Museum.

Throughout the years, the museum had been acquiring funds through gifts and memorials. Those funds were used to purchase equipment and printed materials and to prepare photographs and displays. The funds had reached a point to make the committee self-sufficient. Therefore, the session and diaconate requested that the Historical Committee begin to assume responsibility for the cost of insurance for the facility under these terms: one third in 1986, two thirds in 1987, and total cost in succeeding years. The Historical Committee agreed to assume that responsibility.

The traditional Easter offering of "One Great Hour of Sharing" was received in 1986. Also, the custom of placing memorial Easter lilies in the sanctuary was observed. A different service this year brought the Methodists and Presbyterians together for a Maundy Thursday Passover Seder and Eucharistic Meal. The service, conducted by Rev. James Reeves of the First United Methodist

Commitment and Service to Christ and Community 147

LES JEUNES CHANTEURS — February 17, 1986 Celebration — 1st Row L-R: Tamara Suttle, Christy Traylor, Christy Neale, Kim Yoder, Christy Parse, Angie Williams, Cesarine Hudson, Catherine Ward, Katie Hanks, Gretchen Weise, Michelle Rostan. 2nd Row L-R: Henry Garrou, Jerry Burgin, Michael Bonner, Michael Brown, Nelson Neale, Benton Brinkley, Charles Hildebran, Andy Parse.

CHERUB CHOIR — 1988
L-R: Bridget Blackwell, Jill Mitchell, Katie Farias, John Hunter Mode, Shana Nesbit, Katie Gravel, Wesley Cannon, Catherine Lafferty, Kelly Masterson.

Church and Rev. Parse and Dr. Felker of this church, explained the religious significance of the two meals and their covenant relationships.

The congregation had hoped that we would have the new pipe organ installed for use by Easter of 1986, but the shipment of pipes from Holland delayed the construction and installation. At the time for the installation in July, the old electric organ was moved from the sanctuary and permanently installed in Pioneer Hall. The congregation worshipped there for two weeks while the organ company installed the pipe organ. The first occasion for its use was Saturday, August 9, 1986 at the brief worship service conducted for the Waldensian Festival. August 10 was the first regular worship service utilizing the instrument.

A special Dedication Service was conducted on September 21, 1986 with Dr. Max Smith, organ professor of Appalachian State University, at the console. He was a wise choice because of his expertise and his great assistance as a consultant in this endeavor. The occasion of the dedication was enhanced by "Carolina Brass," a group of five instrumentalists from Charlotte, and by special anthems by the choir. Everyone was pleased with the organ.

The Music Department of the church felt that it was important to acquaint our congregation and the community with the beauty and capability of the new pipe organ. Therefore, a series of Sunday afternoon organ concerts was scheduled with guest artists. They were David B. Richardson, organ instructor at Winthrop College, Rock Hill, South Carolina, on October 26, 1986; Mrs. Libby Alexander, noted organist from Shelby, North Carolina, on November 16, 1986; and on January 18, 1987, Ray Ebert, of Winston-Salem, North Carolina, organist at Centenary Methodist Church and teacher at North Carolina School of the Arts and Salem College.

Two important actions were taken in the fall of 1986. First, the Long Range Committee, under the leadership of John A. Bleynat, suggested that the church begin having two worship services each Sunday morning. This was to alleviate overcrowding of the sanctuary and would permit growth. That recommendation was approved, and dual services were held each Sunday with different choirs singing at the two services. The attendance was good and was increasing, but the congregation was dissatisfied with the arrangement because frequently it divided families, with some members being required to attend one service and some the other. It also kept friends and relatives from seeing one another. At the end of three months' time, the session decided to discontinue the practice and have only one morning worship service.

The second action regarded the service station which stood on church property on the corner of Italy and Main Streets. The property had been donated to the church by Mr. and Mrs. J. P. Rostan, Sr. The diaconate had for years debated whether it should be operating as a landlord. The building was difficult and costly to maintain. A study committee of the diaconate recommended that the building be razed. The proposal was approved, and a display of the master plan for the landscape design of the church campus was also approved. The removal of the service station and the underground oil tanks and the planting of grass in the area proved to be a wonderful enhancement to the appearance of church property and the town in general.

Missionaries Dr. and Mrs. Walter Hull visited the church on November 8 and 9, 1986. A thanksgiving dinner was served on Saturday night with the Hulls reporting on their activities. They also led in worship on Sunday. The dedication of the dynamic couple to the service of the Lord has always been a great witness to the congregation.

On November 16, 1986, Miss Thu Thi Tran and Mr. Quang Quy Nguyen were united in marriage in a beautiful ceremony in the sanctuary of the church. The congregation rejoiced in the marriage of Miss Tran, a member of the Vietnamese refugee family sponsored by the church. The Presbyterian Women gave a reception for the couple in Pioneer Hall. Later that evening, a dinner for the out-of-town Vietnamese guests and intimate American friends was held at the home of Mr. and Mrs. Hugh Fletcher. These events were meaningful to all and added to the joy of the congregation in its relationship with the Tran family.

One could tell that change was occurring in the church in 1987. For the first time in the history of the church, two women held the most important positions. Mrs. Mildred Fletcher was the first woman to serve as Clerk of Session, and Mrs. Elsie Whisenant was the first woman to serve as Chairman of the Board of Deacons. It was a good year, and both women established high standards for their successors.

Dr. Edgar Lane, upon retirement from active practice of medicine, donated various equipment from his office to Dr. Walter Hull, our medical missionary to Zaire. The equipment was packed by members of the church and shipped to Dr. Hull for his use.

With the help of the Strengthening of the Church Committee, the church moved into contemporary times with the purchase of a television and VCR. This equipment would enhance teaching methods and find wide use among the educational units of the church by the use of video tapes.

Dr. Gregory Grana, clergy son of the church, conducted a series of Christian Renewal Services for the church May 24-26, 1987. He led members through a self-evaluation of their spiritual welfare. He also led the church through an appraisal of its ministries and possible areas of service for the future. This was a most enlightening and challenging experience for all.

Various staff changes were to be made during the spring and summer of 1987. Adam Huffman was hired for the second time to direct the youth programs of the church for the summer. In May, Mrs. Dianne Floyd resigned her position as church secretary and bookkeeper. She had served faithfully and effectively for thirteen years as church secretary. She and her family were moving to Columbia, South Carolina where she and her husband had new job opportunities. After a brief search period, Dianne was replaced as church secretary by Mrs. Bess Dean, a recent resident of the area. Mrs. Frances Micol Pascal was to become bookkeeper for several years. After six and a half years, Rev. Jack Parse resigned his position as Associate Minister. The church granted him a sabbatical for six months to pursue a course of study suitable to his special gifts. He went to engage in Clinical Pastoral training at Baptist Hospital, Columbia, South Carolina. After a period of evaluation and discussion, the session concluded that rather than seeking another Associate Minister, the church would seek to secure a Director of Christian Education.

In the fall, a significant planting was done on the Main Street lawn. For years that lawn had been graced by a huge evergreen tree which was a landmark in the downtown area. In recent years, the church had granted permission for the town to decorate the tree with colored Christmas lights for the season. In 1986, however, a workman, unable to reach the top of the tree in his cherry picker, had topped the tree destroying its symmetry. Then, within a few months, lightning struck the tree killing a large section of it and making it completely unusable for decorating in the future. Dr. Ben Garrou, a horticulturist by avocation, offered the church three large evergreen trees to be planted in a grouping where the dying tree would be extracted. The offer was gratefully accepted, and professional workers planted the three large trees. For Christmas, the town decorated the trees with small white lights. Coupled with the white lights the town also placed in the dogwood trees of the park area, they provided a beautiful seasonal setting for the church. The favorable response to this would lead to an annual decoration by the town.

Trees seemed to assume significance in the life of the church in 1987. Under the direction of Mrs. Linda Rostan, the church had its first angel tree in December. A tree was placed in Pioneer Hall and decorated with angels, each identified for a boy or girl of a specific age. The congregation took the angels, bought appropriate gifts, and returned them in time for distribution to needy families at Christmas. The venture had such appeal that it became an annual service project of the church.

In decades past, the Waldensians of Valdese and the Moravians of Winston Salem had felt some kinship. Seeking to capture something of that former relationship, Dr. Felker made arrangements with the Rev. Scott Venable of New Hope Moravian Church, Hickory, who came to our church on December 13 with several of his lay leaders to conduct a typical Moravian Love Feast. The candlelight service included scriptures, familiar carols, and the serving of sugar cookies and sweetened coffee. The ritual dates back to the eighteenth century observances of the Moravians in the United States.

January 1988 was significant for the Men of the Church. Some years prior, the Men of the Church had ceased to exist because leaders could not be found. This year it was reorganized, and Horace Brown was elected as its new president. Monthly meetings were held with various men volunteering to prepare the dinners. It was determined that from time to time specific projects should be undertaken by the organization.

The February celebration of the Edict of Emancipation of the Waldenses was not held at the church in 1988 but at the Old Rock School. The delicious catered meal was served in the Waldensian Room. Since the Old Rock School had been renovated recently and designated as a cultural center of the community, the program centered about the history of the school. Recognition was given to those who had built the school and to the graduates of the high school from 1924 to 1938. One interesting feature was the display of photographs of various classes and athletic groups. Following the program, there were tours of the refurbished auditorium, the art museum which was relocated there, and a newly established dental museum.

One speaker for the occasion was our friend, Pastor Giuseppe Platone, pastor of the Serre and Pra Del Torno Churches in Italy. Having visited in Valdese several years earlier, he was serving a sabbatical year as a foreign pastor at a retreat in Stoney Point, New York. He brought greetings from the Waldensian Church of Italy at the Saturday night dinner, and on Sunday he delivered the sermon.

Some years prior to this time, the congregation had approved a pastor's equity allowance which served to assist him toward building equity for retirement housing. As a part of the contract, he was given option to purchase the manse. In the spring of 1988, selected officers approached Dr. and Mrs. Felker to determine their interest in the purchase of the manse. They expressed an interest, if acceptable terms could be reached. The result was that the Felkers purchased the manse for $84,082. The money derived from the sale was in turn invested with the income from the same to go towards the minister's housing allowance which became a part of his new call, which was executed by congregational action. With that, the church removed itself from the responsibility of maintaining a home for its pastor.

Flowers were placed in the sanctuary on May 8 in honor of Alexis Guigou on his 100th birthday. Mr. Guigou was the only survivor of the original twenty-nine Waldenses who came to Burke County. (Alexis Guigou died on March 6, 1990, at the age of 101.)

In June 1988, a call was extended to Mr. James Kirkpatrick for the position of Director of Christian Education. Currently a resident of Charleston, West Virginia, he had formerly served both the Newton and Morganton First Presbyterian Churches of this presbytery. He was known by many in the congregation and would be well received. The call was extended to him; and he, his wife Kelly and sons Forrest and Reid moved to Valdese in August. With special gifts in youth ministry and recreation, Jim Kirkpatrck quickly became an asset to the church.

For some years, many in the congregation had been saying that we needed to improve the landscaping around the church. With the approval of an overall plan, the Men of the Church decided that it should undertake small planting projects, one at a time. The first area chosen for improvement was the horse-shoe drive off St. Germain Avenue. Under the direction of Commander Edward

Bleynat and Dr. Benjamin Garrou, the men planted the area with dogwood and weeping cherry trees, azaleas, and other shrubs and annuals. In one day's time, the area was transformed from a nondescript site to a place of beauty. It was a great improvement which led to other planting projects over the next several years.

July 13 became the occasion for a wonderful meal sponsored by the Witness Committee. Served at McGalliard Falls park, 120 people enjoyed a fish fry prepared by the Charles Farris family.

In August 1988, the church entered a new era with the anonymous donation of a computer on which church records were to be kept. In the following year, two additional computers were purchased, and the staff moved toward complete operation and record keeping by computer.

With the denomination holding its 200th anniversary, a special observance was held in October 1988 at Davidson College, sponsored by Concord Presbytery. The observance known as "Celebrate the Journey" featured worship, short dramas, and displays by the various churches and institutions of the presbytery. Waldensian Presbyterian Church had a special display of items from the

Volunteers Stuffing Envelopes at Grandfather Home for Children — 1989 — Clockwise: Marie Tise Bollinger, Frances Micol Pascal, Jack Burns, Donald Martinat, Helen Bleynat Warlick, Annie Mae Lancaster Pons, Aline Garrou Marchetti, Emma Ball Pons, Sylby Pons Martinat, Evelyn Pons Bronson.

museum and a distribution of printed literature on Waldensian history. A number of our people attended the festive event. Then as a part of the denominational bicentennial celebration, a special worship service was held on November 6, 1988, noting God's blessing upon the denomination during the 200 years.

In years past, the church leaders had been on television in brief interviews regarding Waldensian history, the annual festival, and other events of interest. The Waldensian Presbyterian Church was to "make it big" on international television when the church was visited by an Italian television crew in October 1988. The crew of three photographed various activities in the church and community and interviewed a number of individuals. The taping included a tour of the museum and a worship service. The film, which relates how the Waldensian heritage was being kept alive in Valdese, North Carolina, was shown on Italian television.

In November, a new feature was added to the ritual of the worship services. Jim Kirkpatrick was asked by the Christian Education and Worship Committees to be responsible for having a "Children's Message" each Sunday during the worship service. This would mean much to the children and added a note of informality and spontaneity to the worship. This would be a regular feature during the years to come, with lay volunteers assuming the responsibility when Jim Kirkpatrick was away.

On Maundy Thursday 1989, the Upper Room Communion Service was conducted in Pioneer Hall. This service is particularly meaningful for people since they go forward in family groups, sit around tables, and receive the elements of bread and wine. The season was climaxed with Easter Sunrise service, breakfast, and 9:00 and 11:00 A.M. worship services.

A happy and significant event in the life of the church occurred on April 29, 1989 when an elder of the church , Louis Vinay, Jr., married the Rev. Beth Ann Miller, a minister of Western North Carolina Presbytery and Associate Pastor of the First Presbyterian Church, Morganton, North Carolina. Both congregations rejoiced in this happy union.

A staff change occurred in April 1989 when the church secretary, Mrs. Bess Dean, resigned. She and her husband moved to Dunn, North Carolina. She was replaced by Mrs. Kevin Duckworth (Nadine Pons), a lifelong member of the church. Within a short time, she was to also assume the duties of bookkeeper, relieving Mrs. Frances Micol Pascal of that duty. Nadine's knowledge of the church history and her familiarity with the congregation were to be a great asset to her.

For some time, committees within the church and the town had been making plans for the centennial observance of the church and town in 1993. At the session meeting in May 1989, approval was given to the concept of a memorial fountain to be placed somewhere on the main street portion of the church property. The session also established a Centennial Fund for use in carrying out various activities and programs the centennial year.

The annual observance of Vacation Church School was conducted June 11-15 in the evening hours. This provided the first opportunity for adults to be in attendance at the three classes which were provided for them on various subjects.

A new funeral pall was given to the church as a memorial gift on July 16, 1989. The beautiful pall is white brocade with gold gadroon border, and bears the seal of the Presbyterian Church (U.S.A.) in gold brocade couched in red and blue thread.

For some time, the presbytery had urged the churches to prepare church banners which could be used locally and also at large presbytery events. Mrs. Victor Garrou, Sr. (Ann Bills) designed and made a beautiful church banner, which bears the Waldensian seal on a white brocade background and with gold braid trim. The banner was used the first time at the worship at the Waldensian Festival on August 12, 1989 and was dedicated at the worship service on August 13. The banner is on permanent display in the Waldensian Museum and is used on festive occasions of the church. James Edward Garrou made a beautiful walnut standard bearer upon which the banner is displayed. This was a very fitting gift for the 300th anniversary of the Glorious Return of the Waldenses. A catered dinner was held in Pioneer Hall honoring the occasion.

Also, at the August 13 worship, Miss Catherine Dalmas was honored for her untiring effort to minister to the needs of persons in the community and for her decades of work as a member of the Historical Committee, many of those years as secretary. She was given a plaque noting the honor and was formally recognized by the Historical Committee.

For several years, the Long Range Committee had been studying the space needs of the congregation for worship. Much work had been done in evaluating needs and determining various courses of action. On November 19, 1989, a special service was held from 10:30 A.M. to 12:00 Noon for the purpose of hearing a presentation of the

Long Range Committee, reviewing the preliminary drawings by the architect, and having a question and answer period. John A. Bleynat, Chairman of the Long Range Committee, made the presentation. Two other informational meetings were scheduled but not really necessary since the congregation was pleased with the plan. On December 3,1989, at a congregational meeting, Chairman Bleynat proposed "that the congregation approve the concept of enlarging the sanctuary and making improvements, as proposed by Mr. Lawrence Evans, church architect, and shown on the sketches and drawings presented to the congregation." If the proposal was accepted, the committee would carry out the second part of its charge: "to plan a financial campaign and appoint a building committee." The proposal authorized a capital funds campaign for $670,000 plus the $94,000 on hand in the Church Building Fund. Pledges were not to exceed six years, and the amount to be borrowed was not to exceed $406,000. When the vote was taken by secret ballot, there were 184 votes in favor and 36 against. Thus the first step was taken toward achieving a long-time goal of enlarged sanctuary facilities.

The first big event in the year 1990 was the observance of the Edict of Emancipation of the Waldenses in 1848. The dinner was held in the Waldensian Room of the Old Rock School, and the program which followed was held in the auditorium. A video documentary, "The Waldensians: a History of Heritage," was shown by Myelitia and Terry Tarleton, who had produced the film. Funding for the project had come from the Rockefeller Foundation, Historic Valdese Foundation, and donations by individuals and groups from the area. Relating the history of the people, the film also showed scenes from the Waldensian Valleys of Italy and familiar scenes in Burke County. The program was well received, and numerous people bought copies of the video for their family video libraries.

The congregation met again in formal session to hear an informative report from the Long Range Planning Committee. The committee outlined the anticipated financial needs of the building program and proposed: (1) a series of informational cottage meetings, (2) personal canvassing of each household by volunteers from our officers and congregation at large, (3) the timing of the campaign in February and March and a thanksgiving meeting at the family night supper on April 4, 1990, and (4) the session to nominate a Building Committee to the congregation with construction to begin in June. The proposals were approved by the congregation. The congregation met again in March to approve the five names as presented by the Long Range Committee to serve on the Building Committee. They were John A. Bleynat, Chairman; William Brinkley, Victor Garrou, Sr., Edward Pascal, and Charlie Vinay. At another meeting in March, the congregation formally requested approval of the Presbytery of Western North Carolina to permit the church to encumber its property to borrow money for construction purposes.

On Palm Sunday 1990, Ms. Yvone Lenard Rowe, a professor at the University of California, Los Angeles, gave a historical presentation with slides, produced by her husband, Dr. Wayne Rowe. She discussed the persecution of the Waldenses in Provence, France, in the 16th century. She encouraged the participation of the Waldenses of Valdese in a special gathering of Waldenses in France in 1992.

On April 22, the church was visited by Pastor Hugo Malan, Moderator of the Waldensian Churches of Uruguay and Argentina. He brought greetings from those sister churches.

Father's Day 1990 was special in that John A. Bleynat and George Williams, Jr. were honored with the "Churchman's Award" for their devoted service to the church in various capacities. This was the first time such awards were given by the Presbyterian Men. It was to become an annual practice.

The fall of 1990 saw the beginning of the construction program. On August 29, 1990, the construction crew began to remove the brick pavers from the patio in front of the church and the walkway to the educational facilities. The sanctuary extension was staked off, and the maple trees which were in the way were cut down. Since the basketball court was at the site of the new parking lot, it became necessary to remove it during site preparation in September. When weather permitted, the concrete slab for the extension of the sanctuary was poured. It was in November of 1990 that a temporary wall was built inside the entrance end of the sanctuary; this would permit the demolition of the south wall of the sanctuary at the proper time. It soon became evident that the congregation could not enter the sanctuary through the extension while it was under construction; therefore, the last window on the west side was removed, and a temporary entrance was utilized on the west side of the sanctuary. While the structure temporarily lost its beauty and stateliness, the congregation accepted each inconvenience with grace and endurance.

Mrs. Fern Abernethy Brinkley, who had served as church organist for some years, submitted her resignation in mid-September 1990. For over six months, the church utilized several interim organists until an organist could be employed.

The generosity of the people was evident in the fall of 1990. A gift of $1,000 was given to Cliffhaven, a home for battered women being organized in Burke County. An anonymous challenge gift of $1,000 for missionaries Dr. and Mrs. Walter Hull was matched and exceeded. With the advent of troop movements to the Persian Gulf, in November 1990, the church sent "care packages" to those of our area who were serving in the conflict. The church offered special prayers as troops were deployed and engaged in war with Iraq beginning January 17, 1991.

Over the past several years, members of the Historical Committee had been at work preparing a pictorial genealogy of the first families of Valdese. A series of albums was completed and placed on view in the Waldensian Museum. Supplementing that pictorial genealogy, the committee in 1990 chose to publish a book they had compiled, *Genealogy of Waldensian Settlers in Valdese, North Carolina, 1893-1990*. Waldensian descendants were especially grateful to receive much data which they did not possess personally.

December found the church doing something new. Because of our construction program and inadequate space in the sanctuary, the Christmas Cantata was given in the auditorium of the Old Rock School. The Chancel Choir and the sixteen-piece orchestra gave a beautiful musical program which included the Christmas portion of Handel's *Messiah*. Because the service was held in a public building, the service attracted many who would not normally join in worship in a church sanctuary.

During December 1990, the angel tree was placed in Pioneer Hall, but the Chrismon trees were not used in the sanctuary because of the lack of space due to construction work. The angel tree provided a ministry to 75 families and 182 children.

As the church entered the year 1991, little did the staff and congregation realize that it would be one of the most historic years in the life of the church. With the program to enlarge the sanctuary and make other improvements, momentous events were to transpire in a year's time.

With the construction program, the church site was a bee hive of activity with the various work crews. It was amazing that the congregation responded so well to the inconvenience, the dirt, and the clutter. Even the children were cooperative, remaining out of the way of construction and not bothering any of the materials or getting in the way. We were able to continue the Wednesday Youth Club despite the inconvenience of the construction. The only inconvenience was the scheduling of funerals.

It was a year which was very trying for the church staff, attempting to carry on their daily responsibilities despite construction noise and interruptions. It was decided that finances would permit the removal of the tower on the Educational Building so that it would not compete with the sanctuary, and the brick Educational Building would be stuccoed. The removal of the tower was one event which practically drove the church staff to distraction. The demolition of the tower could not be done with a wrecking ball and chain. Instead it necessitated the use of a jack hammer and wrecking bar. Everyone seemed to know that the inconvenience, dirt, and noise were all worth the effort to achieve our goal of enlarged and enhanced facilities.

The year 1991 began with a bang on January 5 and 6 with a visit from our missionaries to Zaire, Dr. and Mrs. Walter Hull. This was their last visit before returning to Zaire in June. A Saturday night dinner honored them in Pioneer Hall. Then they led in worship on Sunday. The financial drive for the Hulls, conducted during November and December 1990, had resulted in a total collection of $2,911.40 to go toward building a permanent school building at Tshikaji, Zaire. The check was presented to Dr. and Mrs. Hull, who rejoiced in the generosity of the church. When the Hulls left Valdese, we assumed that it would be four years before they visited with us again. How wrong we were! The nation of Zaire experienced a political uprising beginning in September. In mid-October, all missionaries had to be evacuated for their physical safety. Thus, the Hulls visited in Valdese again on November 23 and 24, 1991 to report on their escape from Zaire and the political and economic situation there.

The Waldensian Emancipation was celebrated on February 16, 1991 at the Old Rock School. The catered dinner in the Waldensian Room was followed by a presentation by Dr. Cathy Pons, a descendant of this settlement and a professor of linguistics at Indiana University. Having done her doctoral thesis on "Language Death Among Waldensians of Valdese, North Carolina," she spoke on "What Do You Have to Know To Be A Waldensian?" A copy of her

Laying of Cornerstone for Sanctuary Enlargement
February 17, 1991

PARTICIPANTS IN SERVICE — L-R: John A. Bleynat, Jim Kirkpatrick, Rev. J. Clyde Plexico, Glenn R. Yoder, Rev. Walter H. Styles, Hilda Ogle Jones, Rev. Paul H. Felker, Carol Price Felker, Rev. Caroline B. Gourley, Executive Secretary, Presbytery of Western North Carolina.

John Mode, Director, and Chancel Choir

thesis was placed in the museum library for use by anyone doing research or study.

Sunday, February 17, 1991, on the 94th anniversary of the laying of the first cornerstone of the church in 1897, a special worship service was conducted in the sanctuary. Then the congregation went in a procession to the site of the sanctuary extension for a special service of the laying of the cornerstone. Assisting Dr. Felker with the service were the Rev. Caroline Gourley, General Presbyter of Western North Carolina Presbytery, and former pastors of this church, now retired, the Rev. Walter H. Styles and the Rev. J. Clyde Plexico, Jr. At the laying of the cornerstone, two time capsules were placed in the stone. The intention was that these time capsules will be opened in 2041, fifty years after their placement. (A complete listing of the items in the time capsules is given in Part II, Chapter 15.)

Palm Sunday 1991 was more low key than normal because of restraints of the facilities. Because of construction, the noonday Holy Week Services were held at the First United Methodist Church. On Maundy Thursday, the Upper Room Communion Service was conducted in Pioneer Hall with one hundred in attendance. Despite the surroundings, nothing could dampen the enthusiasm of the congregation when celebrating the resurrection of the Lord. On Easter, the Sunrise Service was conducted in the church cemetery with sixty-seven people who then went for breakfast in Pioneer Hall, prepared by Men of the Church. Dual services were conducted at 9:00 and 11:00 A.M. with music by the chancel choir accompanied by a brass quartet. Three hundred fifty-eight were in attendance for the two services.

There has always been a good spirit between the Waldensian Presbyterian Church and the sister churches of the community. This was made evident when it became necessary to vacate the sanctuary during the construction program. Both First United Methodist Church and First Baptist Church offered the use of their facilities during that time. The Worship Committee preferred that the worship be held on site if possible; therefore, the worship services were held in Pioneer Hall for several weeks.

As a part of our ecumenical cooperation, the Methodist and Presbyterian churches of Valdese conducted a "Festival of Christian Unity" on May 5, 1991. The elders and their spouses of the Presbyterian Church and members of the administrative board and their spouses of the Methodist Church, and special guests met at

Pioneer Hall for a joint dinner. Then the group journeyed to the First United Methodist Church where a communion service was conducted. Bishop Bevel Jones of the Methodist Church and the Rev. Caroline Gourley, General Presbyter of Western North Carolina Presbytery, conducted the service, assisted by the Rev. Cameron West, pastor of the Methodist Church, and our pastor, Dr. Paul Felker. The Methodist mode of receiving communion was used, with the congregation going to the altar to receive the elements. It was a very festive service containing both Presbyterian and Methodist elements of worship and with the processional being led by a Scottish guest musician playing the bagpipes, reminiscent of the Scottish heritage of the Presbyterian Church.

Another ecumenical experience came in July 1991 when the Presbyterians attended worship with the Methodists on July 7 and 14. On the first occasion, the Methodist minister and choir conducted a typical Methodist service, with the Presbyterian minister assisting. On the second occasion, the roles were reversed with a typical Presbyterian service being held. A social hour followed the worship service each Sunday, providing opportunity for the two congregations to greet one another.

In April of 1991, Mrs. Rhonda Smith was employed as organist of the church, following the resignation of Mrs. Fern Abernethy Brinkley. A native of Florida, Mrs. Smith graduated from Hobe Sound Bible College in Florida, and holds a Masters in Sacred Music from Bob Jones University, Greenville, South Carolina. She is a multi-talented musician and vocalist.

On June 30, a special patriotic worship service was conducted with Dr. Felker preaching on an appropriate theme. Special patriotic music was incorporated in the service, with Mrs. Smith at the organ, assisted by Mrs. Ann Garrou at the piano, Miss Noelle Garrou playing piccolo, Brian Franklin playing trumpet and Miss Angela Hyde playing drums.

Missions were emphasized by two events in the church during the summer of 1991. Miss Pamela Bonner, a Spanish and French teacher and member of this church, served as a member of a Western North Carolina Presbytery mission team going to Mexico to help build a school dormitory. Director of Christian Education Jim Kirkpatrick accompanied three of our youth as they became a part of a home mission work crew in West Virginia. Kimberly Rostan, Susanne Garrett, and Kristen Hart had a tremendous experience and learned to lay water lines and to roof a barn.

Participants of these two events reported on their activities at church night dinners in the fall.

With the construction of the church in progress in 1991, it seemed an unlikely time to have other financial drives. However, two successful drives were conducted almost simultaneously. An effort to raise money for a new piano to be placed in the sanctuary resulted in $4,028. A new Kawai upright piano was delivered in time for the opening service in the enlarged sanctuary.

The other fund raising effort was to secure funds to beautify the church cemetery. A site plan was approved with a paved walkway running north and south in the cemetery and perpendicular to the roadways. Flowering trees, shrubs, and perennials were to be planted along the walkway. Additional flowering trees would be planted around the perimeter of the cemetery to enhance its beauty. Work on this project was done during the early part of 1992 with $3,800 raised.

The building committee had been led to believe that the construction work could be completed by Easter of 1991. It soon became apparent that was a vain hope. One delay resulted when the plaster ceiling in the original portion of the sanctuary had to be removed for safety's sake. After that delay, it was hoped that the dedication could occur on July 4, which would have been the anniversary of the dedication of the original sanctuary in 1899. Then it was discovered that the completion date was delayed when the additional pews did not arrive.

Upon completion of the sanctuary, the laying of the carpet, and the installation of the old pews, it was decided to hold the first worship service in the sanctuary as soon as possible, with folding chairs being used in the newer portion in lieu of pews. That service was held on September 15, with an observance of the Lord's Supper. Dr. Felker's meditation of the day was appropriately entitled, "Let's Celebrate."

The dedication service was held on October 6, 1991 with the Rev. Walter H. Styles, a former minister, preaching. The service featured a special dedication litany and prayer and appropriate hymns and anthems. Rev. Styles also conducted Renewal Services Sunday night through Tuesday night of that week.

On Sunday, October 20, an open house of the renovated facilities was provided for the public. A special musical service was held in the afternoon with Mrs. Rhonda Smith providing a program of organ, piano, and vocal music with music ranging from Chopin to

DEDICATION OF ENLARGED SANCTUARY — OCT. 6, 1991
Building Committee L-R: Edward Pascal, Charlie Vinay, William M. Brinkley, John A. Bleynat, Chmn., Victor H. Garrou.

Rachmaninoff and Gershwin. A reception in Pioneer Hall followed with a large number of friends from the community in attendance.

The completion of the construction program brought a great sigh of relief to everyone. There was rejoicing at the beauty of the facilities and pride in every accomplishment. Now the sanctuary had been enlarged to accommodate 144 additional seats, a commodious narthex, two rest rooms, a bride's room, and a sound control room. Everyone rejoiced that the beautiful stained glass windows had been duplicated with such accuracy.

On the exterior, a new brick patio provided fellowship space, with the sanctuary accessible to the handicapped. A covered walkway from the sanctuary to the educational facilities and beyond to a porte-cochere made movement between the buildings much more pleasant in bad weather. An elevator, with access from the walkway, made movement to the first and second floors of Pioneer Hall easy for the handicapped and aged. A parking lot, with entrance from Italy Street, now accommodates thirty cars. The support system for the bell in the church tower was reinforced to make it usable for years to come. Now, once again the church bell would peal for worship and special services.

The greatest improvement in exterior appearance was that the yellow brick Educational Building, constructed in the 1950's, was

Waldensian Presbyterian Church after 1991 Renovation

Interior of Enlarged Sanctuary — Easter Sunday, 1992

From St. Germain Street

changed. The tower was removed. The architect of that era had intended that a new sanctuary be built adjacent to it and running east and west, facing the site of the current museum. That plan had been abandoned. With the removal of the tower and the facility being stuccoed to match all the new fiberglass stucco of the other buildings, the complex now matches in exterior materials and gives a unified appearance. Total construction costs and interest charges were approximately $946,560.

As the completion of the facilities was drawing nigh, the Historical Committee became aware of the poor condition of the exterior of the museum. The stucco was badly cracked, and the cement block construction showed through the thin layer of stucco. It was decided that while construction was going on, Temo & McCall Construction Company, which had stuccoed the church facilities, should be employed to improve the museum. A layer of plastic foam was installed over the exterior and then stuccoed. This will prevent deterioration of the stucco job in the near future. Further investigation disclosed that a new roof needed to be installed and interior leaks and repainting done. Funds from accumulated savings of the Historical Committee and anonymous donations from church members made it possible for all this work to be done in 1991. Thus at last, all church facilities now look alike. Another thing which enhances the contribution of the museum to the community is the placement of a historical marker in front of the Waldensian Museum. Purchased by the Historical Committee, it identifies points of interest in Valdese. This is very helpful to visitors of the town and guests of the museum.

In the meantime, the Presbyterian Men were sponsoring several landscaping projects under the direction of Edward Bleynat and Benjamin Garrou. The projects enhanced the landscaping of the church facilities and resulted in a financial saving of several thousand dollars. The projects also provided opportunities for wonderful fellowship as men, women, and youth labored cooperatively. Upon the completion of the parking lot, there was a "work Saturday" when the surrounding area was planted with grass. Bradford pear trees were planted between the parking area and the basketball court. A later project was the replanting of the courtyard area between Pioneer Hall and the sanctuary. The final project was the planting of grass and shrubs from the patio retaining wall south toward St. Germain Street. Later the church received a memorial gift of a patio table and four benches for the courtyard. A final landscaping project was the improvement of the plantings around the museum.

While all these construction projects were being carried out in 1991, the regular church programs continued. A Family Vacation Church School was conducted in July. A wide variety of youth activities enhanced the summer. They ranged from swimming parties to short trips, and many children and youth attended the camps and conference schedule at Camp Grier. In addition, four adults attended the Music and Worship Conference at Montreat and several ladies attended the Women's Conference. In June, the Service Committee hosted, for the third year, a cookout at McGalliard Falls for the residents of AGAPE Retirement Housing.

Several years earlier, a computer system had been installed in the church offices. Church staff had been utilizing the programs as much as possible, but Nadine Pons Duckworth, the secretary and bookkeeper, had found the bookkeeping system very inadequate. Thus, with the approval of the officers, much of the calendar year was spent in switching over to a special program especially designed for use in Presbyterian Churches. The transition required interminable work by the bookkeeper and resulted in inadequate financial reporting during the interim. Everyone, however, looked to the time of its completion and a more adequate system of record keeping and reporting which was achieved in early 1992.

For some months, a town committee had been preparing plans for a town Centennial Park which would be located on the Main Street property of the church. The session had agreed at an earlier time that it would lease that property to the town and that a Centennial Park would be erected at public expense. In early December 1991, the committee appeared before the session, displayed a model of the proposed park and requested church approval of the concept. The session approved with the agreement to lease the property to the town for twenty-five years, with the possibility of a renewed lease if it was agreeable to both parties and if the town had maintained the park properly. The plan was then to be presented to the town council for approval, and the idea was that the park would be built and in place for the centennial with dedication of the park to take place as a part of the festivities on July 4, 1993. The design of the park, as portrayed in the model, featured a three-tiered metal fountain in the center of a park area with paved walks, flowering trees and shrubs, against a low rock wall which would display symbols depicting various events in the history of the town. The park will surely be a spot of beauty and will add much to the attractiveness of the town as well as the church property. The congregation approved the final plans for the park on August 16, 1992.

The ninety-ninth year of the church (1992) proved to be a year of great activity. There was the usual activity with births and baptisms, sickness, death and funerals. There was an abundance of weddings in the new sanctuary, special days for the Boy and Girl Scouts, and for the Presbyterian Women and Presbyterian Men. Each Sunday seemed to have some special activity so that the normal, or traditional worship became somewhat abnormal. The various activities of the church were well supported and financed, with special offerings for a variety of activities. We rejoiced that our funds were coming in well and that the church was not experiencing any difficulties in meeting its budget or its building fund payments.

In the spring, prior to Easter, work was begun to beautify the church cemetery, under the guidance of Mrs. Carol Felker. A concrete walk was laid, concrete benches were installed and antiqued, and a water line was installed. One Saturday, approximately thirty men spent five hours planting numerous trees and shrubs. Certainly the beauty of the site was enhanced, and plans were made for additional plantings in the fall. At the Easter Sunrise Service, the worshippers were pleased to find the Kwanzan cherry trees with scattered blooms.

In 1992, because of the enlarged sanctuary, the session did not feel the necessity for conducting dual Easter services in the sanctuary. A capacity congregation, with numerous friends and relatives, gathered to celebrate the resurrection of Christ with beautiful music by the Chancel Choir and brass ensemble. Those assembled felt it was one of the best experiences of worship possible.

In July 1992, a group of twenty-five from the church and community attended an international gathering of Waldensians in Mérindol, France. In this area in France in 1545, a number of Waldensian villages were destroyed and the people massacred. After the meeting, the group visited the Waldensian Valleys in Italy. At the beginning of the trip, when the group arrived in Frankfurt, Germany, they were met at the airport by a group of Waldensians from nearby Walldorf, Germany, who provided a meal for them. The experiences of this trip show that the ties between Valdese Waldensians and Waldensians in other parts of the world remain strong. The trip was organized and led by Louis D. Bounous, Sr. and CDR Edward L. Bleynat and assisted by travel agent Gennifer Garrou-Albert, great-great granddaughter of Jean Garrou (Bobo), who came to Valdese as a colonist in November 1893.

A second pictorial directory was produced in 1992 to replace the one from 1983. This will enable the newer and the older people of our church to recognize one another. It will also serve as a wonderful record of the enrollment in the centennial year.

The session regretfully accepted the resignation of James W. Kirkpatrick, Director of Christian Education, effective October 1, 1992. Mr. Kirkpatrick resigned to accept a staff position for youth ministry with Holston Presbytery. A farewell dinner for the Kirkpatrick family on September 27 was attended by a large number of church members. The congregation will miss the vitality of Jim Kirkpatrick's ministry to the church for the past four years, especially in his work with the children and youth.

Work continues to be carried out by the various committees of the

**GERMAN WALDENSIANS GREET VALDESE WALDENSIANS
July 8, 1992**
Members of the Waldensian Association of Walldorf, Germany (l.) welcome the Valdese group at the Frankfurt Airport with a sign displaying the Waldensian emblem. On the right are some of the Valdese group: Naomi Bounous Rostan, Barbara Bounous Wall, and René and Enes Durand.

session and diaconate. There is a feeling of great anticipation. Many members of this congregation are engaged in committee work and decision making regarding the church and town celebration of the centennial in 1993. There is much activity with everyone looking forward to a grand and glorious celebration during the centennial year.

It is unusual for a minister in any denomination to remain in a given pastorate as long as Dr. Felker has remained at the Waldensian Presbyterian Church. When outsiders question how this relationship has survived so long, several answers can be given. First, it is evident that the pastor and his wife are well loved and that they love the congregation. The couple appreciates Waldensian history and has become well versed in it. In addition they have worked closely with the Waldensian Museum. In a sense they are adopted Waldensians, and this has endeared them to the people.

Secondly, the minister believes in being thoroughly Presbyterian and "doing things decently and in order." Through the years, he has developed a well-established committee system which carries out the work of the church. With the talents of about 180 people involved in committee work, plus a large number involved in the Sunday School, Youth Club, youth fellowships, and choirs, the majority of the people who are able-bodied are active in some aspect of ministry through the church. When people are involved in the work of the church, they are happier and they feel more a part of the church.

Volunteerism is one of the greatest assets of this church. There is no task which is undertaken without a number of people being capable of carrying out the responsibility. The church has a great wealth of leadership, as well as persons who are excellent supporters of every program. In addition, the generosity of this congregation, in support of the ministry and programs of the church, is indicative of the loyalty of a dedicated people. Once the people are convinced of a need, they will support a program to the fullest.

The Giving Record

Year	Membership	Benevolence	General	Building	Total
1969	657	$36,822	$ 53,987	$ 2,847	$ 93,656
1970	621	40,286	69,767	3,344	113,397
1971	602	44,055	68,569	2,702	115,326
1972	592	46,886	77,638	8,348	132,872
1973	594	40,804	72,639	84,709	198,152
1974	581	39,023	77,839	72,512	189,372
1975	610	35,133	106,054	6,984	148,170
1976	610	35,490	95,029	4,007	134,526
1977	611	34,932	97,418	10,258	142,608
1978	579	71,973	99,295	114,298	285,166
1079	591	48,580	120,575	194,667	363,822
1980	591	59,144	119,249	55,000	233,393
1981	595	47,708	127,839	29,989	197,536
1982	567	66,677	141,367	47,831	255,875
1983	573	48,268	174,187	42,383	264,838
1984	608	67,015	162,953	43,741	273,709
1985	599	74,842	186,926	42,912	304,680
1986	606	65,105	192,875	74,092	332,072
1987	588	58,368	202,069	3,838	264,275
1988	584	65,882	199,772	74,482	340,136
1989	606	66,455	223,444	5,000	294,899
1990	597	71,580	216,152	14,469	428,201
1991	593	61,394	259,294	505,532	876,220

THE CHURCH AT WORK IN 1992

CHERUB CHOIR — Linda York, Director — Bottom Row L-R: Joanna Smith, Coulter Brinkley, Julianna Martinat, Catherine Fletcher, Regan Reynolds, Brittany Robinson. Middle Row L-R: Jessica Smith, Samantha Powell, Sarah Harrison, Shawn Powell. Top Row L-R: Emily Harrison, Matthew Mode, Anna Parsons, Jessica Smith, Anna Heilman, Michael Morse.

YOUTH HANDBELL CHOIR — Mary Louise Pascal Hatley, Director — Front Row L-R: John C. Lafferty, Katie Mastin, Shelley Mastin, Tia Zimmerman, Leslie Sherrill, Matthew Barus, Matt Mitchell. Back Row L-R: Jill Mitchell, Katie Bevis, Snow Sherrill, Mary Louise Pascal Hatley, Laura Stevenson, Will Cannon.

Commitment and Service to Christ and Community 173

1992

LES JEUNES CHANTEURS — John Mode, Director — Front Row L-R: Forrest Kirkpatrick, Radd Nesbit, Amy Church, Shannon Rembert. Second Row L-R: Marian Sherrill, Molly Wellman, Kristen Hart, Kimberly Rostan, Julianne Parse, Stephanie Manfredi. Third Row L-R: Michael Blackwell, John Mode, Choir Director; Seth Harrison, Joshua Duckworth, Tod Blackwell, Sam Jones, Jason Hart.

2ND AND 3RD GRADE SUNDAY SCHOOL CLASS — L-R: Bruce Cannon, teacher, Dustin Powell, Jacob Smith, Josh Smith, Reid Kirkpatrick, Wesley Cannon, Robert Martinat, Marianne Cannon, teacher; Catherine Lafferty.

1992

FRENCH CIRCLE — April 13, 1992 — Seated L-R: Ermeline Grill (Giovanni) Bigotto, Elda Rostan (John) Tessore. 2nd Row L-R: Lora Perrou, Norma Rostan (Reece) Scull, Helen Grill (Joseph) Broverio, Lena Pons (Gus) Whisenant, Aline Garrou (Albert) Marchetti. 3rd Row L-R: Elèna Long (Robert) Michelin, Isabel Dalmas, Ada Pons, Elizabeth Pons (Hal) Harrison, Julia Pascal (Paul) Bardet, Susie Bleynat (Jason) Bridges. 4th Row L-R: Yvette Long (Curtis) Foshee, Catherine Rivoire Cole, Catherine Dalmas, Evelyn (Olin) Stiff, Lois Holder (George) Bleynat.

MEN'S CHOIR ENTERTAINS YOUTH CLUB — February 19, 1992 — First Row L-R: Granville Morrow, David Fletcher, Jack Burns, Marc Mitchell. Second Row L-R: Victor H. Garrou, John A. Guigou, Benton Brinkley, Dr. Benjamin W. Garrou, Dr. Edgar W. Lane, Jr., John Mode, Director.

1992

CENTENNIAL COMMITTEE — Seated L-R: Linda York; Dr. Benjamin W. Garrou, chmn.; Hilda Ogle Jones. Standing L-R: Catherine Rivoire Cole; Dr. Paul H. Felker, pastor; Carol Perrou Brown; Edward Pascal; Evelyn Bounous; Catherine Dalmas; John A. Bleynat.

CHURCH HISTORY COMMITTEE — Seated L-R: Evelyn Pons Bronson; Olga Pascal; Jewel Pyatt Bounous; Rosalba Pascal Shook, chmn.; Naomi Bounous Rostan. Standing L-R: Catherine Rivoire Cole; Carol Price Felker; Dr. Paul H. Felker, pastor; Imogene Pons Hudson; Catherine Dalmas; John A. Bleynat.

THE WORK OF CHURCH COMMITTEES

The major work of the church is done through committees under the authority of the session or the diaconate. A brief summary of the duties of the major committees follows.

The Worship Committee has oversight of all the worship services, the administration of the sacraments, the special preaching missions, and worship for the Christian seasons of Christmas and Easter. It chooses the ritual that will be used in weekly worship, and the types of worship to use on special occasions. As a result of the committee's decisions, the weekly worship usually includes two anthems by two choirs and congregational participation through prayers, scripture readings, creeds, and offerings. We believe it is vital that, rather than being the observers of worship, that all persons be vitally engaged in worship with God as the observer and recipient of our praise. We believe that it is vital for children to be involved; therefore, each Sunday there is a children's message, and children participate regularly through the choirs.

For over fifty years, choral music has been a vital part of the worship of this church, which is known for the accomplished choirs and the outstanding anthems and musical programs presented at Christmas and Easter. Currently the vocal choirs are Chancel Choir (adult), Les Jeunes Chanteurs (junior high and high school age), Junior Choir (grades 4-6), Melody Choir (grades 1-3) and Cherubs (age 3-6 years). In the past decade, handbells have also assumed their importance in worship. Currently there is an Adult Handbell Choir and a Youth Handbell Choir.

The Worship Committee is responsible for planning all the special worship services such as Christmas cantatas, Waldensian observances such as February 17 and August 15. It also plans the annual series of evangelistic or Christian growth services held in the late spring or early fall. During February and August, the congregation normally sings one French hymn each Sunday and the Chancel Choir sings French anthems. This perpetuates the Waldensian heritage of this church.

Baptismal services are conducted as a part of the regular worship. These follow the regular Presbyterian ritual. For each service, a Presbyterian elder, representing the session, stands with the minister and assists with the service in a supportive capacity. The designated elder is normally one who has a close spiritual relationship to the individuals involved. In keeping with Waldensian tradition, godparents are often chosen.

The Lord's Supper is normally observed quarterly during the morning worship and on Maundy Thursday night. A distinctive aspect has been the exclusive use of wine, which was a Waldensian custom. Homemade wine was used until about ten years ago. Then it became more difficult to secure, because fewer members are producing wine for family consumption. In 1991, the decision was made to serve both wine and grape juice since children, and some adults, prefer juice. Communion is normally received in the pew and served by the elders, but on occasion such as the Upper Room Communion in Pioneer Hall, it is served by the minister and an elder as the people are seated at the table in small groups.

Funerals are normally brief and emphasize thanksgiving to God for the life of the deceased, a celebration of faith and belief in the resurrection. Funerals are usually conducted in the sanctuary, but may be held at the funeral chapel or at graveside. The pastor, Dr. Felker, is known and loved for the warm, personal funeral services he conducts. Over the past two decades, it has become customary for our congregation to send memorial gifts to the church, with each bereaved family specifying the church cause. These memorial gifts to the deceased have amounted to as much as $10,000 in a given year!

Church weddings are as varied as the couples united in marriage. They may be small intimate family weddings or grand and glorious with large congregations in attendance. The committee restricts the choice of music to religious or classical music. Vocal music and organ and piano are normally used. Others may choose to use brass or strings. The desire is to make each wedding a Christian worship service which calls upon the couple to be faithful to Christ and their vows. As has been the custom for over thirty years, each newly wed couple is presented a Bible as a gift from the church.

The Commitment and Witness Committee seeks in various ways to lead our people to a deeper commitment to Christ and His church. It is concerned with reaching the unchurched, their visitation, and enlistment. It is responsible for keeping the attendance records through the signing of the friendship pads at worship services. This committee has sought to make ours a friendlier church by encouraging everyone to speak to visitors, invite them to return to church, and visiting in their homes. To provide times to build community spirit, the committee sponsors a monthly church dinner and plans informative and inspirational programs.

The Christian Education Committee has long had an important

task in this church, as evidenced by the employment of a Director of Christian Education or a Minister of Christian Education. This person oversees the work, serves as a resource person, and works closely with this and other committees. This committee provides for the Sunday School, the youth fellowship groups, the Youth Club, library, audio visual room, and nursery. Just recruiting leadership for these numerous activities is demanding. Over sixty people are required for these functions.

The Christian Relations Committee is responsible for providing a wide scope of activities. Leaders are recruited to assist with such programs as the annual Vacation Church School, provide liaison to Boy and Girl Scouts, plan confirmation and new member classes, provide vocational guidance for senior highs, and see that the outdoor nativity scene is produced. Other responsibilities are assigned to this committee as needs arise.

The Historical Committee has the responsibility of preserving the heritage of our church and the Waldensian people. This includes the maintenance and operation of the museum, the scheduling of its use, and providing docents for museum tours throughout the year. Numerous school and church groups visit annually, as well as local and out-of-town visitors, sometimes on an impromptu schedule. For these reasons, this is the largest committee in the church with approximately seventy-five members. This committee also plans for special Waldensian observances such as February 17, festival day in August, and for visits of persons interested in Waldensian history or culture. Not only is this committee responsible for the physical cleaning of the museum, it is responsible for the financial investments which make it financially independent from church support.

The Stewardship and Finance Committee is responsible for developing the liberality of the people, educating them concerning the financial needs of the church courts and the local church, planning the budget, developing the annual financial campaign, and having oversight of the expenditures and distribution of the gifts. It also seeks to encourage the giving of memorials, bequests and trusts. This congregation has for years been recognized as a very benevolent church which has little or no difficulty in meeting its requests. It consistently ranks fifth or sixth in the presbytery in benevolent gifts. In addition to the higher courts, the church provides local benevolent funds to Valdese Hospital Chaplaincy , United Christian Shelter, Burke United Christian Ministries, the

Commitment and Service to Christ and Community

Life Enrichment Center, Flynn Home, Options (for battered women), and Hospice.

Through the years, the congregation has been encouraged to give memorial gifts when a member or loved one dies. In years when there are a number of deaths, the memorial gifts increase. Memorials may be made to a variety of funds, such as the Building Fund, Museum Fund, Museum 2000 Fund, Organ Fund, Ruth M. Williams Music Scholarship Fund, and Service Committee.

The Service Committee is a very active committee. The committee of over twenty persons does a tremendous amount of visiting among the sick and shut-ins, the bereaved, and those with special needs. It provides a semiannual clothing drive and the distribution of clothing to a variety of agencies. An average of a ton of clothing is collected and distributed each year. In addition it administers the distribution of about $5,000 each year to the sick, needy, and indigent who come to the church for aid. This is one of the finest ministries of the church, one that few other churches in this area do to this extent. The actual distribution of the funds is carried out by the staff and the chairpersons under the direction of the committee. In addition to these activities, the committee mails seasonal and birthday cards to the elderly and sympathy cards to the bereaved. Each year "care packages" are mailed to the college students at exam time, and each year the committee sponsors a patient at Western Carolina Center.

Other committees utilized by the church organization are: Maintenance, Cemetery, Ushering and Funeral Ushers, Computer, Van, Campus Design, Personnel, and Festival. In addition, there may be ad hoc committees established for one-time events. As is evident, this is a working church. If a member is not working in some capacity, it is because the individual is too infirm or chooses not to become involved.

Postscript: The account of the preceding era, 1969 - 1992, was written mainly by Dr. Paul Felker. His natural modesty prevented him from calling attention to his personal influence and responsibility for the work done during those twenty-three and one-half years. Dr. Felker has served his God and this congregation for almost one quarter of the church's history. His loving personalty, his sympathetic counsel, his inspiring sermons, his ability to ease the burden of bereaved families, and his love for his fellow Christians has had a tremendously positive effect on the lives of this congregation. His attention to the details of organization and his ability to negotiate reasonable solutions to difficult challenges has endeared him to all who have had occasion to work with him. His ability to stand for his principles yet hear opposing views has earned him the respect of this congregation and of his peers in the work of Presbytery. We are deeply indebted to him for his service to his Lord and to this congregation and for his invaluable help and counsel in the completion of this book.

The Book Committee

CHAPTER 8

THE PROMISE OF THE FUTURE

*"Let us hold fast the profession of our faith
without wavering; (for he is faithful that promised;) . . ."*
Hebrews 10: 23

We look to the challenge and opportunity of the future.

The future of the Waldensian Presbyterian Church cannot be told with assurance; only the Lord knows for certain what it will be. Yet there are certain things that we can forecast for the future.

Valdese is a very stable community. Over the past thirty years, there has been little numerical growth. With the Waldensian practice of holding to the land which is owned by the family, there is little possibility of great growth. This stability means a lack of church growth. Therefore, there is no foreseeable need for additional buildings or improvements to the church facilities. Over the next twenty-five years, it should be a matter of simple maintenance of the facilities.

There are foreseeable changes among the staff. Dr. Felker has reached the time of retirement. When he does retire, there will be the necessity for choosing a new minister. Following a lengthy pastorate such as Dr. Felker's, it is frequently suggested that there be a twelve- to eighteen-month interim pastorate. During that transitional period, the congregation will evaluate its goals and ministries and determine the direction for the future. Certainly, whoever is chosen as the minister will have a different style of ministry and operation. This means that the new clergy person will also influence the direction of the future.

Once the new minister is secured, it is likely that in addition to a Director of Christian Education, the people will see the necessity for an Associate Minister to assist with preaching, visitation, counseling, and the myriad of other duties the pastor must assume.

Because there is a great love for music in this congregation, it is also predictable that in the future the church will move toward a full-time Director of Music. This would enhance the music program, and such a person could assume the leadership of several of the choirs. Additional support staff will also be needed. It is currently too difficult for one person to do secretarial work and the bookkeeping. It would be well to employ a receptionist/secretary. With the variety of programs provided, it may also be necessary to hire an additional custodian to assist in maintenance.

While the aforementioned things will require additional financing, so will new programs which may be started. If more mothers are working, the church may be led to provide a day care for children, or an after school program. With a large percentage of the membership over fifty-five years of age, it will certainly necessitate a good senior citizen program. In fact, it is hoped that this program can be instituted within the next year.

This church will continue to provide a good ministry of service to the community. There are an increasing number of community-wide programs asking for good leadership, and members of this church have been at the forefront in the past. In all likelihood, there will continue to be a great amount of volunteerism from among our retirees and others not engaged in public work. It is also hoped that we will have an increasing number of men and women who will volunteer their service to work at the presbytery level.

One of the most important things to do in the future is to emphasize evangelism and visitation. Unless there are strong programs followed in these areas, the church will not even maintain the status quo. It is certain, however, that the church will continue to be a strong ecumenical leader in the community. It is the driving force in the support of ecumenical programs such as Burke United Christian Ministries and the Valdese Hospital Chaplaincy Program.

One of the dramatic changes that will occur in the church is a reduction in the number of people with Waldensian heritage. Currently there are only four full-blooded Waldensians in their forties. The majority are in their sixties and older. As these people pass away over the next twenty-five years, there may be less support of the Waldensian Museum and less interest in maintaining Waldensian heritage. The leadership of the church will have to work to maintain that heritage as an important asset in the future life of the church.

Who holds the future? It is the Triune God. He holds the future in His hands. Therefore, let us rejoice. We know that by His great mercy He will preserve His church. May He bless this congregation in the next one hundred years as He has the first one hundred years.

PART II

HERITAGE
and
PEOPLE

CHAPTER 9

PASTORS OF THE WALDENSIAN PRESBYTERIAN CHURCH

The Reverend Doctor Charles Albert Tron
1893, 1894

Dr. Tron was born in 1850 in Massello, Italy to Jean Jacques Tron and Susanne, née Rostan. After studying at the Faculty of Theology in Florence, Italy, he married Florida Galay with whom he had a son, Stanley, who died not long after becoming a doctor of medicine.

Dr. Tron's background included the following positions: aide of P. Geymonat at Florence, Italy (1874); pastor at Rodoretto 1876-1879; pastor at Perrero (1876-1879); and the Committee of Evangelization, Torino (1880-1889). From 1889-1905, he was in San Germano involved with the reconstruction of the temple, the construction of the schools for girls of the Chiabrandi, of the Combina and of the Chenevière, and the construction of the Asilo dei Vecchi (1894).

In May 1893, after much deliberation and preparation, eleven families and Dr. Tron set sail on the *S.S. Zaandam* for America. After arriving in Burke County on Monday, May 29, 1893, Dr. Tron helped the settlers with many legal and financial matters. He had interviews and correspondence with American churches and societies interested in opportunities for missionary work in Valdese. He also tried to secure a regular pastor for the church, one who could take over the responsibilities of the newly formed colony.

Dr. Tron departed for Italy in July 1893 but kept in touch with the colonists and was called on for advice and help. When the Valdese Corporation was dissolved in January 1895, there was a debt of $1500. Pastor Soulier informed Dr. Tron of the situation, and Dr. Tron sent his own personal money to pay the debt.

Dr. Tron returned to Valdese for brief visits in 1894 and 1922. On his last visit in 1922, he arrived in time for the dedication of C. A.

Tron Hall in his honor.

In 1920, Dr. Tron retired after holding pastorates in San Germano, Florence and Torre Pellice, Italy. In addition to his pastoral duties, he had been a leader in many of the activities of the Waldensian Church. He served as its delegate abroad on twenty-five occasions. He was for many years Vice-Moderator of the Venerable Table. For eight years, he was the Director of *L'Écho des Vallées*. He founded many schools and institutions. His greatest monument is the Old People's Home of San Germano, Italy, which he founded in 1894.

In 1930, in memory of their son Stanley (1883-1913), Dr. and Mrs. Tron gave a new wing of the hospital in Torre Pellice, which was dedicated in 1932.

Dr. Tron's last years were spent at the Home in San Germano, Italy, where he contributed his labors and interest in the work of the home until his death on June 18, 1934.

Pastor Enrico Vinay
1893-1894

Pastor Vinay arrived in July 1893 to become the first regular pastor of the Waldensian colony. He was born in 1856 in the Waldensian Valleys. Vinay was a man of talent and leadership. The Waldensian Church of Italy sent him to Sicily on missionary work for a short time; then the Venerable Table decided to send him to North Carolina to assist the colonists.

Pastor Vinay remained in North Carolina for one year, and during that time, he assumed full responsibility for supervising the clearing of fields and building of homes for the colonists. Many early settlers recalled the pastor, armed with a revolver to keep off wild animals and marauders, directing the labors of the immigrants as if they were a gang of contract laborers.

In October 1893, Pastor Vinay, in addition to his pastoral work and other activities, attended the meeting of the Synod of North Carolina of the Presbyterian Church in the U.S. and wrote a long article for the *Morganton Herald*. At the Synod meeting held in

Tarboro, he was introduced as a member of the Waldensian Synod, and he gave an address in French.

Pastor Vinay left Valdese for California in the spring of 1894. He was employed by the Board of Home Missions of the Presbyterian Church in the United States of America as missionary in the Italian Mission, San Francisco. For the church year 1894-1895, he served nine months there as stated supply and continued in this post until his death during the summer of 1896.

Pastor Barthélemy Soulier
1894-1900

Pastor Soulier was born on April 20, 1865, in Pramollo, Italy. He studied at the Waldensian Seminary and did post-graduate work in Edinburgh, Scotland. He and his bride Amélie Vinçon (1878-1947) arrived in Valdese in June 1894.

Pastor Soulier was a practical man of affairs and intensely in love with his mission. He served as a public secretary, interpreter and justice of the peace. During his years as pastor, he contributed his time and talents to developing the community and to disentangling the financial affairs of the colony. He and his wife taught the children and adults to speak English, and he made changes in the organization of the colony. Pastor Soulier led the colonists in building the church. When he left the colony in 1900, no debt remained on the church.

While in Valdese, Pastor and Mrs. Soulier had two sons to die in infancy. Both children were buried in the Waldensian Cemetery. These deaths and the impaired health of Mrs. Soulier caused the pastor to resign his pastorate and return to Italy on September 20, 1900.

On his return to Italy, he became pastor at Rio Marina, Island of Elba (1900-1901), Revere, Mantua (1901-1903), Massello (1903-1904), Villa Secca (1904-1916), and Villar Pellice (1916-1930). After retiring, he lived in Turin from 1930 to 1932 and then became director of Asilo Valdese per Vecchi (Home for the Aged) in San Germano Chisone from 1935 to 1942. He died in Turin in 1946. Mrs. Soulier died in 1947. Pastor and Mrs. Soulier had two other children in addition to the two infant sons who were born in Valdese. They were son Dino, born and died in 1902, and a daughter Letizia, born in 1903. This daughter, Letizia Soulier Gay (widow) is now living in Asilio Valdese in Luserna San Giovanni. When she was visited in July 1992 by Catherine Rivoire Cole, she was delighted to see someone from Valdese.

Pastor Henri Garrou
1900-1903

Pastor Garrou was born August 9, 1870 in Prali, Italy. He was the son of one of the first colonists, Jean Garrou (père), and the brother of Jean and François Garrou. Early in December 1900, pastor Garrou sailed from Italy to become pastor of the Waldensian Church in Valdese. He arrived in time for the Christmas celebration.

Pastor Garrou found the colony in good condition. The houses were well built, and most of the land was under cultivation.

It was during Pastor Garrou's pastorate that much of the property belonging to the church, including the pastor's farm, the quarry and the lots between the railroad and the Morganton highway, which had been turned over to the church at the time of the dissolution of the Valdese Corporation, was sold. Pastor Garrou, while here in America, also helped his brothers, Jean and François, in the hosiery mill by serving as adviser and bookkeeper.

Garrou served as pastor from December 19, 1900 to May 31, 1903 when he resigned to accept a position at McDonald, Pennsylvania. He later returned to Italy and married Adèle Gay on January 9, 1908. He served as pastor of the Waldensian Church of Perrier-Maneille until his death on May 6, 1915.

Pastor Filippo Enrico Ghigo
1903-1906 and 1916-1917

Pastor Filippo E. Ghigo became the pastor of the Waldensian Presbyterian Church on November 28, 1903. He was born on December 20, 1869 in Ghigo, Prali, Italy, the son of Jean Isaac Ghigo and Marie Madeleine, née Rostan. He completed his courses of study at the following institutions: the College of Torre Pellice, Italy; the Waldensian Theological Seminary in Florence, Italy; and the Universities of Berlin and Leipzig, Germany. Before arriving in Valdese, he had served as a missionary in Switzerland and had been pastor of churches in Uruguay and Argentina.

Pastor Ghigo was hampered in his work in Valdese due to ill health; however, he was able to carry on the regular program of work, and he also devoted much time to the collection of funds for the erection of a new school.

In 1906, Pastor Ghigo resigned his pastoral service to accept a position in Scranton, Pennsylvania. In 1915, he became professor of Italian at the Theological Seminary in Bloomfield, New Jersey.

On April 6, 1916, Pastor Ghigo returned to Valdese to serve a second pastorate. During this time, he helped raise funds for mission work in Italy, the orphanage in Torre Pellice and the Waldensian Soldiers' Station in Turin.

He died on December 16, 1917 in Asheville, North Carolina and was buried in the Waldensian Church Cemetery.

Pastor Ghigo was married to Juliette Louise, née Rosso, and had two children: Anita, who was until her death in 1956, assistant choir director and pianist at the Waldensian Presbyterian Church and an outstanding French teacher at Valdese High School; and Dr. Francis Ghigo, who became professor of Romance languages at Davidson College in Davidson, North Carolina.

The Reverend John Pons
1907-1909 and 1918-1925

Rev. Pons was born in Massello, Italy on November 18, 1877. His parents were Barthélemy Pons and Marie, née Pons. He was educated at the college of Torre Pellice, the Waldensian Seminary of Florence, Italy, and the University of Genoa, Italy, where he received the degree of Bachelor of Divinity.

Before coming to America, he served as pastor of three churches. His first church was at Rodoretto, and then he spent six months at Rio Marina, Elba, and two years at the church of La Maddalena, Sardinia.

Rev. Pons arrived in Valdese on January 21, 1907, and while here he met and married Lydia Jacumin, daughter of Jean Jacques Jacumin and Virginie, née Peyronel. Shortly after their marriage on October 28, 1909, Rev. and Mrs. Pons left for Scranton, Pennsylvania where he preached for four months. In 1910, he went to Brooklyn, New York to become pastor of the Rockaway Avenue Presbyterian Church, and later he moved to Rochester, New York to help build a new church there. With his determination and aggressiveness, Rev. Pons dedicated himself to the work of evangelization and persuaded the authorities of the church to erect the first Italian Presbyterian Church in Rochester. The work began in 1911.

In 1918, Rev. Pons returned to Valdese to become again the pastor of the Waldensian Presbyterian Church, a position he held until 1925. At the same time, he served as professor of foreign languages at Rutherford College, where he continued his duties for fourteen years.

Even after his active pastorate, Rev. Pons served as French pastor of the church and conducted monthly services in French for the benefit of the older Waldensians. He could preach in English, French or Italian, and he also taught Greek and Latin.

Rev. Pons wrote *A History of the Waldenses*, which deals with the trials and tribulations of the Waldensians from the Middle Ages to 1848. It first appeared as articles in the *Morganton News Herald* in 1937. Then it was compiled into a book and presented to the session of the Waldensian Presbyterian Church by Rev. Pons' children as part of the 75th anniversary (1893-1968), commemorating the arrival of the Waldensians in Valdese.

Rev. Pons was secretary and treasurer of the Valdese Building and Loan Association and held this position until his death. A leading Mason, he was a member of the Lovelady Lodge No. 670 and was associate patron of the order of the Eastern Star Lovelady No. 147. He entered the Royal Arch and Commandery and was buried with Masonic honors. He was also a member of the Waldensian society of Le Phare des Alpes.

Rev. John Pons and Lydia Jacumin Pons were parents of five children: Arnaldo Albert, Edward, Evelyn Marie, Walter, and Marguerite Albertine. He died in Valdese, North Carolina on November 11, 1944 and was buried in the Waldensian Church Cemetery.

Pastor Émile Henri Tron
1913-1916

Pastor Tron was born on June 16, 1884 in Ciamp-La-Salse, Massello, Italy. He was educated at the College of Torre Pellice, the Waldensian Theological Seminary in Italy, and in Edinburgh, Scotland.

He married Laura Vigliano of Genoa, Italy. They sailed for America and arrived December 10, 1913 to accept the pastorate of the Waldensian Presbyterian Church. Pastor Tron was joyfully received by the colonists of Valdese, North Carolina due to their having been without a regular pastor for four years. Many accomplishments were made during his ministry, including the renovations of the church, the renewal of the observance of the Waldensian Emancipation of February 17, and the adoption of the latest regulations of the Mother Church.

Pastor and Mrs. Tron left Valdese in April 1916 to respond to Italy's call to the military service in World War I. Upon his arrival there, however, his services were not required in the army.

Pastor Tron accepted the pastorate of the Waldensian Church of

Rodoretto in the Valleys in 1916. Toward the end of the war, he was for several months in active service as a chaplain. From 1919 to 1920, he was director of the Gould Institute in Rome (an orphanage and school). Due to ill health, he left the orphanage and spent a year in the Valleys recuperating and working as a supply pastor.

In 1922, Pastor Tron became pastor of the Waldensian Church of Luserna San Giovanni in the Valleys. He remained there, except for a period when he was sent on a mission to England, until his death at age forty-six on January 18, 1931 in San Giovanni.

Pastor Émile Tron and wife Laura Vigliano had three children born in Italy: Lucille (1917), Silvio Alfredo (1919), and Gustavo Giovanni (1926), who married Frances Elizabeth Hern of Valdese, North Carolina, daughter of Joseph A. Hern, Sr. and Nelle Garrou Hern. Gus and Frances Tron are now members of the Waldensian Presbyterian Church.

The Reverend Joseph Armand Verreault
1925-1931

Rev. Verreault came to Valdese from New Iberia, Louisiana in 1925. He was the first non-Waldensian pastor of the Waldensian Presbyterian Church. Being bilingual, he conducted two services each Sunday, one in French and one in English.

Rev. Verreault was born March 28, 1871 at St. Jean Port Joli, St. Laurence River, Quebec, Canada. He was the son of Pamela Duprey and Pamphille G. Verreault, senator in the Canadian House of Parliament. He was educated at St. Ann College, graduated from Levis College and the Theological Department of Laval University, Quebec.

During his early years he was an educator in Canada. He came to the United States in 1901 and studied at the Moody Bible Institute in Chicago, Illinois.

He was married to Malvina Brunette of Houma, Louisiana. They had three children: Joseph Armand, Jr., who married Sarah Teal; John Francis, who married Jeanette Garrou; and Jeanne Nellen, who married John Laird Jacob.

Rev. Verreault was a member of the New Orleans Presbytery, and from 1910 to 1925, he did extensive work in Home Missions in Southern Louisiana among the French people. His home was in New Orleans and later in New Iberia, Louisiana.

He was pastor of the Waldensian Presbyterian Church from 1925 to 1931. In 1927, his friend, the Rev. J. G. Bruner, pastor of the Advent Moravian Church, Winston-Salem, North Carolina, and his congregation were invited to join in the August 15 celebration of the Glorious Return. The following June the Waldensian Church was invited to join the Moravian Church in the Love Feast celebration. These joint celebrations continued for several years.

While Rev. Verreault was pastor, he used to walk several days a week to visit his parishioners, since he did not have a car. If the visits were not too far from their home, Mrs. Verreault would accompany him.

The Verreaults lived in the second manse (located where the museum stands today), which was remodeled in 1927, during their stay. A central heating system and indoor plumbing were installed. The house was changed from a two-story to a one-story brick veneered structure.

In December 1930, Rev. Verreault resigned his pastorate due to declining health. He continued to serve several months as a pulpit supply while the church was securing a minister.

From 1932 to 1936, Rev. and Mrs. Verreault lived in their former home in New Iberia, Louisiana. They returned to Valdese in 1936 and lived here the remainder of their lives. Mrs. Verreault preceded her husband in death by four weeks. She died November 19, 1960, and Rev. Verreault died December 16, 1960.

The Reverend James Henley Caligan
1931-1938

Rev. Caligan was born in Red Springs, North Carolina on October 31, 1903, son of Rev. James Alexander Caligan and Eleanor Smith Caligan. He attended Davidson College (1923-24) and the University of South Carolina (1924-25). He returned to Davidson in 1925 and graduated with a Bachelor of Arts in 1927. He received the Bachelor of Divinity degree (1931), the Master of Theology (1949) and the Doctor of Theology (1950) from Union Theological Seminary in Richmond, Virginia. On July 10, 1931, he was ordained by Concord Presbytery.

Rev. Caligan began his ministry as a supply pastor at the Waldensian Presbyterian Church on August 1, 1931. In May 1932, he was elected to remain as the regular pastor and continued to serve until May 1, 1938. Rev. Caligan was the first minister of the Valdese church to conduct services entirely in English. He alternated Sundays with Rev. John Pons, who preached two services a month in French. This arrangement continued for two years, and then the French service was held once a month to comply with the wishes of the older Waldensians of the church.

On June 9, 1934, Rev. Caligan married Emily Léger, a descendant of Jean Léger, historian of the 17th Century who wrote *Histoire Générale des Églises Évangéliques des Vallées de Piemont; ou Vaudoises* in 1669. After James Caligan's resignation in 1938, he and Mrs. Caligan spent a year traveling and studying abroad and visiting the Waldensian Valleys. In October 1938, he attended and addressed the Waldensian Synod in Torre Pellice, Italy as a fraternal delegate of the Presbyterian Church in the U.S.A.

After returning to the United States, Rev. Caligan became a supply pastor at St. John's Presbyterian Church in Miami, Florida from 1942 to 1948. Then he became temporary pastor at Uleta Church from 1955 to 1957 and officially retired in 1970. He died January 29, 1972 in Miami, Florida.

The Reverend Sylvan Stephen Poet
1939-1941

Rev. Poet was born in Torre Pellice, Italy in 1905. He was educated at the College of Torre Pellice. He served eighteen months in the mountain artillery of the Italian Army and later was secretary to the Italian Consulate in Monsul, Iraq. He was also vice-consul until he decided to enter the ministry.

He came to the United States and received his Bachelor's Degree from the Theological Seminary of the Reformed Church in New Brunswick, New Jersey and received his Master's Degree from Princeton University. He served for a time as pastor in charge of the

Italian work of the New Utrecht Reformed Church in Brooklyn, New York.

While in New York, Rev. Poet met and married Elizabeth Verdoja on January 21, 1936. Their son Paul, born August, 1937, is at present on the faculty of Friends Seminary in New York City as professor of history. Shortly after the marriage, the Poets moved to Chicago where Rev. Poet was pastor of the Waldensian Presbyterian Church there.

In February 1939, the Rev. Poet accepted the pastorate of the Waldensian Church in Valdese. While serving as pastor, he was appointed fraternal delegate to the Waldensian Synod, and in 1940, he represented the Waldensian Church at the General Assembly held in Chattanooga, Tennessee. He also wrote a short history about the Waldensians: *A Waldensian Colony in the United States, Valdese, North Carolina.*

During the summer of 1941, Rev. Poet and his wife left Valdese for Middletown, New York. He served in a church there, and then at the outbreak of World War II, he worked for awhile at the Stock Exchange on Wall Street. Rev. Poet and his wife separated and were later divorced. His second marriage was in 1951 to Irene Vastine of Brownell, Kansas.

Here is an excerpt from a letter written by Rev. Poet to Catherine Dalmas on May 22, 1992. It tells about his life from 1943 to the present day.

> When Mussolini fell in 1943 and the Resistance movement against the Axis Powers began in the subjected countries, I sought admission to the OSS, the parent of our CIA. I thought that with my knowledge of the Valleys and of their languages and dialects, I could act as a liaison officer between the Allies and the Partisans. Dr. R.W. Anthony, then Secretary of the AWAS had some contact in Washington. Though I was a naturalized American, and probably more anti-Fascist than most (as were most of the Waldenses over here because of their heritage of resistance to unlawful authority and for freedom of

conscience), I was turned down because Italy was still technically at war with the USA.

For about two years I had no news from the Valleys. Then came the news through the Red Cross that both my younger brothers had died in the struggle; the youngest (Pouluch) as leader of one of the "brigades" of the "Action Party" was killed in ambush.

In 1946, as soon as possible by freighter (all ships were used to return the GIs) I went for a visit. I found that the house had been partly burned with the attached barn, as well as 75 percent of all rural homes in all the Valleys during Nazi reprisals; that my older brother as tough as a rock, had been badly beaten more than once (he died not many years later).

When I returned, I moved to Colorado, where I found a second wife who liked the mountains, though born and raised on the Kansas prairie. It was a happy choice. We served churches (cooperative parishes and yoked fields) in S.E. Missouri, Northern and Southern Kansas and Nebraska until retirement in 1971 when we moved here to build our own house for retirement. I lost her in 1987 to "massive encephalic infection."

Since then I have been doing what most people my age do: griping about the government — local, state and national — sometimes with some good reason, for never listening to what we told them all along was wrong with the country! Words! A fairly common virtue, especially with preachers, lawyers and politicians, if not everybody!

I am not quite as old as Valdese — twelve years short! So it is fitting to wish the town and the church at least another century of life, if not as "the fastest growing town in North Carolina" as it was when I was there!

Rev. Poet now lives in Arroyo Seco, New Mexico.

The Reverend Watson Munford Fairley, D.D. 1941-1945

Dr. Fairley was born in Manchester, New York in 1873. He was a graduate of Davidson College, Davidson, North Carolina and Union Theological Seminary in Richmond, Virginia. He was ordained July 26, 1900 by Fort Worth Presbytery in Texas and served many pastorates in Texas and North Carolina. He retired from his pastorate in Raeford, North Carolina on June 1, 1940 due to ill health.

Dr. and Mrs. Fairley moved to their home in Montreat, North Carolina, and as his health improved, he was recommended by officials of Concord Presbytery to the Waldensian Presbyterian Church as a temporary supply pastor.

Dr. Fairley came to the Waldensian Presbyterian Church in October 1941, and during his ministry, a real growth in membership began. Vast plans were made for remodeling the sanctuary.

The congregation was so impressed with his work and Mrs. Fairley's contribution that they decided to keep them as long as his good health continued. They remained until 1945.

Dr. and Mrs. Fairley retired to their home in Montreat, North Carolina and remained there until his death on June 6, 1955. He was buried in Tarboro, North Carolina. His wife, the former Alice Rollwage of Forrest City, Arkansas was at the Presbyterian Home in High Point until her death.

The Reverend Albert Bonner McClure, Sr.
1945-1950

Rev. McClure was born on July 16, 1905 in Toccoa, Georgia. He was graduated from Union Theological Seminary, Richmond, Virginia in 1934. Before coming to Valdese, he was pastor of the Lincolnton Presbyterian Church, Lincolnton, North Carolina for eight years.

On October 16, 1945, Rev. McClure was received from the Presbytery of Kings Mountain, North Carolina and was installed as minister of the Waldensian Presbyterian

Church on October 28, 1945.

During his ministry in Valdese, he placed emphasis on the youth, the choir, and the gathering and preservation of items brought by the colonists from Italy.

During the fall of 1949, Rev. McClure received a call to assume the superintendency of the Barium Springs Home for Children at Barium Springs, North Carolina. He resigned on November 6, 1949 and preached his last sermon January 8, 1950.

Rev. McClure remained at Barium Springs until his death on October 22, 1972 in Statesville, North Carolina. He was married to Mary McGehee. They had three children when they came to Valdese: Mary Emma, Albert Bonner, Jr., and Beverly Kate. Their fourth child, Emily Sue, was born in Valdese.

The Reverend Walter Hugh Styles
1950-1958

The Rev. Styles was born on July 20, 1917 in Paint Gap, North Carolina. He was educated at Toccoa, Georgia and Columbia Theological Seminary in Decatur, Georgia.

Rev. Styles came to the Waldensian Presbyterian Church in March 1950 from the Black Mountain Presbyterian Church in Black Mountain, North Carolina. During his pastorate here, the Educational Building was erected, and a full-time staff person serving as both secretary and Director of Christian Education was employed.

On December 14, 1958, after eight and three-fourths years of serving the church, Rev. Styles accepted a call to the Faith Presbyterian Church in Tallahassee, Florida. During his ministry in Tallahassee, a new educational building and sanctuary were built. More than 1700 members joined the church. Rev. Styles was also elected Moderator of the Synod of Florida in 1968.

In 1975, Rev. Styles left Faith Presbyterian Church and spent the last years of his pastorate in small churches. He served two and one-half years in Douglas, Georgia and four years in Havana, Florida. Rev. Styles retired in 1981.

In 1985, Rev. and Mrs. Styles moved back to Black Mountain, North Carolina where he first began his ministry in 1945. Since his retirement, he has been a supply minister for numerous churches. He has preached more than four hundred times in thirty-eight different churches.

Rev. Walter Styles married Mertis Brooks from Cumming, Georgia. They have two children: Walter Brooks and Frances Makemie (Kemie).

The Reverend James Clyde Plexico, Jr.
1959-1968

Rev. Plexico was born on July 14, 1921 in Sharon, South Carolina, son of Rev. and Mrs. J. Clyde Plexico, Sr. He was educated at King College, Bristol, Tennessee and Asheville College, Asheville, North Carolina where he earned the Bachelor of Science degree in education. He attended Columbia Theological Seminary, Decatur, Georgia where he received the Bachelor of Divinity, Master of Divinity and Master of Theology degrees.

Before coming to Valdese, Rev. Plexico had served the First Presbyterian Church in Enterprise, Alabama (1946); First Presbyterian Church, Dalton, Georgia (1948); Seneca Presbyterian Church in Seneca, South Carolina (1949-1954); and First Presbyterian Church in Cartersville, Georgia (1954-1959).

Rev. Plexico came to the Waldensian Church in Valdese, North Carolina on May 6, 1959. During his ten years as pastor, many changes occurred. The Cherub, Melody, Junior and French Choirs were organized; a new manse was built on North Laurel Street; and a Ruth M. Williams Music Scholarship Fund was established. Rev. Plexico also organized the Chaplaincy Program at the Valdese General Hospital.

In 1968, Rev. Plexico resigned his position to accept a call to Metairie, Louisiana where he remained until 1973. Then he served the Deer Creek Presbyterian Church, Cumming, Georgia (1974-1977); St. Paul's Presbyterian, Chester, South Carolina

(1977-1980), and Presbyterian Home of South Carolina in Summerville, South Carolina, as Chaplain Administrator (1980-1986).

Rev. Plexico retired in July 1986. Since then, he has supplied twenty-one churches and was interim minister of the Summerton Presbyterian Church, Summerton, South Carolina (1987-1988). Now Rev. Plexico is a supply minister of Westminster Presbyterian Church in Asheville, North Carolina.

Rev. Plexico is married to Miriam Easter Clark. They have three children: Sandra Ruth Salvaggio Walker, James Clark Plexico, and Rebecca Dale Scott.

The Reverend Doctor Paul Henley Felker, Jr.
1969-

Dr. Felker was born on August 1, 1926 in Kannapolis, North Carolina, son of Paul Henley Felker, Sr. and Connie Estelle Rodgers. He received the Bachelor's degree from Davidson College, Davidson, North Carolina, the Bachelor of Divinity (1954) and Master of Divinity (1971) degrees from Columbia Theological Seminary in Decatur, Georgia. In 1978, he received the Doctor of Ministry degree from McCormick Theological Seminary in Chicago, Illinois.

Dr. Felker served pastorates in Filbert Presbyterian Church and Beersheba Church in York, South Carolina (1954-1960) and the Mulberry Presbyterian Church in Charlotte, North Carolina (1960-1969). Then he came to the Waldensian Presbyterian Church on January, 16,1969. His pastorate is the longest in the history of this church.

During the twenty-four years Dr. Felker has spent as pastor of the Waldensian Presbyterian Church, many changes have been wrought in church life. The church is more highly organized with an increasing number of people involved in the decision-making of the church. The choir program has been strengthened, the Christian Education program enhanced, and the youth activities broadened. There has been an increased amount of service to the community, through financial support of community social agencies and programs. More work of compassion has been done by the Service Committee, including the clothing drive, monetary help for the needy, and food for the hungry.

Dr. Felker has led the congregation through three successful financial/construction programs. The first was for the construction of the present museum in the early part of the 1970s, followed by the renovation of the educational buildings in the latter portion of the 1970's, and finally the campaign to enlarge the sanctuary and provide other improvements. With these programs completed and the enhancement of the facilities by lovely plantings, the church complex stands as one of the most beautiful structures anywhere.

On four occasions—1959, 1965, 1979, and 1992, Dr. Felker was a commissioner to the General Assembly of the Presbyterian Church. In August 1970, he attended the Waldensian Synod at Torre Pellice, Italy as a fraternal delegate of the Presbyterian Church U.S.

Dr. Felker has been an active presbyter in each presbytery served and has worked on most major committees and chaired many of them. They include the following committees: Women's Committee, Stewardship and Finance, Christian Education, Presbytery Council, Candidates Committee, and Mission Committee. He has been a member of the Committee on Ministry for the past seven years and served as chairman for three years.

In the community, Dr. Felker has been a member of the Valdese Rotary Club and president of the Old Colony Players. He has also served on the Board of Directors of Grandfather Home for children in Banner Elk, North Carolina.

Dr. Felker is married to Carol Jean Price, and they have three children: Mark Butler, married to Wendy Lee Donahoe; Alan Carlton, married to Lesa Anne Ratliff; and Eric Paul, married to Sandra Lynn Day.

CHAPTER 10

THE VALDESE CORPORATION

After the arrival of the colonists on May 29, 1893, Pastor Charles Albert Tron immediately began work to organize the colonists' land transaction, and working with a group of advisers from Morganton, the Valdese Corporation was chartered on June 8, 1893. The incorporators were Charles Albert Tron, Isaac T. Avery, Marvin F. Scaife, William C. Ervin and Samuel T. Pearson. The corporation was empowered to engage in the following enterprises: to buy and sell real and personal property; to own, hold, control, improve and develop its real estate; to lease or bond mineral interests in lands; to conduct any and all mining operations; to conduct and operate sawmills and do any and all things necessary for carrying on a lumber business; to build any kinds of factories; to act as immigrant agents and colonize their lands; to do any or all things necessary to promote or conduct the colony; and to borrow money and issue coupon bonds or other evidence of indebtedness and secure the same by mortgage or deed of trust on any or all its property. The duration of the corporation was to be sixty years. The capital stock was $25,000 divided into shares of $100 each, with the privilege of increasing the stock by an amount not exceeding $5,000. The stockholders were not to be individually liable for the debts, contracts, or torts. A board of directors was named whose members were Charles A. Tron, President; the pastor who should replace Dr. Tron, Vice-President; Philippe Richard, Secretary; Samuel T. Pearson, Treasurer; Messrs Jaubert Micol, Albert Pons, the Reverend John M. Rose, Jr. and W.C. Ervin.

A word about the incorporators and advisers would be in order. Dr. Tron, of course, was the leader of the settlers. Mr. Scaife has been mentioned earlier as the industrialist/benefactor of the settlers. Mr. William C. Ervin and Isaac T. Avery were attorneys in Morganton, and Mr. Samuel T. Pearson was the cashier of the Piedmont Bank in Morganton. The Rev. John M. Rose, Jr. was the pastor of the First Presbyterian Church in Morganton and served as adviser and friend to the settlers for several years during his tenure in Morganton.

The Corporation was set up to purchase the property in order to sell to the settlers. Settlers were assigned acreage after mutual agreement as to where they would locate. They were then to redeem the bonds to cover the value of their acreage. The Corporation would then prepare a deed for the specified acreage, delivering ownership free and clear of any mortgage. Although the Corporation was drawn up to hold property in common, there was the provision for individual ownership as soon as the family could get enough money to redeem the bonds sufficient to cover their property value.

It became apparent after a short period of time that the Corporation/commune organization would not work. It also became apparent that the settlers had much more land than they could manage or pay for. An approach was made to the Morganton Land and Improvement Company to renegotiate the amount of land being purchased.

Dr. Matteo Prochet, Chairman of the Committee of Evangelization of the Waldensian Church, visited in Valdese and Morganton during Christmas of 1893. Dr. Prochet was evidently a very perceptive man who saw immediately the seriousness of conditions in Valdese. He set about to rectify matters. He spoke to the Morganton Land and Improvement Company officials about reducing the size of the land commitment and thereby reducing some of the financial pressures. He also visited in Charlotte and struck an agreement with John Meier, the superintendent of a hosiery mill in Charlotte, to set up a mill in Valdese using only Waldensian labor. In return, the colony would help prepare a building for his factory, and, at the end of five years of satisfactory operation, the building would be his. The contract was approved by the colony on May 30, 1894.

Negotiations with the officials of the land company had continued, and in June 1894, while the Rev. C.A. Tron was making an extended visit to Valdese, the acreage in the agreement was reduced to 5,000 acres. After the reduction, Dr. Tron calculated the financial condition as follows: Owed to Morganton Land and Improvement Company $18,000 for land, $1,387.48 for materials, equipment and farm animals, for a total debt of $19,387.48. The individual settlers had purchased land for which they owed $14,780.49 and had accounts at the Corporation Store in the amount of $846.84, making a total owed the Corporation by individuals $15,627.33. This left a deficit for the Corporation of $3,760.15. However, this only meant the debt had been transferred to individual settlers rather than the Corporation. The individual families were beginning to experience real difficulties in making ends meet.

The Rev. Barthélemy Soulier and his bride arrived in Valdese in late June 1894 to minister to the settlers. They found the colony in dire straits with problems becoming worse as time progressed. The Rev. Soulier was a very capable and thoughtful man. He set about to solve the problems of the colony and worked at it diligently for the next seven years. He probably deserves more credit for the ultimate success of the venture than any other single person.

By November 1894, the conditions in the colony were becoming desperate. Mr. Soulier arranged a meeting with the officers of the land company and worked out arrangements with them to further reduce the obligations of the colony. The proposal provided that: (1) The corporation would deliver all its land as well as the sawmill, ox teams, and other personal property. (2) The company would then sell to each individual the lands which had been assigned by the Valdese Corporation, accepting notes at five percent. The prices should be those fixed by Dr. Prochet in January, 1894, to which should be added a proportionate part of the debt owed by the Valdese Corporation. (3) All redeemed bonds held by the colonists should be surrendered, the par value of said bonds to be credited on the purchase price of the farms. (4) Four large tracts containing 1,463 acres would be taken back by the land company at the rate of $2.50 per acre. The ox teams, wagons, and lumber already sawed would be taken by the company at a value to be set by Mr. Soulier and the surveyor, Mr. Robert Ervin. (5) The unimproved town lots on the north side of the railroad tracks, except those which had already been sold, assigned, or built upon, should be conveyed to the officers of the Waldensian Church. The burial ground should be held perpetually as a colony cemetery. Sites should be selected for a church and a school and should be held permanently for those purposes. The remainder of the town lots should be held in trust by the church for sale with a clause prohibiting the manufacture and sale of intoxicating liquors or beverages other than native wines, and with such other restrictions as the officers should determine. The proceeds of all sales should be applied to the maintenance of the church and school. (6) The hosiery mill (built for John Meier) should be conveyed to the company at a price of $450. (7) The company would continue to operate the sawmill until January 1, 1896, and would employ as far as possible Waldensians at a rate of not less than forty cents a day. (8) The mortgage given by the Valdese Corporation to the Piedmont Bank and all outstanding bonds should be canceled and the Valdese Corporation dissolved. (9) The proposition would be withdrawn unless it was accepted by every stockholder and director of the Corporation by January 1, 1895.

On December 24, 1894, thirty-eight stockholders and directors agreed to the stipulations, and on January 1, 1895, a deed was executed between the Valdese Corporation, the Morganton Land and Improvement Company, and the Piedmont Bank by which, on consideration of the cancellation of all its outstanding bonds, the Corporation conveyed to the Company all of its real estate holdings. This deed, signed by the Rev. John M. Rose, Jr., Jean Jacques Léger, George P. Erwin (President of the Piedmont Bank) and S.T. Pearson, was filed and registered by the Register of Deeds of Burke County on March 2, 1895 (Volume A-2 pages 261-266).

At the time the Valdese Corporation was dissolved, it was found that the Corporation owed the Morganton Land and Improvement Company $2,000. The Company reduced this to $1,500. Mr. Soulier wrote to Dr. C.A. Tron asking for his help in clearing this debt. Dr. Tron, a man of means, promptly sent the $1,500 and enabled the settlers to clear the Corporation debt.

This account of the formation and experiences of the Valdese Corporation comes from Dr. George B. Watts' book, *The Waldenses in the New World*.

Thus ended the experiment in corporate/communal living. Each individual family was now on its own, although the Christian love and concern for others in the church family would always see that care was given to people in the church who needed help.

CHAPTER 11

BUILDING AND RENOVATION PROGRAMS

The Waldensian Presbyterian Church has undergone many changes and improvements since its dedication July 4, 1899.

The first repair or improvement took place in 1914-15. Quoting from the church minutes, the congregation voted on July 7, 1914 to undertake the following work:

a) To replace the floor, taking care to leave under it an airspace of about two feet and to make vents in the walls so that air can circulate under the floor to help preserve it.
b) To stain the ceiling with oak stain.
c) To stain the benches with crude oil.
d) To repair and whitewash the exterior of the church.
e) To adopt a system of gas lighting and to take up a collection to cover the cost of installation. (The collection was begun on the spot by Mrs. Grant who offered $5. Mrs. Grant had come to help educate the children very early in the life of the settlement and stayed to make her home.)
f) To heat the church with coal, using the stove the church now owns plus another as the session sees fit.

It was reported to the session on October 13, 1915 that the work had been completed, and it was decided to have the church yard cleared and ground worked so grass might be sowed in the spring.

The next major change in the physical plant occurred in 1921-22. At a meeting on June 5, 1921, the congregation charged the session to resolve the question of heating the church. From these simple instructions evolved present day Tron Hall.

The session in its meeting July 22, 1921 had this statement:

> The Session given the mandate received from the Church assembly on June 5, 1921, given the great need for a building annexed to the church for the development of various church programs, and given also that the only means of heating the sanctuary is to install a steam heating system and that in order to do that a building is absolutely necessary, the Session voted unanimously to

have an annex added to the church, 45 feet long and 28 feet wide, in stone. Begin as soon as possible.

The construction of this annex caused considerable discussion in the church. The addition necessitated the removal of a small room attached to the north east corner of the sanctuary and the closing of a window in the same corner. The building of the annex provided for a basement in the building large enough to install a steam boiler fired with coal. This heating system was used for a number of years until Pioneer Hall was constructed. There are no figures available on cost.

The next change in the structure of the church occurred in 1927. This is a change which no one seems to recall, although many people living today were present at that time. When the church building was originally constructed, the north end of the church did not have the gable end as we now see it. Instead, the gable end of the church was the wall that also serves as the north end of the present sanctuary and contained a door still in use as the entrance from that area of the building. The roof across the end of the church was a slanted roof from the wall toward Main Street and from the bell tower to the north east corner. The ground level on this end of the building was several feet higher than at present.

The above information is given to help the reader understand the changes that were made in 1927. The Rev. P.E. Monnet, a retired minister who was active in the church, offered to pay for the changes if the congregation would agree to move the entrance from the south end of the building to the north end. Mr. A.M. Kistler of Morganton also donated $500 to put nine new windows in the remodeled north end. The congregation agreed to the proposal, and a building committee was appointed, consisting of Mr. Frederick Meytre, chairman, John Long, Pierre Emmanuel Micol, John Guigou and John P. Rostan, Sr. There is no explanation in the minutes of the session or of the congregational meeting as to why the authorized changes were not carried out. Instead, the north end of the building was changed to its present configuration. The yard ground level was lowered to its approximate present level.

A major building program was authorized in 1938, when the congregation voted to build what is known as Pioneer Hall. This building provided additional Sunday School classrooms, plus a pastor's study and a kitchen and fellowship hall on the second floor. In addition, the heating system for the entire complex of buildings was located in the partial basement. Steam pipes were run underground to provide heat for the sanctuary. The heat was provided by two steam boilers fired by coal. These were later converted to oil burners. This system provided the heat for the buildings at that time as well as for the Educational Building built in 1953-54. The oil-fired boilers were used until a major renovation in 1977-78.

The next major addition to the building complex was approved in 1952 when authorization for the Educational Building was given. This was a three-story yellow brick building connected to Pioneer Hall by an arched covered walkway. This building was designed to house Sunday School classrooms and the administrative offices of the church. It has been in use since January of 1955. It was designed on the south end to attach a new sanctuary, but this idea was never developed. A tower designed to support a steeple was provided.

A major refurbishing of the entire complex took place in 1976-78. The heating system was converted to heat pumps to provide heat or air conditioning for all buildings, new carpets were installed in the sanctuary and many improvements were made in the fellowship hall. Ceilings in the Educational Building were lowered to accommodate air conditioning ducts. An overall landscape plan was adopted, which has been implemented in stages since then. Building interiors were painted, and windows were re-caulked and repainted. A brick patio was laid in front of the sanctuary.

In 1990 a project which had been discussed for years was approved. The congregation approved the enlarging of the sanctuary. An additional 144 seats were added to the sanctuary with an enlarged narthex and a sound control room and space for a bride's room provided over the narthex. A covered walkway was built from a porte-cochere on the east side of the building complex to the sanctuary. An elevator was installed for Pioneer Hall to provide handicapped access. The bell tower base on the south end of the Educational Building was removed to roof level and the entire building complex was restuccoed to give the appearance of one continuous building. The building process was completed in October of 1991, having taken fifteen months to complete.

WALDENSIAN PRESBYTERIAN CHURCH
VALDESE, NORTH CAROLINA
1992

CHAPTER 12

WALDENSIAN CUSTOMS AND TRADITIONS

THE WALDENSIAN EMBLEM (Of Biblical Inspiration)

The lighted candle signifies "The Word of God." The blue field represents "Darkness." The seven stars represent the "Seven Churches of the Book of Revelation." The Latin motto LUX LUCET IN TENEBRIS means "A Light Shines in Darkness," or "The Burning Word of God Is Bringing Light and Splendor among Men." The two branches, one of green oak and one of green laurel, tied together at the bottom with a blue ribbon, complete the emblem.

The green oak means "Hope and Strength or Power." The green laurel means "Hope and Glory." Thus we have Hope, Power, and the Glory of God.

In 1640, on the frontispiece of a theological publication, there appeared for the first time the Waldensian emblem, which has since been used by the Waldensian Church.

In the Waldensian Presbyterian Church, the tradition of using the Waldensian emblem as a reminder of the heritage of this congregation remains strong. The emblem is displayed in a stained glass window over the entrance to the sanctuary and also in a full-length window in the sanctuary, along with emblems of other Protestant faiths throughout the world.

The Waldensian emblem is found over the entrance to the Waldensian Museum. Inside the museum on the wall to the left of the entrance is placed a unique version of the emblem handcarved in walnut by Edward Garrou and donated to the museum on February 17, 1974. The window in the center of the west wall of the museum has the Waldensian emblem in stained glass at the top, above one of the original sanctuary windows. This window was a gift of Dr. Robert Pascal, who, with his sister Olga, worked actively for many years in the establishment of the museum.

Church printed materials frequently use the Waldensian emblem. It is found on church bulletins, in the church newsletter, on church stationery, in the church directory, and on printed programs for special events. Prominently centered on the church banner is the Waldensian Emblem painstakingly created in needlework by Mrs. Victor Garrou (Ann Bills). By using the emblem so often, the congregation is reminded of its Christian mission to be "a light shining in a dark world."

THE WALDENSIAN TRADITIONAL DRESS

The traditional dress of the Waldensian women is made of silk, wool or cotton of dark material, with a collar edged with white lace. The sleeves are long and full with an edging of white lace at the wrist. The skirt falls in even folds to the ankles. A shawl, preferably of silk or wool, is worn with the dress and is usually in colors of red, violet, dark blue, crimson, black or white, with embroidery of gay colored flowers, and edged with long fringes. An apron is an integral part of the Waldensian dress. It is made of taffeta of changeable colors, showing various hues.

The Waldensian bonnet—"coiffe" in French, "cuffio" in Patois and "cuffia" in Italian—is the principal element of the ensemble. It is made of starched embroidered lace fabric. It gently frames the face. A long white silk ribbon streamer encircles the back part of the coiffe and is tied in a bow at the back, then falls along the shoulders.

The coiffe is an "emblem of purity." It is to be worn only for church functions and therefore is not worn at any frivolous affairs, such as for dancing.

In the Waldensian Valleys when a young girl reaches the age of thirteen or fourteen, she starts a course in catechism which lasts for two to four years. While attending these catechism classes, she wears a black or navy coiffe. Then, when she joins the church and receives her first communion, she wears the white coiffe for the first time. Traditionally, the white coiffe was worn for a young lady's wedding. Oftentimes when a woman died, she was dressed in her cherished Waldensian attire.

In Valdese, most women of Waldensian descent have a Waldensian ensemble. It is sometimes worn for the Waldensian celebrations and for other special occasions. Brides sometimes wear the white lace coiffe as their headpiece with a white wedding gown.

BAPTISM, WEDDINGS, FUNERALS

Baptism: The service of infant baptism was customarily held in the home in the early years of the colony. Waldensian infants were usually baptised prior to the age of one year. The service was performed by the pastor assisted by an elder in the presence of the family of the infant and close relatives, godparents, if any were chosen, the pastor's family, members of the session and invited close neighbors and friends. After the service, a photograph would be taken of the group, and all present would enjoy a sumptuous dinner in the home to celebrate the occasion. This was a custom carried over from the Waldensian Valleys. Presently, except in rare circumstances to accommodate the family of the infant to be christened, baptisms are held in the sanctuary.

Wedding Customs: Marriage ceremonies in the early years of the Waldensian settlement in Valdese were held in the home of the bride. Attending the wedding were the immediate families of the bride and groom, maternal and paternal grandparents, and oftentimes cousins if space would accommodate them. After the vows were exchanged, the wedding party and guests would enjoy a memorable dinner of celebration.

From 1893, the year the Waldensians emigrated from their ancestral homes to Valdese, through 1902, there were only seven marriages. The first was the marriage of Marguerite Gaydou to John Long that occurred in the bride's home on April 29, 1894. Twenty-five years later, the elder daughter of that union, Mary Long, was married to the Reverend Aurelio Mangione on April 29, 1919, in the Waldensian Church sanctuary. This was the first formal wedding in the church. The Mangionies lived to enjoy their sixty-second wedding anniversary.

Since the first wedding in the church sanctuary, many marriages have taken place there. When any occur on the anniversary of the first wedding, April 29, the couple is reminded of the historic date.

Funeral Customs: The Waldensian settlers continued the burial customs of their homeland. In Valdese prior to the availability of funeral establishments, the bodies of the deceased were readied for burial in the homes where death occurred and then were placed in wooden caskets made by friends called on to assist. The caskets were lined with linens from the home. Funeral services were held in the home and attended by the immediate family and all who could be present. Then, the casket was placed on a wagon, which was pulled by horses to the cemetery, with a cortege following on foot.

Prior to the funeral in the home, it was customary for neighbors to assist in all-night vigils until the day of burial. Caskets were draped with the black funeral pall that is now on display in the Waldensian museum. It is recalled by one family that as late as 1912 when an infant daughter died, the family rode in the family wagon with the casket, pulled by their grey horse guided by the father. Distance from the home to the cemetery, in many cases, was quite an undertaking on foot.

The first funeral held in the sanctuary was in 1917 when Pastor Filippo Ghigo died in a sanitarium in Asheville, North Carolina. The body could not be taken to the manse due to the illness of one of the pastor's children. After the church service, Pastor Ghigo's body was transported to the hillside cemetery in a wagon drawn by a team of horses. The second funeral service held in the sanctuary was in 1918 when two deaths occurred at opposite areas of the settlement. Relatives, neighbors and friends who lived near each family of the deceased gathered in that home for an initial service. Then, the procession followed the two wagons to the sanctuary for a combined service.

The first motorized funeral hearse was used in 1919 when the body of Fanny Tron Berry (Mrs. Cicero Berry), daughter of Pierre and Louise Pons Tron, was driven to the sanctuary for the funeral service and from there to the Waldensian Church Cemetery. After that time, the place for the funeral service became a matter of choice. Taken into consideration were the distances, the conditions of the roads, the weather, and the means of transportation.

WALDENSIAN CELEBRATIONS

The anniversaries of two important events in the history of the Waldensians have been celebrated for many years in the Waldensian Valleys. The August 15 celebration commemorates the date in 1689 when an army of Waldensian men successfully fought their way back to the Valleys to reclaim their homeland after a three-year exile in Switzerland. The Edict of Emancipation of February 17, 1848 granted the Waldensians equal civil and political rights held by other Italians. Remembering these two events gives Waldensians on both sides of the Atlantic cause for giving thanks and rejoicing in their heritage.

In Valdese, the Waldensians continued to celebrate Emancipation Day, February 17. The celebration gradually took on a more religious nature and was held in various locations, including the

Waldensian Customs and Traditions

meeting house, the Le Phare des Alpes clubhouse, the Rock School and, about 1917, the second floor of the newly built Co-operative Store.

One of the February 17 suppers was prepared by Jacques Henri Bounous and Jean Pons (Bienvenue). They prepared veal stew with vegetables and potatoes in a large pot. Two young girls, Margaret Pascal (Mrs. Peter Meytre) and Zeline Pons, served the meal by going around the tables, one carrying the pot and the other dipping the food from the pot to the guests' plates.

After the meal, a few short talks in French or patois on the significance of the celebration were given by some of the men. Then, Henry Clot played the accordion, while the guests danced the courenta and had an enjoyable time, even though the floor was unfinished. Mr. Henry Clot of the colony and Mr. J. Gordon Queen of Morganton organized a band composed of Waldensian men and boys about 1917. Thereafter, for several years the Waldensian colonists had a band to play for them at their celebrations.

The band practiced on Sunday afternoons in "the Pines," across the street from the sanctuary on Rodoret Street (where the first cemetery had been located). Many gathered there weekly to listen to the band and socialize. The band was well known in the area and was invited to play on numerous occasions. On November 1, 1924, the band had an engagement in Lenoir. As they were returning to Valdese, they stopped by the home of Albert Bleynat, one of the band members, and played to celebrate the birth of his new baby boy born that day. The baby was John A. Bleynat, who grew up to make an outstanding contribution to the life and work of the Waldensian Presbyterian Church.

At other February 17 celebrations in the Waldensian Valleys and in the early years in Valdese, the feast usually consisted of soutisso, boiled potatoes and a salad. This menu is still used on numerous Waldensian occasions today. In the early days, the soutisso had been made at hog-killing time from the recipes brought from their homes in the valleys.

The other celebration was that of the Glorious Return of August 15. For many years, the Glorious Return was celebrated on the Sunday nearest the fifteenth. The families, carrying large picnic baskets, would go to a selected farm where they would have a worship service in a grassy meadow by a stream or spring. After the worship service, the families enjoyed their picnics in family groups. The meal usually included homemade bread, wine, grapes, cheese, brus, and baked or fried chicken. Perhaps there would be potato salad, made with boiled potatoes, parsley, onions and dressing of wine vinegar and olive oil.

Later, this celebration was held in the sanctuary, and the meal was on the church lawn. In the late 1920's, friends from the Advent Moravian Church of Winston Salem, North Carolina joined in this annual celebration. The Waldensian Church then joined the Moravian church in the Love Feast Celebration in Winston Salem. This practice continued for several years. During and following World II, the picnics were discontinued. In recent years, the Glorious Return has been celebrated with a church service and a festival.

WALDENSIAN FOOD

In the early years in Valdese, the colonists' food was much like what they ate in the Waldensian Valleys. At the evening meal, soup was usually the main dish, perhaps with some bread and cheese. In season, the soup was made of mashed turnips and potatoes and milk. At other times fava beans, or lentils, boiled in water, were used. Carrots, celery, and potatoes, with an onion sauteed in butter, were added to the soup.

Another dish was the cornmeal mush, polenta, usually boiled in a cast-iron pot to a thicker consistency than mush. The polenta was eaten with a bowl of milk or tomato sauce. The left-over polenta was sliced and fried the next morning for breakfast and sometimes eaten with cheese.

For a covered dish on special occasions, "la souppa," was made. Bread sticks were broken and placed in a shallow pan. Broth (chicken or beef) was poured over the bread sticks. Specks of butter were put on top of the sticks, which were then sprinkled with parmesan cheese and cinnamon. The dish was then baked in the oven until a crust formed on top.

The usual Sunday meal was a chicken baked with potatoes and onions and served with a green salad.

Another traditional recipe brought from the Valleys and served for special meals was "cagliettas." These contained a mixture of bread sticks, eggs, and cheese, wrapped in a cabbage leaf or grape leaf and boiled in broth. At times, different kinds of meat were added to the stuffing.

Soutisso was always made at hog-killing time and is still a favorite sausage. It was made with fresh ground lean pork, seasoned to taste with plenty of pepper and garlic, then stuffed in casings.

Moustardella was another sausage. It was made by using the blood of the freshly killed hog, the liver, the head meat, cracklings and various seasonings mixed together and stuffed in casings.

Bread was one of the staples of the Waldensian's diet. It was made with flour, water, salt, and yeast, which was sometimes a starter similar to that used today in sourdough bread. After the dough had risen for the second time, it was ready to be placed in pans and baked in the outdoor oven. Another method was to let it rise on floured boards then transfer it to the oven with a wooden peel. Before baking the bread, the oven was heated to the correct temperature, which was about 400 degrees F. Then, the oven floor was cleaned of coals and ashes before the bread was placed in it. The bread was baked until it was crusty.

In the Waldensian Valleys of Italy, the outdoor oven was built in the center of the village. Each family had a certain day to bake their bread. The oven was built by the men of field rock and mud and was shaped like a beehive. The outside top was covered with sand to retain the heat. The floor of the oven was constructed of slabs of stone, and the entire oven was covered by a small shed. When the settlers arrived in Valdese, one of their first tasks was to build a community oven. Later, each district and some families built their own ovens.

Desserts were custards or fruits, fresh, canned or dried, and always served with cheese and wine. Apples were wrapped in leftover dough from the bread making and baked in the outdoor oven. Brus was a home-made cheese similar to cottage cheese.

THE WALDENSIAN DIALECT

The colonists who settled Valdese brought their Waldensian dialect, or "patois," with them from the Waldensian Valleys. There were some differences in the language used in the upper Germanasca Valley from that in the lower Pellice Valley, and there were representatives of both regions among the Valdese settlers. The differences were minimal, however, and the people communicated easily.

The Waldensian dialect has often been described as part French and part Italian, but in origin it belongs to neither language. Research has identified the Waldensian dialects as a variety of Occitan, a family of dialects once spoken across the south of France and in northern Italy. These dialects were derived from Provençal, once the standard language of the region.

In the Waldensian Valleys in the late 1800's, both French and Italian were taught in the schools. French was used for church services. The patois was the conversational language spoken in the home and with neighbors and friends. In Valdese, the same pattern of language use continued in the home and church, with English added to the school program.

In the first thirty years of the colony, a few parents spoke French in the home, for they believed that knowing French would be of educational benefit to their children. Some others insisted on using only English so that their children would be better prepared for the public schools and for life in the United States. The majority, however, spoke patois in the home and neighborhood. Many of the children in the Waldensian neighborhoods spoke no English until they started to school. After that, the children learned English quickly and soon were speaking English among themselves. Often, children spoke patois with parents and grandparents but only English with brothers and sisters. In large families, sometimes the younger children understood patois but did not learn to speak it. For the majority of the generation born in the Waldensian Valleys, except for those who came at a very young age, the Waldensian patois continued to be their primary language for the remainder of their lives. Most of them, however, learned enough English to be able to manage their affairs without assistance.

In the past twenty years, there has been a renewed interest in Waldensian heritage, as evidenced by the erection of the Waldensian Museum, the Waldensian Festival held in August, and the group tours to the Waldensian Valleys. Along with this interest came efforts to revive the use of patois. In 1978 and 1979, Ernest Jahier capably taught the rudiments of patois to two large classes of enthusiastic students.

In spite of this effort, at the present time, very few Waldensians under the age of sixty can converse in patois. Many of the younger people have learned a few phrases which they toss out at Waldensian social gatherings. Even among those who are still fluent in patois, there is little use of the language, except for a greeting exchanged from time to time. The phrases heard most often are "Cum la vai lo?" (How are you?) and "Erveise" (Goodbye). Not more than two or three families of older Waldensians still use patois on an everyday basis. A few families make an effort to converse in patois but revert back to English when expression becomes difficult. On visits to the Waldensian Valleys, fluency in patois has been

Waldensian Customs and Traditions

most helpful in conversing with relatives and friends there.

As the older generation passes on, there is no doubt that the Waldensian patois will disappear from Valdese. When that time comes, future descendants may be helped to recreate the sounds and vocabulary of the language by two studies completed in recent years. In 1980, Dr. Francis Ghigo, son of Pastor Filippo Ghigo, published *The Provençal Speech of the Waldensian Colonists of Valdese, North Carolina*. Cathy R. Pons presented *Language Death Among Waldensians of Valdese, North Carolina* as her doctoral study at Indiana University in 1990. Dr. Pons is the great-granddaughter of Jean Jacques and Madeline Tron Pons, who were in the November 1893 group of colonists.

FARMING AND WINE MAKING

The Waldensians who came to Valdese in the first groups were all small farmers, and they came with the expectation of continuing this line of work. They did not realize the problems they would encounter with rocky land and shallow topsoil. In spite of the problems, some of the settlers were very successful in farming after they learned how to live with the climate and poor soil.

The most successful farmers of Valdese engaged in dairying and small grain farming. Several were also successful in raising large numbers of chickens for laying hens. Having come from an area where a quarter acre of land in one piece was considered a large piece of land, to an area where some fields measured ten to twenty acres or more, the people had to change their methods and expectations drastically. Their experience in small-scale dairying in Italy helped them set up and operate their small dairies. The community soon became dependent on the Henry Martinat, Fred Peyronel, John Henry Pascal, Mrs. Auguste Pascal (Henrietta Martinat), Emanuel Micol, and Albert Tron dairies for their milk and butter. In those days, raw milk was sold and delivered to the doorstep. Each of the dairymen had his own method of delivery. Mr. Emanuel Micol was known for his cheerful whistling as he made his rounds delivering milk and butter in his Ford truck. Mr. Fred Peyronel was recognized by his early model station wagon, which he used as a delivery vehicle. Some children carried milk in a denim, double-sectioned school bag carried over the shoulder and delivered it on their way to school.

Everyone who owned a plot of ground planted grapevines to provide grapes for wine making. The alpine region the Waldensians came from was famous for its grape culture and wine making. The climate of Valdese, although not as suited to grape culture as the Valleys, nevertheless produced some good grapes. A few years after the colonists came to Valdese, there were numerous young vineyards established—some quite large. Over the years Valdese earned a reputation for the fine wines produced here. Almost every family made some wine.

Harvest time for all farm crops is a good time, but the grape harvest was the best. The work of the grape harvest is not as hard and is cleaner than grain harvesting. Also the girls and boys both worked in the grape harvest, which naturally made it more interesting. Bunches of grapes were cut from the vine and placed in baskets for transporting to the cellar, where the wine making began. The grapes were crushed and placed in large vats for fermentation. Contrary to popular belief, they were not mashed by stamping on them with the feet but with crushers made of four-by-four pieces of wood with handles attached for ease of handling. The wine making process was a long, drawn-out affair with the pouring of the crushed grapes in the vats only the first step. Several weeks were required to go through the fermentation and settling process, with regular attention paid to the vat and its contents to prevent the spoiling of the wine. Proper care was required to avoid turning the product into vinegar. When the process was completed, the drawing-off of the wine took place. It was withdrawn through a filter made of matted straw, which had been placed in the vat at the beginning of the process. The new wine was placed into wooden barrels for the aging process. The length of the aging process depended upon the thirst of the owner and his friends and neighbors.

As in all farming communities, much of the work was accomplished through exchanged labor. The farmers helped one another with planting and harvesting when additional help was required. Some of the larger farms would employ a farm hand, who usually lived on the premises and received his room and board in addition to a low wage. Some of these relationships endured for years, and the farm hand was considered almost a family member. A black gentleman named Alphonzo Reece, who worked for the Barthélemy Bounous family, lived in a room in the granary. Mr. Bounous did not speak English, so Mr. Reece learned to speak patois fluently.

SOCIAL LIFE

Active social life and fun times were quite limited due to the hardships endured in the early years by the Waldensian settlers in the New World. Nonetheless, the welfare of the children and of the young adults was of ever-present concern and interest, and despite all obstacles, whenever there were children and young adults, there were fun times. In overcoming the hardships, much gratitude is due to the early missionary teachers in the 1890's and early 1900's. Time, money, reading materials, and recreational items for games were furnished by these teachers. Some of the many donated materials remembered were baseballs, bats, gloves for the boys, and ropes for skipping games for the girls.

As the children grew into adulthood and melded with the natives of the community, on many Saturday nights there were "box suppers," organized to raise funds for school projects. These "box suppers" required much originality on the part of the young ladies to make attractive boxes from shoe boxes or whatever box was available of reasonable size, lavishly camouflaged with various colors of crepe paper and ribbon. Each box was filled with homemade goodies and auctioned off with the highest bidder obtaining the box. Prizes were given for the most attractive box. The young swains would attempt to bid for the box of their favorite girlfriend, if they could guess which was hers, and, if successful, the box supper would be shared with her. In addition, in the summer on Saturday evenings or Sunday afternoons, there would be picnic outings with the delightful treat of homemade ice cream, handcranked right on the spot.

Sunday afternoons were times for neighborly, social get-togethers. There was visiting by the older members of households while children played in the yards or convenient pastures and meadows. About four o'clock, all would gather for "tea time" at a table laden with kitchen delights. Nostalgia for those afternoons runs rife for many who recall dining tables laden with refreshing foods, such as homemade pies, layer cakes amply filled and frosted, homebaked breads, pound-size molds of butter, pitchers of whole milk for the children, and always, the steeped hot tea. These tea-time specials were not limited to Sundays but were a daily practice in most households and provided a work-break and "snack" time after arduous labor in the fields and vineyards. After these "breaks," the menfolk would continue with their labor, while the women and children would busy themselves with the closing chores of the late afternoon, such as preparing the evening meal, feeding the domestic animals and fowl, getting in stove wood, drawing water from the well or carrying it from a nearby spring, and preparing the kerosene lamps. The children of the household played a vital role in performing the many domestic tasks.

Hiking to areas of interest on Sundays and holidays was also a most enjoyable pastime. McGalliard Falls was the "community center" with much activity on special celebration days, Sunday School outings, and oftentimes the fifteenth of August celebration. These fun times at McGalliard Falls in the summer were spent learning to swim and swimming in the pool formed at the bottom of the falls. Dressing rooms as such were nonexistent, so girls dressed in homemade bathing suits of cotton fabric in the privacy of Mr. Meytre's nearby grist mill. The boys sought privacy for changing clothes on the opposite side of the pool beneath an overhanging rock. In addition to McGalliard Falls as a place for swimming, families who had good water sources would permit damming them to be used for outdoor baths and early swim lessons. Later, entrepreneurs built a public swimming pool on the east side of town that was equipped with a real diving board.

Lack of manufactured play equipment did not prevent the children from having fun, for they made their own toys. Mothers were kept busy mending clothes and keeping a supply of baseballs

McGALLIARD FALLS
Scene of many social events in the early 1900's

on hand that were made by raveling old knit socks to form a ball from the threads, or by using strips of worn fabric, and sewing the ends securely so the balls would not fall apart. The bats were made from any board available.

As time went by, many changes took place, and before the advent of the radio and the car came the so-called "talking machine," or Victrola. Lucky was the family who could afford such an item. Many young people would gather in that home at tea time and listen to the current recordings, such as the popular World War I songs "KKK Katy," "Over There," "Keep the Home Fires Burning," and the ever-sad farewell songs. Although the "courenta" is the traditional folk dance of the Waldensians, many of the young were eager to do other dances made so popular by Vernon and Irene Castle, such as the waltz, the fox trot and later the Charleston.

In addition to the hikes to McGalliard Falls, the 1920's brought another hiking destination—the top of Mineral Springs Mountain, where the Crouch family had built a hotel. This was a nice hike during the fall and winter months, as Mr. and Mrs. Crouch would have a fire roaring in the large fireplace of the public hall, where one could get warm before hiking back the three miles to Valdese.

At the end of the Sunday outings, whether hiking or visiting, the young people would attend church for evening vespers. Sunday School groups would meet at five o'clock for play and worship.

When cars became available for a few families, young people, as well as adults, would motor by way of Morganton to Clearwater Beach and Brown Mountain Beach. Many happy hours were spent at these beaches fed by mountain streams. These two popular places of recreation offered swimming, hiking up the creek, and picnics, which were also enjoyed by adults of the church.

Much can be said for the fun times of the "good ole days!"

BOCCIE

One of the customs the early Waldensians of Valdese brought to this country was the playing of "boccie." The game of boccie dates as far back as 5200 B.C. in Egypt. It was a popular game then and was carried to Greece by early Greek armies, then adopted by conquering Roman armies and taken to their homeland. During the fourteenth century, Charles IV banned the game because his soldiers became so absorbed in the matches he felt it hampered their fighting ability. He wanted the soldiers to concentrate solely on making war.

In present times, boccie is played throughout the world, under different names and especially in larger cities. In northern Italy, around Turin, near the ancestral homes of the Waldensians, it is an extremely popular pastime.

The game is played by having one of the team captains roll the small ball or "boucin" out on the court. The team members then see who can place their boccia closest to earn the point. Knocking the other team's boccia out of the match is permitted under certain conditions.

When the Town of Valdese was first settled, a court was laid out where the present dry cleaning and laundromat establishment is located across Rodoret Street from the church. There was a grove of large pine trees, and the court was designed to take advantage of the shade.

About 1927-28, Le Phare des Alpes bought the building presently used as a clubhouse and built courts adjacent to the building. At a later date, two courts were constructed under a shed at the rear of the property so that the game could be enjoyed during inclement weather.

For many years, the game was played on Wednesday afternoons, by those who were so lucky as to have free time on Wednesday, and on Saturday and Sunday afternoons. The game was taken seriously by the contenders, and voices were sometimes raised in disagreement over the measurement and placement of the boccie. One man would oftentimes serve as the official measurer to keep down dissension. His word would be accepted by the contending team members.

In recent years, the game has attracted some followers in North Carolina. There was a tournament held at Nags Head in 1992, and there has been a tournament for several years at a festival in Durham. Here in Valdese, there has been some renewed interest due to the exposure at the outdoor drama *From This Day Forward*. The tournament conducted on church grounds at the August Festival always attracts a number of participants.

THE COURENTA-WALDENSIAN FOLK DANCE

Getting together on Sunday evenings to dance the Waldensian folk dance, the "courenta," was the main social activity of the young people in the Waldensian Valleys. They danced in someone's home or barn to the accompaniment of a fiddle or an accordion. Through love of the lively dance, many of the young men and women became graceful, skillful dancers.

Once the colony in Valdese was established and there was time for occasional social activity and musical accompaniment could be secured, those who had learned the courenta in their youth still loved to dance. The main occasion for dancing was the February 17 celebration. About 1918, the celebrations were held on the top floor of the Valdese Cooperative Store, where dinner was served and music and dancing followed. A community band, made up of some of the Waldensian men, played for the dancers. A photograph of this band hangs in the museum.

In 1925, Francis Perrou and Albert Garrou, Sr. purchased an accordion for James Henry Pascal, who had learned to play the instrument as a young man in the Valleys. He began playing for the dancers on February 17 and on other occasions. For many years, the courenta continued to be a part of the February 17 celebrations. The older Waldensians still enjoyed showing their skill in dancing, and while a few groups of young people were taught the dance, they never quite equaled the older folks.

The most noteworthy of the young courenta teams was organized in 1956 under the direction of Mrs. George Grill (Elfie Bounous) and Peter Meytre. These dancers, accompanied by James H. Pascal on the accordion, performed many times and won awards at folk dance festivals in Asheville, North Carolina and Virginia Beach, Virginia from 1956 to 1958.

Sometime in the early 1970's, about the same time that James H. Pascal was no longer able to play the accordion and the few remaining older dancers were no longer able to dance, the courenta stopped being a part of the February 17 celebrations. A modified version of the dance has survived in the outdoor drama *From This Day Forward*.

Some of the older Waldensians who are well remembered for their dancing skills were Mr. & Mrs. Henry Curville, Philip Perrou, Peter Meytre, Mr. & Mrs. Aldo Martinat, Antoine Grill, Antoine Rostan, Mr. & Mrs. J.P. Rostan, Sr., Madeline Grill, Herman Grill, Mrs. Joe Broverio (Helen Grill), Mrs. Philip Bounous (Elda Gaydou), Mrs. Emile Squillario (Madeline Rostan), Mrs. Jack Bounous (Ida Pascal), Mrs. Auguste Pascal (Henriette Martinat), Laurent Rivoire, Mrs. James Henry Pascal (Marie Ferrier) and Daniel Bounous.

Dancing the Courenta
Peter Meytre (1894-1961) and Elda Gaydou Bounous (1892-1971). Courenta is enjoyed by participants on occasions of historical Waldensian Celebrations.

CHAPTER 13

EARLY ORGANIZATIONS

LE PHARE DES ALPES and
MONT VISO INSURANCE COMPANY

The early days of the church were times when people in distress from sickness or death were dependent entirely on their families and the church for help. As a result of this need, two organizations were formed which were not part of the Waldensian Presbyterian Church but did an admirable job of helping meet the needs of the membership. These two organizations were Le Phare des Alpes and Mont Viso Insurance Company.

In 1909, some of the men of the community saw an opportunity for service to their fellow man, as well as improving their own lot in times of need. The group formed, on May 8, 1909, Le Phare des Alpes (Lighthouse of the Alps). This was a mutual aid society supported by modest dues from the membership and entitling members to medical care paid by the society. The founding members of the group were Daniel Bounous, Sr., Jean Pons (Bienvenue, son of Albert), Antoine Grill, Henri Martinat (Pineburr), François Garrou, Albert Pons, John Louis Garrou, Jean Henri Pascal (Bienvenue), and Auguste Pascal. At organizational meetings on May 9 and May 15, rules of organization were drawn up.

Conditions of membership were that a man be between the ages of 18 and 60 years, that he be Waldensian and be approved by two-thirds of the voting membership. The applicant must be a resident of Valdese or known to the people of the community and be of good character. Some of the older members recall the strict lecture they received as part of their reception as new members regarding the standards of conduct which the society expected of its members.

The original membership fees were $1 as an entry fee and dues of $.50 per quarter. In return, the society promised to pay medical expenses, including doctor, medicines and hospitalization to a maximum of $50. This $50 probably covered most any illness. The members also promised to personally help in the event of sickness or death in a member's family.

The organization contracted with Dr. C.E. Ross to be the official physician of the group. Burke Drug Company was to furnish medicine at a ten percent discount. Since Dr. Ross and Burke Drug

Company were located in Morganton, special arrangements were worked out with the superintendent of the Asheville Division of Southern Railroad to provide for trains #34 and #36 to stop in Valdese when necessary for Dr. Ross to visit patients. Members were permitted to use a physician of their choice as long as the fee was the same as authorized to Dr. Ross. Second opinions were encouraged before submitting to surgery or in the case of grave illness. The society would meet and authorize the additional expense of a second opinion.

The society also provided help in the event of a death of a member. From $15 to $18 was authorized for the purchase of a coffin. That was evidently the only expense associated with a funeral at that time. In this connection, an entry of November 9, 1915 is of interest. A payment of $30 was made to the widow of the Rev. Henri Garrou, a former pastor who had joined the society and had later returned to Italy where he subsequently died. The $30 payment was for two physicians who treated Mr. Garrou for appendicitis and peritonitis and also for the cost of a coffin.

The society was of considerable help to sick members during the early days. It was also very attentive to the need of families not covered under the program. For many years, the men of the L.P.D.A. dug the graves needed for any member of the congregation. They left their own work and spent the day digging the grave in the hard rock of the cemetery. With the advent of funeral homes and modern services for funerals, this practice was discontinued.

Le Phare des Alpes continues until this date and is a thriving organization at present. The value of the insurance is of no consequence, but the society continues as a social organization which meets four times yearly with additional social functions.

The other successful attempt to provide for the unexpected was the formation of Mont Viso Insurance Company. Mont Viso was established in 1915 to provide fire insurance for the property of the settlers. Although there was no official connection between Le Phare des Alpes and Mont Viso, the same leadership started both organizations.

During the very early days of the settlement, the Valdese Corporation had insured the homes of the settlers. There is no indication of how many homes may have been insured between 1894 and 1915.

Mont Viso was founded on July 1, 1915. A second meeting was held on December 27, 1915 when thirty-three home owners signed up for property insurance. The total value of the property insured was $27,575. The insurance took effect January 1, 1916. The average insured value of the homes was $835.60.

There were three categories of buildings listed under Mont Viso Insurance programs. Category one was for stone or brick buildings with a metal roof. This category carried a rate of $2 per thousand. Category two was for buildings of stone or brick with wooden shingle roofs or wooden buildings with metal roofs and carried a rate of $2.50 per thousand. Category three buildings were built of wood with wooden shingle roofs and carried a rate of $3 per thousand dollars of coverage.

It is believed Mont Viso conducted business until the 1930's. It was another instance of hard-working, resourceful people providing for themselves, and this company did provide a much needed service in its time.

Le Phare des Alpes Clubhouse

Le Phare des Alpes — 1990

CHAPTER 14

CHURCH LEADERS

CHARTER MEMBERS

The early residents of the Valdese colony were highly organized in some ways and much less organized in other ways. The small group put a great deal of effort into their worship but were not formally organized as a church when they first arrived judging from the evidence we have. The evolvement into an organized church was a long and sometimes tedious process. Thus, there never appeared a list of "Charter Members," such as we would make today, in the church records. We assume the original group over fifteen years of age were probably all members of one of the churches in Italy and automatically considered themselves members of the church in Valdese. We would, therefore, assume the following would be considered as "Charter Members" of the local church.

Jean Giraud, age 34.

Jean Guigou, 41, and his wife Catherine, née Guigou, age 31.
The Guigou children not considered old enough for church membership were Louis Philippe 10, Étienne 7, Alexis 5, and Naomi 3.

Jaubert Micol, 40, and his wife Jeanne, née Tron, age 38. Their children were Jean, 15, Marguerite, 12, Emmanuel, 7, and Victor, 2. Although Jean was 15, he had not joined a church before coming to Valdese. He joined the church here at a later date.

Albert Pons, 35.

François Pons, 24.

Jean Henri Pons, 29.

Jean Refour, 42, and his son Jean, 15, who was probably already a member in Italy.

Philippe Richard, 33, and his wife Marianna Louise, née Ribet, age 38.
Their sons were Philippe, 9, and Étienne, 4.

François Tron, Jr., 18, and his wife Marguerite, née

Garrou, 31.

Jacques Henri Tron, 44.

Pierre Tron, 39, and his wife Louise, née Pons, 34. Their children were Albert, 5, and Madeleine, 3.

At a congregational meeting on Sunday, May 10, 1896 the following decision was made: "To consider as voting members every male Church member over 21 years old who has contributed according to his means to the work of the Church and who has notified the Session of his desire to be a voting member." It appears that prior to this time only men who had purchased property were considered voters. This, of course, included all the heads of household in the colony.

The members designated as voting members in 1896 were as follows:

Date of Enrollment	Name
September 27, 1896	Antoine Martinat
	Jean Garrou, Sr.
	Henri François Long
	Romeo Tagliabue
September 29, 1896	Jean Jacques Léger
	Albert Pons
	Samuel Pons
	Henri Perrou
	Jean Refour, Sr.
	Jean Jacques Pons
October 4, 1896	Pierre Emmanuel Micol
	Jaubert Micol
	Jean Jacques Barus
October 5, 1896	Jean Daniel Mourglia
	Henri Peyronel
October 7, 1896	Jean Jacques Jacumin
	Philippe Pascal
	François Tron, Jr.
October 8, 1896	Jean Philippe Pons
October 11, 1896	Jean Garrou, Jr.
	Jacques Henri Long
	Antoine Grill
	François Tron, Sr.
	Ippolite Salvageot
	Philippe Perrou
	Jean Henri Pascal (Jean)

Church Leaders

December 1896
J. Prochet
Albert Beux
Pierre Tron
Henri Vinay
Jean Long
François Barus
Jean Guigou
Jean Pierre Peyronel
François Balmas
Henri Grill
Barthélemy Soulier
Jean Thomas Guigou
Jean Henri Tron

WALDENSIAN PRESBYTERIAN CHURCH STAFF

Minister

Rev. Doctor Charles Albert Tron		1893
Rev. Enrico Vinay		1893-1894
Rev. Barthélemy Soulier		1894-1900
Rev. Henri Garrou		1900-1903
Rev. Filippo Ghigo	1903-1906	1916-1917
Rev. John Pons	1907-1909	1918-1925
Rev. Émile Henri Tron		1913-1916
Rev. Joseph Armand Verreault		1925-1931
Rev. James H. Caligan		1931-1938
Rev. Sylvan S. Poet		1939-1941
Rev. Watson Munford Fairley, D.D. (Stated Supply)		1941-1945
Rev. Albert Bonner McClure, Sr.		1945-1950
Rev. Walter H. Styles		1950-1958
Rev. George E. Staples (Stated Supply)		1958-1959
Rev. J. Clyde Plexico, Jr.		1959-1968
Rev. Doctor Paul Henley Felker, Jr.		1969-

Associate Minister

Rev. John C. Parse	1981-1987

Assistant Minister

Rev. Donn Wilson Wright	1965-1967
Rev. Ford F. G'Segner	1970-1974

Director of Christian Education

Ms. Mary Ruth Marshall	1954-1956
Ms. Yvonne Raftelis	1958-1959
Ms. Shirley Gilliam	1960-1963
Rev. J. Clyde Jones	1964-1964
Rev. Donn Wilson Wright	1965-1967
Ms. Cathy Newton	1974-1978
Mr. Steven Lee Mowery	1978-1980
Mr. James W. Kirkpatrick	1988-1992

Director of Music

Mrs. George W. Williams, Jr. (Ruth McQuiston)	1935-1971
Mr. Steven Lee Mowery	1971-1980
Mr. John Eric Mode	1980-

Organist

Mrs. George W. Williams, Jr. (Ruth McQuiston)	1935-1971
Mr. John Bridges	1971-1972
Mr. James Benton Brinkley, Sr.	1972-1975
Mrs. Philip Steve Stewart (Carol Corriher)	1976-1981
Mrs. Fern Farris Abernethy (Mrs. James B. Brinkley, Sr.)	1981-1990
Mrs. David E. Smith (Rhonda Brush)	1991-

Church Leaders

Business Manager

Mr. Roscoe Lee Pyatt	1965-1966

Secretary

Mrs. Joe A. Hern (Ann Long) (Part-time)	1959-1962
Mrs. Daniel B. Bounous (Hazel Coley) (Part-time)	1962-1974
Mrs. K.P. Floyd (Dianne Smith)	1974-1987
Mrs. Carl Dean (Bess Baptist)	1987-1989
Mrs. Kevin Duckworth (Nadine Pons)	1990-

Treasurer/Bookkeeper

Mrs. George Carpenter (Emily Pascal) (Part-time)	1971-1980
Mrs. K.P. Floyd (Dianne Smith)	1980-1987
Mrs. Edward Pascal (Frances Micol) (Part-time)	1987-1990
Mrs. Kevin Duckworth (Nadine Pons)	1990-

ELDERS OF WALDENSIAN PRESBYTERIAN CHURCH

The following men and women have served the Waldensian Presbyterian Church as elders since its beginning in 1893. Many of them have served numerous terms. In the earliest years, terms of office were five years and a man could serve any number of consecutive terms. Mr. Jean Henri Pascal (Bienvenue) served five consecutive terms or twenty-five years.

In later years, the term of office was reduced to three years, and consecutive terms were no longer permitted. At the present time, a two-year rest is required between three-year terms of service.

Some items of interest are:

> April 1, 1935, Mr. Julius M. Ramsay, Sr. became the first non-Waldensian elder of the church.
>
> March 2, 1947, Mr. Daniel B. Bounous, Sr. was elected Elder for Life.
>
> In 1964, Mrs. J. Laird (Jeanne Verreault) Jacob became the first woman elder in the Waldensian Presbyterian Church and also the first woman to serve as a session representative to a meeting of Concord Presbytery.

The names below are listed in sequence relating to the date of their first election to office.

Name	Year
Antoine Martinat	1893
Jean Garrou (père)	1894
Henri F. Long	1894
Albert Beux	1896
Jean Henri Pascal (Gardiole)	1896
Henri Vinay	1901
Jean Henri Pascal (Bienvenue)	1902
Pierre Ribet	1908
Henri Martinat (Pineburr)	1910
Jean Henri Pascal (Balsille)	1910
Jean Refour, Jr.	1922
John A. Pons	1922
Jacques Henri Bounous	1922
Henri F. Martinat	1922
Henry F. Garrou	1925
Philip S. Grill	1928
Albert F. Garrou	1928
Daniel B. Bounous, Sr.	1929
John D. Guigou	1935
Frederic H. Pons, Sr.	1935
Julius M. Ramsay, Sr.	1935
Arthur W. Baker	1939
Louis Philip Guigou	1939
Edward Micol, Sr.	1939
Ben Pons	1939
John P. Rostan, Sr.	1939
Antoine Grill	1941
Edward Pons	1941
George W. Williams, Jr.	1942
Earl B. Searcy, Sr.	1944
J. Armand Verreault, Jr.	1945
Loy Ray Burris, Sr.	1946
Emmanuel Richard	1946
Reese Scull	1946
R.E. Spainhour	1946
W.J. Cotten	1947
J. Francis Tron, Jr.	1947
Henry P. Perrou	1948
Lacy M. Hall	1949
George D. Carpenter	1951
Louis E. Deaton	1951
Carl C. Long	1952

Church Leaders

Auburn H. Setzer	1952
T. Edward Burney	1953
Daniel B. Bounous, Jr.	1953
James C. Farris	1954
Peter A. Meytre	1955
John A. Bleynat	1956
Henry Grill, Jr.	1958
Edward Pascal	1958
Leon E. Guigou	1959
Clyde N. Young, Sr.	1959
W. Harold Mitchell	1960
M. Haynes Rutherford	1961
Valdo S. Martinat	1962
Louis W. Garrou	1963
Mrs. J. Laird (Jeanne Verreault) Jacob	1964
Henry J. Pascal	1964
Walter Pons	1964
J. Edward Garrou	1965
Mrs. Lacy M. (Iula Britt) Hall	1965
Robert E. Micol	1965
Richard C. Neale, Sr.	1965
Edgar W. Lane, Jr.	1966
Philip H. Garrou	1967
W.D. Owens, Jr.	1967
Mrs. A. Olin (Evelyn Senter) Stiff	1967
J. Ellis Zimmerman	1967
Mrs. Arthur W. (Rassie Grisette) Baker	1968
John C. Little	1968
Claude J. Shaffer	1968
Robert A. Pascal	1969
Earl B. Searcy, Jr.	1969
Mrs. John A. (Margaret Fulbright) Bleynat	1970
Benny Ray Powell	1970
J. Henry Bounous, Sr.	1971
Mrs. Leroy (Evelyn Pons) Bronson	1971
John Harvey Guigou	1971
Paul Edward Bardet	1972
Benjamin W. Garrou	1972
Mrs. John P. (Naomi Bounous) Rostan	1972
C. Frank Gaddy	1973
Glenn R. Yoder	1973
Rene A. Durand	1974
Mrs. J. Edward (Doris Campbell) Garrou	1974
John A. Guigou	1974
Mrs. Daniel B. (Hazel Coley Bounous, Jr.	1975
Carlton E. Caruso, Sr.	1975
H. Benjamin Perrou	1975
J. Hugh Fletcher	1976
Victor H. Garrou, Sr.	1976
Mrs. Robert E. (Frances Deal) Micol	1976
Ernest Jahier	1977
Mrs. M. Haynes (Vera Berry) Rutherford	1977
John Rostan (Chicago)	1977
Mrs. Paul C. (Harriet Bleynat) Hastings, Sr.	1978
Mrs. J. Hugh (Mildred Price) Fletcher	1979
J. A. Grisette	1979
Granville W. Morrow	1979
Mrs. Richard C. (Yvonne) Neale, Jr.	1979
Edwin A. Bowditch	1980
John S. Heilman	1980
Mrs. Walter (June Harrison) Pons	1980
Edward L. Bleynat, Sr.	1981
Mrs. John A. (Betty Lou Mitchell) Guigou	1981
Joseph A. Hern	1981
Mrs. Edward (Frances Micol) Pascal	1981
Hugh A. Blackwell	1982
Mrs. W. Harold (Pat Melvin) Mitchell	1982
Mrs. Stephen (Hattie Reynolds) Rostan	1982
Mrs. Herbert N. (Betty Bumgarner) Garrou	1983
Mrs. I. Wayburn (Hilda Ogle) Jones	1983
Mrs. Billie (Betsy Dodd) Pittman	1983
Mrs. Horace (Carol Perrou) Brown	1984
Warren A. Ward	1984

Mrs. Edwin (Elizabeth McFarland) Bowditch	1985	Henry E. Perrou	1988
Donald M. Brittain	1985	Mrs. Kenneth (Rosalba Pascal) Shook	1988
Lee R. Suttle	1985	Frank J. Grill	1989
Mrs. J. Henry (Jewell Pyatt) Bounous	1985	John Lafferty, Sr.	1989
Horace Brown	1986	Louis D. Bounous, Sr.	1990
Louis Vinay, Jr.	1986	Mrs. Jack (Agnes Ramsay) Burns	1990
Mrs. John C. (Sara Turner) Little	1987	Marcus W.H. Mitchell	1990
Eric Parsons	1987	David B. Wiese	1990
Mrs. George (Edith Rainey) Perrou	1987	Michael Kaufman	1991
Marion D. Arnold	1988	Mrs. John C. (Kathy Eisenhart) Parse	1991
		Julius C. Pons, Jr.	1991

Church Leaders

DEACONS OF WALDENSIAN PRESBYTERIAN CHURCH

The following is a list of the men and women who have served the Waldensian Presbyterian Church as deacons since its beginning in 1893. The first approximately fifty years of church life the elders (session) and the deacons met together. About 1942 during the pastorate of Dr. Watson Fairley, the two bodies began meeting separately due to the insistence of Dr. Fairley.

In 1964, Mrs. Leroy (Evelyn Pons) Bronson became the first woman to serve on the diaconate. In 1987, Mrs. Richard F. (Elsie Mull) Whisenant became the first woman to serve as Chairwoman of the Diaconate.

The names are listed in sequence relating to the date of their first election to office. Many have served several terms.

Name	Year	Name	Year
Jaubert Micol	1896	Fred Searcy	1946
Antoine Grill	1901	George F. Squillario	1946
Pierre Emmanuel Micol	1905	Valdo S. Martinat	1947
Jean Louis Garrou	1910	Robert E. Micol	1947
François A. Perrou	1913	Eric Thierfelder	1947
Jean Long	1916	John A. Bleynat	1948
Auguste Pascal	1917	Edward Pascal	1948
Jean Garrou (Bobo)	1921	Daniel B. Bounous, Jr.	1948
Frank Pascal	1922	John Harvey Guigou	1948
Filippo Ghigo	1929	J. Edward Garrou	1949
John P. Rostan, Sr.	1931	J. Laird Jacob, Sr.	1949
Edward Micol, Sr.	1931	Louis D. Bounous, Sr.	1950
John D. Guigou	1932	Walter Pons	1950
Henry Grill, Jr.	1935	Julius A. Grisette	1951
Ben Pons	1935	Leon E. Guigou	1951
Frederick Ribet	1939	Donald H. Martinat	1952
M. Haynes Rutherford	1939	W. Harold Mitchell	1952
George W. Williams, Jr.	1939	Julius M. Ramsay, Jr.	1952
Ben Grill	1939	Philip H. Garrou	1953
Earl B. Searcy, Sr.	1941	Hall E. Williams	1953
Reese Scull	1941	John A. Guigou	1953
Wade H. Stemple	1942	Arnaldo A. Pons	1953
J. Armand Verreault, Jr.	1942	Ted Starnes	1954
Peter A. Meytre	1942	Earl B. Searcy, Jr.	1954
James C. Farris	1942	Loy Ray Burris, Jr.	1955
Henry J. Pascal	1942	J. Ellis Zimmerman	1955
Onesime H. Pons, Sr.	1942	John P. Rostan, Jr.	1955
J. Francis Tron, Jr.	1944	T. Edward Burney	1956
Erwin Williams	1944	J. Henry Bounous, Sr.	1956
C. Frank Gaddy, Jr.	1945	Edgar W. Lane, Jr.	1956
Julius Deal	1946	W.D. Owens, Jr.	1957
Louis W. Garrou	1946	Robert A. Pascal	1957

J. Dallas Brinkley, Jr.	1958	Mrs. George D. (Emily Pascal)	
Worth Campbell	1958	Carpenter	1974
Charles L. Briggs, Sr.	1960	James H. Rostan	1974
Thomas E. Hollingsworth	1960	Jerry R. Wilkinson	1974
Ray C. Fletcher	1961	Donald M. Brittain	1975
Granville W. Morrow	1961	Jack Burns	1975
Gerald N. Baker, Sr.	1962	Billie E. Pittman	1975
Carlton E. Caruso, Sr.	1962	John Harvey Wilson	1975
J. Hugh Fletcher	1962	Hugh A. Blackwell	1976
H. Benjamin Perrou	1962	Edward L. Bleynat, Sr.	1976
I. Wayburn Jones	1963	Steven Demiter	1976
Charlie Vinay	1963	Mrs. Frank (Melany Bounous)	
Glenn R. Yoder	1963	Grill	1976
Benny Ray Powell	1964	Bruce Cannon	1977
Mrs. Leroy (Evelyn Pons)		Steve Masten	1977
Bronson	1964	Mrs. Granville W. (Alma	
George H. Bleynat	1965	Whisenant) Morrow	1977
Victor H. Garrou, Sr.	1965	Frank J. Grill	1978
Elmo J. Pascal	1965	Lee R. Suttle	1978
Henry E. Perrou	1965	Mrs. Richard F. (Elsie Mull)	
John Stephen Perrou	1965	Whisenant	1978
Herbert N. Garrou	1966	James B. Brinkley	1979
Mrs. Paul C. (Harriet		Mrs. L.R. (Doris Pons) Burris, Jr.	1979
Bleynat) Hastings, Sr.	1966	Mrs. Victor H. (Ann Bills)	
Mrs. Stephen (Hattie		Garrou, Sr.	1979
Reynolds) Rostan	1966	Mrs. Braxton (Maxine Briggs)	
P. Paul Deaton	1967	Hightower	1979
Benjamin W. Garrou	1967	Marcus W.H. Mitchell	1979
John Rostan (Chicago)	1967	Warren A. Ward	1979
David R. Burnette	1969	Kendall Hanks	1980
H. Lindy Hudson	1969	Stephen H. Martinat	1980
John S. Heilman	1970	Mrs. John (Rose Perrou) Rostan	1980
Mrs. John C. (Sara		Mrs. J. Henry (Jewell Pyatt)	
Turner) Little	1970	Bounous, Sr.	1981
Phife C. Ross	1970	Horace Brown	1981
John P. Rostan III	1970	Julius C. Pons, Jr.	1981
Richard F. Whisenant	1970	Louis Vinay, Jr.	1981
Mrs. Herbert N. (Betty		John R. Williams	1981
Bumgarner) Garrou	1971	Mrs. John A. (Margaret Fulbright)	
James L. Hatley	1971	Bleynat	1982
Joseph A. Hern	1971	Mrs. Catherine Rivoire Cole	1982
Hedrick R. Powell	1971	Eric Parsons	1982
William M. Brinkley	1972	Mrs. Warren (Jan) Ward	1982
Lee Roy Huffman	1972	Mrs. Louis (Viola Newton)	
John Thomas Pons	1972	Vinay, Sr.	1982
Mrs. J. Hugh (Mildred Price)		Mrs. Jack (Agnes Ramsay) Burns	1983
Fletcher	1973	Mrs. Benjamin W. (Audrey Taylor)	
John Henry Shell	1973	Garrou	1983

Church Leaders

John M. Heilman	1983	Kevin Farris	1988
Spottswood P. Neale	1983	Robert Heilman	1988
Mrs. Edward L. (Meredith Brady) Bleynat, Sr.	1984	Mrs. Rick (Susan Rhoney) Smith	1988
		Mrs. Mary Beth Wilkinson	1988
Mrs. James L. (Mary Louise Pascal) Hatley	1984	Walter G. Church, Jr.	1989
		Gene Garrett	1989
John E. Mode	1984	Steve L. Mullis	1989
B. Wesley Garrou	1985	Mrs. Harold (Kathy Jones) Wellman	1989
Harold Wellman	1985		
David B. Wiese	1985	J.J. David Fletcher	1990
Mrs. John R. (Carolyn Pascal) Williams	1985	Mrs. W. Joseph (Sharon Christie) Jacumin, Sr.	1990
Ms. Evelyn Bounous	1986	Mrs. Gregory (Jennie Lucas) Mastin	1990
T.M. Rembert	1986		
John F. Black	1987	W. David Owens, III	1990
Ms. Rachel Bowditch	1987	G. Parks Sherrill, Jr.	1990
Gregory Mastin	1987	Ms. Pam Bonner	1991
Cam C. McNeely	1987	David Hart	1991
Athos Rostan, Jr.	1987	Mrs. James W. (Caroline Hunt) Kirkpatrick	1991
Mrs. Robert (Gwendolyn Pons) Bonner	1988		
		Charles M. Young	1991

SUNDAY SCHOOL

Sunday School was an important part of the life of the children in the early days of the settlement. From the very beginning, Sunday School was conducted each week. For the first ten or twelve years, the lessons were conducted entirely in French. They consisted primarily of Bible verse memorization and teaching from the Bible.

The first Sunday Schools were held in the frame building used as a headquarters for the settlement and also used as a church on Sundays until the sanctuary was completed and dedicated in 1899. After the completion of the sanctuary, the Sunday School was held in the church building. The classes were divided by age and met in the four corners of the building.

After the completion of C.A. Tron Hall in 1922, classes were held in this room. The classes were divided by curtains of burlap hung on wires so they could be pushed back out of the way when the room was needed for larger gatherings.

An assembly of the entire Sunday School started the program each week. There was scripture reading, comments by the superintendent and several songs. The classes were then dispersed to their assigned area for their studies and reassembled at the end of the class for more singing and a prayer of dismissal. In the 1920's, after English was used in class, leaflets concerning the lesson were used as aids to learning. Beautiful posters illustrating some central thought of the lesson were often used.

Rewards for perfect attendance received much recognition in the first forty or fifty years of existence. Attendance certificates and promotion certificates were presented each year at Rally Day. Perfect attendance pins were also awarded. A first year of perfect attendance merited a pin, the second year merited a wreath to encircle the pin and each succeeding perfect attendance year merited a bar to attach below the pin. Much effort went into earning these awards, and they were valued highly by the recipients.

Prior to 1940, we have very few written records listing our Sunday School superintendents in the church minutes. We found one listing showing Mr. W.C. Coley as superintendent in 1932. It is possible there should have been other people listed.

1893 through 1903	Henri F. Long
1904 through 1919	John Henry Pascal (Bienvenue)
1920 through 1931	Louis Philip Guigou
1932	W.C. Coley
1933 through 1938	Louis Philip Guigou

Church Leaders

1939 through 1951	John D. Guigou
1952 through 1955	George W. Williams, Jr.
1956 through 1960	Edward Pascal
1961 through 1962	Carlton E. Caruso, Sr.
1963	Thomas E. Hollingsworth
1964 through 1965	Granville W. Morrow
1966 through 1967	Glenn R. Yoder
1968	Charlie Vinay
1969	John C. Little
1970	Ray C. Fletcher
1971	Richard F. Whisenant
1972 through 1974	Lee Roy Huffman
1975	John R. Williams
1976 through 1977	Mrs. Hugh (Mildred) Fletcher
1978	Mrs. John A. (Margaret) Bleynat
1979 through 1980	Granville W. Morrow
1981 through 1982	Stephen H. Martinat
1983 through 1986	Donald M. Brittain
1987 through 1989	Donald M. Brittain and T.M. Rembert
1990	T.M. Rembert
1991	T.M. Rembert and M. Kevin Farris
1992	M. Kevin Farris

WOMEN OF THE CHURCH PRESIDENTS 1931-1987
PRESBYTERIAN WOMEN MODERATORS 1988-

The year given indicates the year term began. Some women served two years consecutively then served another term later. In recent years the term of office has been one year with adjustment for changing from ending year in September to December.

1931	Mrs. Albert F. Garrou (Louise)
1932	Mrs. Joe Hern (Nelle)
1934	Mrs. John A. Pons (Janie)
1935	Mrs. Frederic H. Pons (Iola)
1936	Mrs. John D. Guigou (Louise)
1937	Mrs. Ben Pons (Marianne)
1938	Mrs. O.H. Pons (Essie)
1939	Mrs. Earl B. Searcy, Sr. (Mae)
1940	Mrs. Haynes Rutherford (Vera)
1942	Mrs. Frederic H. Pons (Iola)
1943	Mrs. Watson Fairley (Alice)
1945	Mrs. Frederic H. Pons (Iola)
1946	Mrs. J. Francis Verreault (Dolly)
1947	Mrs. Albert McClure (Mary Emma)
1948	Mrs. Henry Grill (Louise)
1950	Mrs. Leon Guigou (Nell)
1952	Mrs. J.P. Rostan, Jr. (Naomi)
1954	Mrs. George Carpenter (Emily)
1956	Mrs. Frederic H. Pons (Iola)
1957	Mrs. I.W. Jones (Hilda)
1959	Mrs. Louis W. Garrou (Betty)
1960	Mrs. Louis E. Deaton (Bertha)
1961	Mrs. Haynes Rutherford (Vera)
1962	Mrs. J. Francis Verreault (Dolly)
1963	Mrs. J. Edward Garrou (Doris)
1964	Mrs. Earl Searcy, Jr. (Jonnie)
1965	Mrs. J. Laird Jacob (Jeanne)
1966	Mrs. Arthur W. Baker (Rassie)
1967	Mrs. Herbert Garrou (Betty)
1968	Mrs. Olin stiff (Evelyn)
1969	Mrs. Ray Fletcher (Rheta)
1970	Mrs. Granville Morrow (Alma)
1971	Mrs. Edward Pascal (Frances)
1972	Mrs. Ben Huffman (Selenah)
1973	Mrs. John Bleynat (Margaret)
1974	Mrs. J. Henry Bounous (Jewell)
1975	Mrs. Glenn Yoder (Phyllis)
1976	Mrs. Richard Whisenant (Elsie)
1977	Mrs. John A. Guigou (Betty Lou)
1978	Mrs. Edward L. Bleynat (Meredith)
1979	Mrs. John Rostan (Rose)
1980	Mrs. Harold Mitchell (Pat)
1981	Mrs. Billie Pittman (Betsy)
1982	Mrs. James Hatley (Mary Louise)
1983	Mrs. Horace Brown (Carol)
1984	Mrs. Steven Demiter (Ann)
1985	Mrs. Hugh Fletcher (Mildred)
1986	Mrs. Victor Garrou (Ann)
1987	Mrs. Louis Vinay (Viola)
1988	Mrs. Horace Brown (Carol)
1989	Mrs. Duane Robinson (Rheta)
1990	Mrs. John A. Guigou (Betty Lou)
1992	Mrs. Steve Mullis (Ann)

WOMEN OF THE WALDENSIAN PRESBYTERIAN CHURCH HONORARY LIFE MEMBERSHIPS

Mrs. Benjamin Perrou (Rachel)	1992	Mrs. J. Frances Verreault (Dolly)	1982
Mrs. Harold Mitchell (Pat)	1991	Mrs. Leon Guigou (Nell)	1981
Mrs. Emmanuel Richard (Romilda)	1990	Mrs. Robert Micol (Frances)	1981
Mrs. Earl B. Searcy, Jr (Jonnie)	1990	Mrs. A.W. Baker (Rassie)	1980
Mrs. Catherine Cole	1989	Mrs. Gus Whisenant (Lena)	1980
Mrs. Pete Meytre (Margaret)	1989	Mrs. J.A. Hern, Sr. (Nelle)	1979
Mrs. Steve Rostan (Hattie)	1989	Mrs. Marshall Warren (Rachel)	1979
Mrs. Edgar Lane (Jane)	1988	Mrs. Frederic H. Pons (Iola)	1978
Mrs. Herbert Garrou (Betty)	1987	Mrs. Olin Stiff (Evelyn)	1978
Mrs. Billie Pittman (Betsy)	1987	Mrs. John A. Bleynat (Margaret)	1977
Mrs. Edward Pascal (Frances)	1986	Mrs. Haynes Rutherford (Vera)	1977
Mrs. John Rostan (Rose)	1986	Mrs. J. Laird Jacob, Sr. (Jeanne)	1976
Mrs. Hugh Fletcher (Mildred)	1985	Mrs. John D. Guigou (Louise)	1968
Mrs. Granville Morrow (Alma)	1985	Mrs. Edward Micol, Sr. (Margaret)	1968
Mrs. Richard Neale, Jr. (Yvonne)	1985	Mrs. Ben Pons (Marianne)	1968
Mrs. John P. Rostan, Jr. (Naomi)	1985	Mrs. J.P. Rostan, Sr. (Irma)	1968
Mrs. Daniel Bounous (Hazel)	1984	Mrs. George Williams, Jr. (Ruth)	1958
Mrs. Paul Felker (Carol)	1984	Mrs. Edwin Bowditch** (Elizabeth)	1952
Mrs. Frank Grill (Melany)	1984	Mrs. L.P. Guigou (Lillian)	1950
Mrs. Paul Hastings (Harriet)	1984	Mrs. Albert F. Garrou (Louise)	1949
Mrs. Leroy Bronson (Evelyn)	1983	Mrs. Watson Fairley* (Alice)	1944
Mrs. I.W. Jones (Hilda)	1983		
Mrs. John Pons (Lydia)	1983		

* Presented by Concord Presbytery
** Presented by Holston Presbytery

SPECIAL AWARDS
Presented by the
WALDENSIAN PRESBYTERIAN CHURCH

AWARD OF APPRECIATION
to
COMMANDER EDWARD L. BLEYNAT
January 1980

A plaque was presented to him in appreciation for his excellent leadership as Building Committee Chairman for the renovation work done during 1978 and 1979. To further express appreciation a check for $1,000 was sent in his honor to his alma mater Lees-McRae College, Banner Elk, N.C.

AWARD OF APPRECIATION
to
MRS. LOUISE GAYDOU GUIGOU
February 28, 1982

A plaque of appreciation was presented to her for her faithful sixty years as a member of the church choirs.

AWARDS OF APPRECIATION
to
MISS OLGA PASCAL
and
MRS. NAOMI BOUNOUS ROSTAN
February 17, 1986

Plaques of appreciation were presented for their many years of devoted service to the Waldensian Historical Museum.

AWARD OF APPRECIATION
to
JAMES EDWARD GARROU
1988

The plaque was presented in grateful appreciation for his twenty-five years of faithful service as the Senior High Sunday School teacher.

AWARD OF APPRECIATION
to
MISS CATHERINE DALMAS
August 13, 1989

The plaque noted her devoted service to the Waldensian Museum and to the citizenry of this town.

AWARD OF APPRECIATION
to
JOHN A. BLEYNAT
October 6, 1991

The plaque was presented in grateful appreciation for his faithful service as chairman of the Long Range Planning Committee and the Building Committee in the renovation of the sanctuary.

PRESBYTERIAN CHURCHMAN'S AWARD

John A. Bleynat	June 17, 1990
George W. Williams, Jr.	June 17, 1990
Edwin Bowditch	June 16, 1991
Valdo Martinat	June 16, 1991
James C. Farris	June 21, 1992
Glenn R. Yoder	June 28, 1992

This is the highest honor that can be given to a man, by Presbyterian Men, for outstanding leadership and work in the church.

CHAPTER 15

THE (SECOND) CORNERSTONE SERVICE CONDUCTED FEBRUARY 17, 1991

The following is a listing of the articles which have been placed in the time capsules which were sealed in the cornerstone of the sanctuary extension. These items relate to the history and organization of the church and are representative of the times in which we live. It is intended that in the year 2041 the materials in the time capsules should be removed, viewed and reinterred. Placed in the cornerstone on February 17, 1991.

CAPSULE # 1

GENERAL INFORMATION ON CHURCH AND TIMES

Organizational plan of Western North Carolina Presbytery
Picture of Sanctuary 1922
Picture of Sanctuary, Tron Hall and School 1923
Postcards of Church — c. 1960
Pictures of Congregation, Palm Sunday, April 8, 1990
Pictures of Nursery Classes January 1991
Church bulletin showing interior of church, December 9, 1990
Church bulletin of February 17, 1991
1991 Officers Book (listing all committees, officers, duties, and budget).
1991 Building Committee Report
Church Roll of February 17, 1991
Choir Materials: cantata bulletin of December 16, 1991
               choir pin given and choir certificates
               given to senior girls and boys from Les Jeunes Chanteurs
               Audio tape of Chancel Choir music
A New Testament — *Good News for Modern Man* (today's English version)
Materials from drama *From This Day Forward*:
               post card of Tron House
               drama brochure from 1991 season
               program brochure from 1991 season
               script of the drama

Front page of Charlotte Observer, February 17, 1991
List of armed service personnel in Middle East war related to our members
Timex watch showing time and date of cornerstone laying
Uncirculated 1990 United States coins

CAPSULE # 2

CHURCH ORGANIZATIONS

Commitment & Witness Committee — report on activities
Service Committee — report on activities
Strengthening the Church Committee:
 report given to church September 30, 1990
 evaluation report of 1990
 1991 — structure of committee
 1991 — Christian Education staff listing
 1991 — Sunday School roster
 1991 — Youth Club roster
  art work of each Youth Club Class
Historical Committee
 1990 — committee report
 1991 — committee assignments
 1991 — program of Emancipation Celebration
 Booklet explaining symbolism of church windows
 Booklet, "The Waldenses of Burke County"
  by Fred Cranford
 French hymnal currently in use
 Necklace with Waldensian seal and explanation
 Handpainted broach with Waldensian seal
 Handpainted broach with Waldensian lady in costume
 Video of each display area in the Museum
  produced by Commander Edward Bleynat with
  Miss Catherine Dalmas as guide
 Printed tour guide of museum.
Presbyterian men — report
Presbyterian Women
 Letter on activities & greetings to members in 2041
 year book of 1990-1991
 picture of French Circle in costume
 hand written French Bible lesson by the late
  Mrs. Irma Ghigo Rostan

Youth Fellowships
        program calendars
        February 13, 1991 newspaper, "The Evening Herald," listing of honor roll students
        Youth Fellowship roster
        Popular audio tape of M.C. Hammer

RESOURCES

Allix, Peter. *The Ecclesiastical History of the Ancient Churches of Piedmont and the Albigenses.* 1690-92. Gallatin, TN: Church History Research and Archives, 1989.

Book of Minutes and Documents Relative to the Founding of the Valdese Corporation, 1893-1894, No. 1. Trans. W. W. Kibler.

Church of Valdese, N.C., Minutes of Proceedings, No. 2. Trans. Cathy R. Pons, 1987.

Église de Valdese, N.C. Procès Verbaux, No. 2. Available at the Waldensian Presbyterian Church, Valdese, NC.

Faber, George Stanley. *The History of the Ancient Vallenses and Albigenses.* 1836. Gallatin, TN: Church History Research and Archives, 1990.

Ghigo, Francis. *The Provençal Speech of the Waldensian Colonists of Valdese, North Carolina.* Valdese: Historic Valdese Foundation, 1980.

Grill, Antoine. "List and History of the Waldensians that Landed at Valdese in 1893 and Later Comings." Unpublished work, 1941.

Guigou, Mrs. Louis Philippe (Lillian Sweeney). *Historical Sketches of the Waldenses and the Waldensian Presbyterian Church* and *History of the Women of the Church, Waldensian Presbyterian Church, Valdese, N.C.* Unpublished work, 1934-1954.

Historian, Women of the Church. *History of the Women of the Church.* Valdese, NC: Waldensian Presbyterian Church, 1955-1990.

Historical Committee of the Waldensian Presbyterian Church of Valdese, NC. *Genealogy of the Waldensian Settlers in Valdese, North Carolina, 1893-1990.* Charlotte: Delmar, 1990.

Livres des Procès Verbaux et des Documents se référant à la Fondation de la Valdese Corporation, 1893-94, No. 1. Available at the Waldensian Presbyterian Church, Valdese, NC.

Perrin, Jean Paul. *History of the Ancient Christians*. 1619. Gallatin, TN: Church History Research and Archives, 1991.

Pons, Cathy R. *Language Death Among Waldensians of Valdese, North Carolina*. Dissertation, Indiana University, 1990.

Salvageot, Ippolito. "Memoirs." Unpublished work, 1894-1903.

Session minutes of the Waldensian Presbyterian Church of Valdese, North Carolina. 1931-1992.

Tourn, Giorgio. *The Waldensians: The First 800 Years*. Torino, IT: Claudiana, 1980.

Tourn, Giorgio, et al. *You are My Witnesses: The Waldensians Across 800 years*. Torino, IT: Claudiana, 1989.

Waldensian Herald. Valdese, NC: Waldensian Presbyterian Church, 1969-1992.

Watts, George B. *The Waldenses in the New World*. Durham: Duke UP, 1941. Charlotte: Delmar, 1990.

——————————. *The Waldenses of Valdese*. Charlotte: Heritage, 1980.

Worship bulletins of the Waldensian Presbyterian Church of Valdese, North Carolina. 1941-1992.

INDEX

A

Adult Handbell Choir 176
AGAPE Retirement Housing 138, 144, 145, 167
Albert, King Charles 11
American Missionary Society 19, 25, 26, 27
American Waldensian Aid Society 87, 96, 115, 116, 134
American Waldensian Society 142
Anderson, Mrs. Catherine 87
Anderson, Rev. Dr. John 127
Angel tree 151, 158
Arbuthnot, Dr. Charles 134
Arnaud, Henri 8, 9
Avery, Isaac T. 203

B

Baker, Gerald 113
Balsiglia 9
"Balsille" 28
Baptismal service 176
Barium Springs Home for Children 47, 81, 82, 87, 198
Bazaar 50, 63, 65, 81
Beckwith, General Charles 10
Bethany Church, Philadelphia 30, 33
Bleynat, CDR Edward L. 133, 152, 166, 169, 246
Bleynat, John A. 105, 120, 125, 148, 156, 157, 215, 247
Bollinger's Chapel 16, 25
Bonner, Miss Pamela 162
Bouchard, Moderator Giorgio 134
Bounous, Jean 14, 97
Bounous, Jeanette 71
Bounous, Jr. Mrs. Daniel B. 104, 125
Bounous, Louis 97
Bounous, Sr., Daniel B. 236
Bounous, Sr., Louis D. 169
Boy Scouts 78, 79, 93, 140, 168
Boys Choir 108, 121
Bridges, John 122
Brinkley, Mrs. Fern Abernethy 136, 158, 162
Brinkley, Sr., J.D. 79
Brinkley, Sr., James Benton 122, 128

Brinkley, William 157
Bronson, Mrs. Leroy 110, 113, 191, 239
Broughton, the Honorable J. Melville 79
Brown, Miss Sylvia 135
Building and Renovation Programs 207
Building the church 28-34, 187

C

C.A. Tron Hall 62, 63, 74, 112, 113, 117, 122, 185, 207, 242
Caligan, Reverend James Henley 69, 70, 72, 81, 193
Calvin, John 4
Camp Grier 103, 116, 119, 167
Catechism lessons 62, 212
Cemetery 17, 18, 44, 47, 65, 68, 74, 78, 85, 108, 119, 163, 168, 215
Centennial Fund 155
Centennial observance 155, 170, 175
Centennial Park 167
Chancel Choir 90, 108, 114, 117, 122, 123, 144, 158, 168, 176
Chanforan, Angrogna 5
Chanteurs, Les Jeunes 144
Chapel district 28, 38
Cherub Choir 142, 147, 172, 176
Children's choirs 102, 131
Children's Message 154
Chrismon Tree 120, 158
Christian Education Committee 122, 177
Christian Endeavor Society 64, 65, 70
Christian Relations Committee 178
Christian Union 44, 48
Christmas Cantata 122
Christmas scene 103, 111
Church library 68, 78, 112
Churchman's Award 157
Comba, Reverend Guido 85
Commitment and Witness Committee 177
Committee of Synodical Home Missions 40, 45
Communion 63, 68, 154, 161, 162, 177

Congregational Church 19, 25, 26, 27, 40
Cornerstone 30, 128, 160, 161
Courenta 224
Courenta Dance Team 100
Cranford, Fred 114, 142

D

Dalmas, Miss Catherine 155, 247
Dean, Mrs. Bess 150, 154
Dedication of enlarged sanctuary 163-164
Dedication of the church 33, 128
Deodato, Achille 118
Dial-A-Prayer 103
Dickey, Rev. Ann Garrou 125, 129, 131, 132, 134, 137, 145
Dickey, Rev. David 137
Duckworth, Nadine Pons 154, 167
Duke of Savoy 6-9

E

Easter Sunrise Service 74, 115, 127, 161
Edict of Emancipation 11, 30
Edict of Emancipation Celebration 39, 48, 68, 88, 89, 96, 115, 118, 119, 125, 126, 151, 156, 214
Edict of Nantes 7
Edict of Tolerance 9
Educational Building 97-100, 102, 143, 159, 164, 198, 209
English choir 58
Ervin, Jr., Sam J. 79, 114
Ervin, William C. 203
Erwin, George P. 206
Evangelical Waldensian Church 27
Every Member Canvass 50, 58, 77
Exile in Switzerland 7

F

Fairley, D.D., Reverend Watson Munford 77-81, 196, 239
Fairley, Mrs. 77-82
Farris, James C. 144, 247

Felker, Jr., Doctor Paul Henley 115-182, 200
Felker, Mrs. Carol 121, 152, 168
Fiftieth Anniversary Celebration, 1943 79
First Baptist Church 79, 114, 118, 161
First Presbyterian Church in Morganton 203
First United Methodist Church 118, 146, 148, 161, 162
Fletcher, Hugh 137
Fletcher, Mrs. Hugh (Mildred) 149, 243
Floyd, Mrs. Dianne 125, 150
Franklin 25, 26
French language 6, 16, 18, 26, 27, 33, 44, 57, 58, 59, 61, 64, 69, 74, 78, 112, 176, 187, 190, 194, 218, 242
French choir 45, 58, 104, 107
French Circle 81, 128, 129, 174
From This Day Forward 114, 117, 127, 142, 224, 225

G

G'Segner, Rev. Ford 117, 120
Gardiole 25
Gardiole district 28, 38
Garrou, Dr. Benjamin Wesley 150, 153, 166
Garrou, Edward and Doris 124, 129
Garrou, François 38, 39, 188, 227
Garrou, James Edward 124, 126, 133, 155, 211, 246
Garrou, Jean (Bobo) 38, 188
Garrou, Jean (père) 37, 38, 188
Garrou, Jean Louis 45, 227
Garrou, Mr. and Mrs. Albert F. 106, 128
Garrou, Mrs. Albert F. 70, 86
Garrou, Pastor Henri 38-40, 45, 188, 228
Garrou, Philip H. 103
Garrou, Sr., Albert 225
Garrou, Sr., Mrs. Victor 155, 212
Garrou, Sr., Victor 157
Gay, Dr. Teophilo 14
Gaydou, Marguerite 21, 213

Genealogy of Waldensian Settlers in Valdese, North Carolina, 1893-1990 158
Ghigo, Dr. Francis 71, 112, 132, 189, 219
Ghigo, Miss Anita 57, 72, 78, 85, 189
Ghigo, Mrs. Juliette 42, 57, 58
Ghigo, Pastor Filippo Enrico 41-43, 45, 50, 132, 189, 214, 219
Giampiccoli, Pastor Neri 118
Gibson, Rev. Frank 142
Gilliam, Miss Shirley 104, 107, 108
Girl Scouts 78, 79, 168
Glorious Return 8, 9, 12, 36, 69, 118, 127, 129, 155, 193, 215
Gourley, Rev. Caroline 161, 162
Grana, Rev. Dr. Gregory 97, 100, 109, 110, 112, 117, 145, 150
Grant, Mrs. Marguerite S. 26, 38, 40, 43, 45, 55, 207
Grill, Antoine 18, 26, 38, 39, 40, 45, 79, 80, 86, 225, 227
Grill, Mrs. Melany (Bounous) 140, 143
Guigou, Alexis 138, 152, 231
Guigou, John D. 101, 208, 243
Guigou, Louis Philippe 23, 58. 231, 242
Guigou, Mrs. John D. 86, 117, 136, 246
Guigou, Mrs. Leon 81
Guigou, Mrs. Louis Philippe 26, 41, 81, 82, 83, 86

H

Handbell choir 121
Harris, Rev. M.I. 79
Hatley, Mrs. Mary Louise 141
Heilman, John 117, 137
Heilman, Mrs. John 108
Hern, Jr. Mrs. Joe 104
Hern, Mrs. Joe 81, 83, 192
Historical Collection Committee 86
Historical Committee 113, 117, 122, 123, 136, 146, 155, 158, 166, 178
Historical Register 139
History of the Ancient Christians 3
History of the Waldenses 137

History of the Women's Auxiliary and the Women of the Church 26, 41
Holy Week Services 118, 142, 161
Home Circle 81
Honorary Life Membership Awards 82, 140
Huffman, Robert O. 74
Hull, Dr. and Mrs. Walter 117, 119, 123, 135, 136, 149, 158, 159

I

Italian television 154

J

Jacob, Sr., Mrs. J. Laird 110, 121, 236
Jacumin, Lydia 190
Jahier, Ernest 135, 218
Jahier, Michel Auguste 19, 25, 26
Janavel, Josué 8
Janavel, Rev. Alfred 87, 129
Jones, Bishop Bevel 162
Jones, Hilda 135
Jones, Rev. Clyde 109, 110
Junior Choir 78, 79, 82, 85, 91, 92, 176

K

Kibler, W.W. 35
Kindergarten 99, 111
Kirkpatrick, James W. 152, 154, 162, 169
Kistler, Andrew M. 67, 208

L

Léger, Jean Jacques 18, 31, 33, 70, 206
L'Écho des Vallées Vaudoises 34, 186
Ladies Aid Society 63, 67, 68
Ladies' Auxiliary 68, 70
Lamberth, Jr., Dr. Clements E. 133, 139
Lane, Dr. Edgar 149
Language Death Among Waldensians of Valdese, North Carolina 159, 219
Le Phare des Alpes 224, 227

Le Phare des Alpes clubhouse 215, 229
Le Témoin 13
Legal Board 21
Les Jeunes Chanteurs 147, 173, 176
Les Jeunes Chanteuses 123
Livre des Procès Verbaux et des Documents se référant à la foundation de la Valdese Corporation. 1893-94 No. 1 18
Long, Henri 38, 40, 43
Long, John 21, 58, 79, 208, 213
Long, Marguerite Gaydou 58
Lord's Supper 163, 177
Louis XIV of France 7, 8

M

Mérindol, France 5, 168
Malan, Pastor Hugo 157
Manse 23, 26, 43, 47, 55, 58, 65, 66, 68, 70, 84, 102, 103, 108, 112, 118, 152, 193, 199
Marshall, Miss Mary Ruth 97
Martinat, Antoine 17, 18, 26
Martinat, Henri (Pineburr) 45, 46, 64, 80, 86, 219, 227
Martinat, Mrs. Henri F. 45
Martinat, Valdo 117, 125, 247
Maundy Thursday 119, 154, 161
Maze Coffee House 112, 118
McClure, Sr., Reverend Albert Bonner 83-87, 111, 122, 197
Meeting house 16, 26, 215
Meier, John 204
Melody Choir 176
Memorial Funds 179
Men of the Church 71, 105, 115, 119, 151, 152, 161
Methodist Campground 125
Meytre, Mrs. Peter 44, 215
Micol, Jaubert 18, 37, 203, 231
Micol, Miss Rachel 116, 120
Micol, Mrs. Edward 86
Miller, D.D., Rev. Samuel 3, 4
Miller, Rev. Beth Ann 154
Missionary teachers 38, 40, 45, 221
Mitchell, W. Harold 101, 105, 136
Mode, John 134, 139

Monnet, Rev. Pietro Enrico 46, 63, 67, 68, 208
Mont Viso Insurance Company 228
Moore, Miss Lois Grier 107, 109
Moral Board 21, 23, 25
Moravian Church 68, 69, 151, 193, 216
Morganton Herald 186
Morganton Land and Improvement Company 15, 204, 206
Morganton News Herald 190
Morrison, the Honorable Cameron 79
Mowery, Steven Lee 120-134, 145
Munroe, Dr. C.A. 45
Museum 2000 Fund 136
Museum Building and Planning Committee 112

N

Napoleon 10
Neff, Felix 10
Newton, Miss Kathy 125, 128, 131, 132

O

Old Rock School 43, 151, 156, 158, 159, 215
Olivetan 5
Organ 45, 58, 65, 72, 86, 107, 135, 139, 148
Outdoor oven 16, 217

P

Palmer, Miss J.C. 40, 43, 55
Parse, Reverend John C. 135, 150
Pascal, Dr. Robert 118, 212
Pascal, Edward 113, 134, 157, 243
Pascal, James Henry 225
Pascal, Jean Henri (Balsille) 45, 46
Pascal, Jean Henri (Bienvenue) 40, 44, 45, 46, 47, 68, 227, 236, 242
Pascal, Jean Henri (Gardiole) 38, 44, 46, 86
Pascal, Miss Olga 124, 136, 146, 212, 246
Pascal, Mrs. Frances Micol 150

Pastor's Farm 45, 47, 48, 57, 188
Pearson, Samuel T. 203, 206
Perrin, Jean Paul 3
Perrou, Étienne 26
Perrou, Emmanuel 78
Perrou, Jr., John Stephen 110
Pictorial directory 137, 169
Piedmont Bank 203, 205, 206
Piedmontese Easter 7
Pioneer Hall 73, 74, 79, 83, 112, 131, 148, 154, 164, 208, 209
Platone, Pastor Giuseppe 140, 152
Plexico, Jr., Reverend James Clyde 102-114, 161, 199
Poet, Reverend Sylvan Stephen 73, 74, 194
Pons, Albert 18, 43, 203, 227, 231
Pons, Dr. Cathy R. 35, 46, 159, 219
Pons, Edward 120
Pons, Lydia Jacumin 138, 191
Pons, Mrs. Ben 86
Pons, Mrs. O.H. 82
Pons, Rev. John 43, 45, 57, 64, 66, 72, 78, 79, 110, 137, 190
Pons, Sr., Mrs. Frederic H. 82, 100
Prangins 25
Presbyterian Board of Home Missions 27, 43, 47, 58
Presbyterian Church (U.S.A.) 138, 155
Presbyterian Church in the United States 21, 26, 27, 28, 40, 43, 58, 71, 81, 99, 105, 118, 121, 138, 186
Presbyterian Church U.S.A. 99
Presbyterian Men 157, 166, 168
Presbyterian Women 168
Prochet, Dr. Matteo 13, 19, 38, 41, 43, 204, 205
Provençal Speech of the Waldensian Colonists of Valdese, N.C., The 132, 219
Pyatt, Mr. R.L. 111

R

Raftelis, Miss Yvonne 101, 102
Ramsay, Reverend James Alston 34
Ramsay, Sr., Julius McNutt 34, 236
Ribet, Lee 79

Richard, Louis 14
Rose, Jr., Reverend John M. 30, 33, 203, 206
Rostan, Jr., Mr. and Mrs. John P. 123
Rostan, Mrs. Linda 151
Rostan, Mrs. Naomi Bounous 146, 246
Rostan, Sr., John P. 117, 208
Rostan, Sr., Mr. and Mrs. J.P. 111, 149, 225
Rostan, Sr., Mrs. John 123
Rowe, Ms. Yvone Lenard 157
Ruth M. Williams Music Scholarship Fund 109, 199
Rutherford, Haynes 113

S

Sale of the church lots 37, 39
Salvageot, Ippolite 27, 31, 37, 39
Sbaffi, Pastor Aldo 126
Scaife, Marvin F. 13, 14, 19, 31, 203
Schoolhouse 42, 64
Schubert, William D. 139
(Second) Cornerstone Service 249
Service Committee 138, 140, 179, 201
Seventy-fifth anniversary 113, 191
Smith, Mrs. Rhonda 162, 163
Smith, Rev. John D. 101
Soulier, Pastor Barthélemy 21-36, 187, 205, 206
Spence, Dr. Thomas 117
Statistical reports 99, 105, 112, 113, 114, 171
Stemple, Mrs. Wade H. 78, 81
Stewardship and Finance Committee 178
Stewart, Mrs. Carol 128, 136
Stiff, Mrs. Evelyn 137
Stoney, A.B., State Representative 79
Styles, Rev. Walter H. 93-102, 161, 163, 198

T

Tarlton, Myelitia and Terry 156
Tenebrae service 127
Thanksgiving Service 119
Tourn, Giorgio 134

Town district 28, 38
Tran family 133, 137, 149
Tron, Dr. Charles Albert 13-21, 62, 185, 203, 204, 206
Tron, Pastor Émile Henri 47-56, 191

U

Upchurch, Mr. 47

V

Vacation Bible School 67, 73, 78
Vacation Church School 155, 167
Valdese Corporation 16, 19, 28, 37, 43, 185, 203, 228
Valdese General Hospital 78, 108, 135, 199
Valdese High School 43
Valdese Manufacturing Company 47, 57, 59, 97
Valdese Ministerial Association 118, 127
Valdese Shoe Corporation 64, 65
Van 139
Venerable Table 46, 186
Verreault III, Joseph A. 104, 137, 145
Verreault, Reverend Joseph Armand 66-69, 79, 110, 137, 192
Vested choir 72
Vinay, Charlie 157, 243
Vinay, Henri 38
Vinay, Jr., Louis 154
Vinay, Pastor Enrico 18-21, 186
Vocational Guidance program 107
Voting members 28, 30, 50, 232

W

Waldenses in the New World, The 137, 206
Waldenses of Valdese, The 13, 27
Waldensian Bakeries 123
Waldensian Church of Italy 3, 13, 14, 17, 28, 43, 46, 47, 50, 59, 69, 78, 116, 118, 126, 134, 152, 211
Waldensian Festival 127, 140, 148, 155, 216, 218, 224
Waldensian Herald 115

Waldensian Hosiery Mill 38
Waldensian Museum 113, 122, 123, 125, 127, 128, 141, 146, 148, 154, 155, 158, 166, 170, 178, 182, 211, 218
Waldensian Tavola 11
Waldensians: The First 800 Years, The 134
Waldo, Peter 5
Watts, Dr. George B. 13, 21, 27, 126, 136, 206
Wednesday night Bible Class 122
West, Rev. Cameron 162
Whisenant, Mrs. Richard F. 149, 239
William of Orange 8
Williams, Jr., George W. 93, 101, 157, 243, 247
Williams, Jr., Mrs. George 72, 78, 85, 109, 120
Woman's Board of the Presbyterian Church in the United States of America (Northern) 41
Women of the Church 93, 101, 119, 120, 128, 140
Women's Auxiliary 71, 73, 78, 79, 80, 83, 84, 85
World War I 50, 57, 191
World War II 77, 83, 216
Worship Committee 132, 161, 176
Wright, Rev. Donn W. 108, 111, 112, 113
Wright, William 31
Wurttemberg region of Germany 9

Y

Yoder, Glenn R. 137, 243, 247
Youth choir 57, 115, 130
Youth Club 122, 159
Youth Handbell Choir 144, 172, 176

Z

Zaandam 14

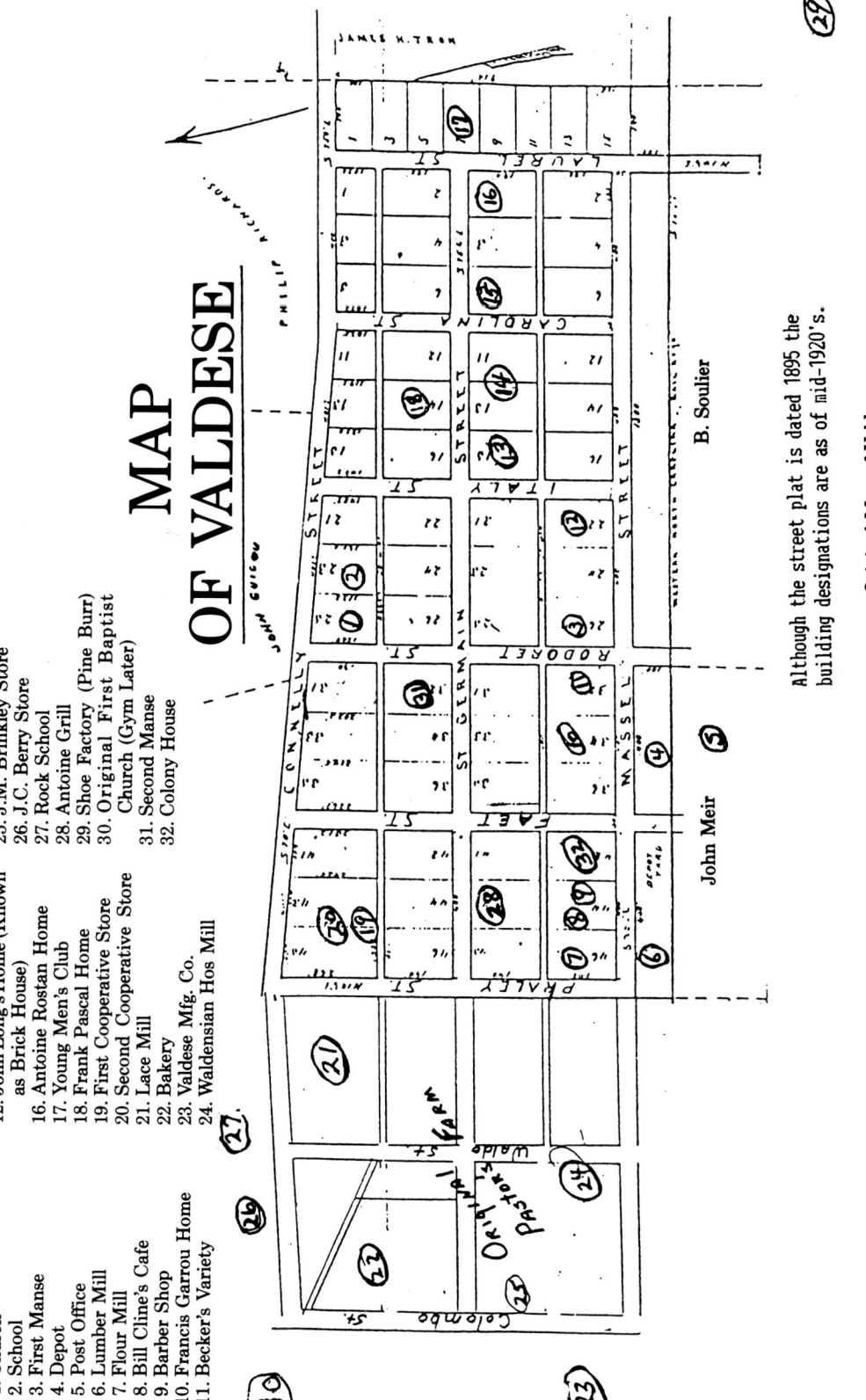